Programs for Asian Global Legal Professions Series Ⅲ

How Civil Law is Taught in Asian Universities

Edited by
KEIGLAD

Keio Institute for Global Law and Development

The publication was produced by KEIGLAD
KEIGLAD - Keio Institute for Global Law and Development
Keio University, 2-15-45 Mita, Minato-ku, Tokyo 108-8345 Japan
http://keiglad.keio.ac.jp/en/

Copyright © 2019 KEIGLAD

All rights reserved. No part of this book may be reproduced in any form or by any electronic or mechanical means, including information storage and retrieval systems, without the prior written permission of KEIGLAD, excepting brief quotes used in reviews.

Distributed by KEIO UNIVERSITY PRESS INC.
2-19-30 Mita, Minato-ku, Tokyo 108-8346 Japan
http://www.keio-up.co.jp/kup/eng/

ISBN 978-4-7664-2589-5
Printed in Japan

PREFACE

In October 2016, Keio University Law School and partner universities from countries in the Mekong region launched a collaborative legal education program, the Program for Asian Global Legal Professions (PAGLEP), to foster legal professionals who can solve cross-border legal issues, which are becoming increasingly complex and confusing.

To make the PAGLEP a more productive and effective program, it is essential to deepen our understanding of the legal education curricula in Japan and countries in the Mekong region. The 2016 research project focused on clarifying the basic information of curricula for legal education at each university and comparing the differences. The results were published in the first volume of the PAGLEP series, "Comparative Legal Education from Asian Perspective."

Studying law abroad is a useful approach to understand legal issues on a global scale. The 2017 project focused on the international exchange programs at each university and discussed the difficulties students face while studying law abroad at Asian universities, not only in their coursework but also in their daily lives, including language barriers. The results were published in the second volume of the PAGLEP series, "Challenges for Studying Law Abroad in the Asian Region."

Based on the general comparative study of legal education programs provided at home and abroad, the project in 2018 focused more specifically on the concrete content of legal education curricula. We started from exploring how civil law is taught in each university (Part I). We also sought to reveal the similarities and differences in the application of civil law provisions across countries by arranging the same legal topics, which we call "common topics" (Part III), together with the characteristics of each country's legal system as the background information (Part II). The third volume of the PAGLEP series will include the remarkable outcomes of the 2018 project.

Sharing the knowledge of unique curricula, teaching method, and characteristic application of relevant provisions of civil law to common topics, with deepening the understanding of legal system in the countries of our partner universities will greatly promote our joint study to improve legal education so as to foster the global legal professionals from Asian universities.

Isao Kitai

Dean, Keio University Law School

31 January 2019

CONTENTS

PREFACE

Isao Kitai i

PART I: HOW CIVIL LAW IS TAUGHT IN ASIAN UNIVERSITIES

Chapter 1:   HOW CIVIL LAW IS TAUGHT
IN JAPANESE LEGAL EDUCATION PROGRAMS

Hiroshi Matsuo 3

    1. Introduction
    2. At University (1): Undergraduate Level
    3. At University (2): Postgraduate Level
    4. At the Legal Training and Research Institute
    5. Conclusion

Chapter 2:   TEACHING CIVIL LAW IN THAILAND:
A Case Study of Thammasat University

    Munin Pongsapan/ Junavit Chalidabhongse/ Viravat Chantachote 35

    1. Introduction
    2. Thammasat University's Monopoly on Legal Education
    3. The Dominant Role of the Thai Bar, the Institute of Legal Education of the Thai Bar, and the Judicial Committee in Reshaping Legal Education in Thailand
    4. Law Degree Programs Entirely in English: Innovative Experiments
    5. Teaching Civil Law at Thammasat University
    6. Conclusion

Chapter 3:   HOW CIVIL LAW IS TAUGHT
AT UNIVERSITY OF YANGON

Khin Phone Myint Kyu 53

    1. Introduction

2. Undergraduate Program (LLB)
3. Postgraduate Program
4. HRD Course
5. Conclusion

Chapter 4: A PRACTICAL EXAMPLE OF TEACHING
AND APPLYING CIVIL LAW IN CAMBODIA:
A Law school's Perspective

            Kong Phallack/ Mao Kimpav 69

Introduction
1. Law Programs and Teaching Civil Law at PUC-FLPA
2. Teaching Methodolgy: Cases And Analysis Applying Cambodidan Law
Conclusion

PART II: INTRODUCTION TO LEGAL SYSTEMS IN ASIAN COUNTRIES

Chapter 1: GROUP LITIGATION (CLASS ACTION)
IN JAPAN

            Toshitaka Kudo 79

1. Prologue: Defining "Group Litigation" and "Class Action"
2. Group Litigation in Japan
3. Special Procedural Measures for Consumer Protection
4. Epilogue

Chapter 2: OVERVIEW OF THE VIETNAMESE LEGAL SYSTEM

            Phan Thi Lan Huong 99

1. The Influence Factors of the Legal System in Vietnam
2. Sources of Law
3. The Court System
4. Legal Professionals

Chapter 3: USING CASE LAW IN LEGAL EDUCATION
IN VIETNAM

            Nguyen Ba Binh 121

1. The Need for Using Case Law in Legal Education in Vietnam
2. The Current Situation of Using Case Law in Legal Education in Vietnam
3. Some Suggestions for Using Case Law in Legal Education in Vietnam

CONTENTS

Chapter 4: GENERAL VIEW OF THE LEGAL SYSTEM
IN VIETNAM

Nguyen Ngoc Dien   129

    Introduction
    1. New Concepts of Sources of Law
    2. New Concept of Subjective Rights
    3. Redefinition of Judicial Functions in the Context of a New Concept of Subjective Rights

Chapter 5: THE LAO LEGAL SYSTEM:
Structures, Challenges and Legal Education
toward Strengthening the Rule of Law

Alounna Khamhoung   141

    1. Overview of Lao People's Democratic Republic
    2. Constitutional Architecture of the Legal System
    3. Legal Policy and Challenges on Legal Development in Laos
    4. Summary on Progress and Challenges in Legal Education towards Strengthening the Rule of Law in Lao PDR

Chapter 6: INTRODUCTION TO THAI LAW:
A Historical Survey

Munin Pongsapan   165

    1. Introduction
    2. A Brief History of Thailand
    3. Sources of Thai Law's Pre-codification
    4. Traditional Thai Private Law
    5. Administration of Justice before Reform in the 19th Century
    6. Modernization of Thai Law
    7. Conclusion

Chapter 7: MYANMAR'S CURRENT LEGAL SYSTEM AND INHERITANCE
UNDER THE MYANMAR CUSTOMARY LAW

Khin Phone Myint Kyu   197

    Introduction
    1. History of Myanmar's Legal System
    2. The Current Legal System (2011–Present)
    3. Inheritance under the Myanmar Customary Law
    Conclusion

PART III: USE OF COMMON TOPICS TO IMPROVE COMPARATIVE LAW AND LEGAL EDUCATION

Chapter 1: USE OF COMMON TOPICS TO IMPROVE COMPARATIVE LAW AND LEGAL EDUCATION IN ASIA

Hiroshi Matsuo   243

1. Introduction
2. Creating Common Topics
3. Use of Common Topics and Its Outcomes

Chapter 2: USE OF COMMON TOPICS TO IMPROVE COMPARATIVE LAW AND LEGAL EDUCATION:
Application of Japanese Law

Hiroshi Matsuo   255

1. A Group of Persons as a Subject of Right
2. Transformation of Property Rights: Acquisition of Immovable Property
3. Contractual Liabilities
4. Non-contractual Liabilities, Succession, Status of the Fetus

Chapter 3: USE OF COMMON TOPICS TO IMPROVE COMPARATIVE LAW AND LEGAL EDUCATION:
Application of Vietnamese Law

Doan Thi Phuong Diep   265

1. General Introduction to Civil Law in the Bachelor's Degree Program at University of Economics and Law (UEL), National University-Ho Chi Minh City, Vietnam
2. Sample of Common Topics

Chapter 4: USE OF COMMON TOPICS TO IMPROVE COMPARATIVE LAW AND LEGAL EDUCATION:
Application of Cambodian Law

Kong Phallack/ Mao Kimpav   273

Chapter 5: USE OF COMMON TOPICS TO IMPROVE COMPARATIVE LAW AND LEGAL EDUCATION:
Application of the Lao Law

Alounna Khamhoung 275

1. A Group of Persons as a Subject of Right
2. Transformation of Property Right: Acquisitions of Immovable Property
3. Contractual Liabilities
4. Non-contractual Liabilities, Succession, Status of the Fetus, etc.

Chapter 6: USE OF COMMON TOPICS TO IMPROVE COMPARATIVE LAW AND LEGAL EDUCATION:
Application of Thai Law

Munin Pongsapan/ Junavit Chalidabhongse 285

1. A Group of Persons as a Subject of Rights
2. Transformation of Property Right: Acquisitions of Immovable Property
3. Contractual Liabilities
4. Non-contractual Liabilities, Succession, Status of the Fetus, etc.

Chapter 7: USE OF COMMON TOPICS TO IMPROVE COMPARATIVE LAW AND LEGAL EDUCATION:
Application of Myanmar Law (1)

Khin Khin Su 297

1. A Group of Persons as Subjects of Rights
2. Transformation of Property Rights: Acquisition of Immovable Property

Chapter 7: USE OF COMMON TOPICS TO IMPROVE COMPARATIVE LAW AND LEGAL EDUCATION:
Application of Myanmar Law (2)

Khin Phone Myint Kyu 303

3. Contractual Liabilities
4. Non-contractual Liabilities, Succession, Status of the Fetus

ON-SITE REPORT

FROM LAW CLASSROOM IN ASIAN UNIVERSITIES:
A Short Report on the Collaboration Program in Cambodia in 2018

Hitomi Fukasawa 313

SAMPLES OF TEACHING MATERIALS FOR CIVIL LAW

- JAPAN   333
- VIETNAM   335
- LAOS   337
- THAILAND 342
- MYANMAR   345

INDEX   347

ABOUT KEIGLAD   349

ABOUT THE AUTHORS   350

PART I
HOW CIVIL LAW IS TAUGHT IN ASIAN UNIVERSITIES

Chapter 1

HOW CIVIL LAW IS TAUGHT IN JAPANESE LEGAL EDUCATION PROGRAMS

Hiroshi Matsuo*

(Keio University)

"What is sowed in private law is reaped in public law and the law of nations. In the valleys of private law, in the very humblest relations of life, must be collected, drop by drop, so to speak, the forces, the moral capital, which the state needs to operate on a large scale, and to attain its end. **Private law ... is the real school of the political education of the people**, and if we would know how a people, in case of need, will defend their political rights and their place among the nations, let us examine how the separate members of the nation assert their own right in private life".[1]

1. Introduction

After we have jointly conducted the general comparative study of legal ed-

---

* Professor, Keio University Law School; Director, Keio Institute for Global Law and Development (KEIGLAD).

[1] Rudolph von Jhering, *Der Kampf ums Recht: The Struggle for Law*, translated from the Fifth German Edition, by John J. Lalor, Second Edition, Chicago Callaghan and Company, 1915, pp. 99–100 (emphasis added).

ucation in domestic curriculums and international legal exchange programs in Asian universities[2], it is now time to do a more specific comparative research on the *concrete content* of legal education for its further improvement. This shift of analysis from macro to micro comparison was predicted in our original plan of comparative legal education.[3] Then, we believe that it is most fruitful to begin with the comparative study of how to teach "Civil Law", in the sense of the general private law[4], in the unique context of legal development within each country.

Civil law as the general private law is an indispensable part of legal education in Asian countries because it defines the private rights of the citizen, such as personal and property rights, stipulates the requirements for the transformation of private rights, and provides for the legal effects of those rights to be implemented or to protect the substantial interests of the citizens, all of which have

---

[2] See KEIGLAD (ed.), *Comparative Legal Education from Asian Perspective: Programs for Asian Global Legal Professions Series I*, Keio University Press, 2017; id., *Challenges for Studying Law Abroad in the Asian Region: Programs for Asian Global Legal Professions Series II*, Keio University Press, 2018.

[3] Hiroshi Matsuo, "Why and How Should Comparative Legal Education Be Promoted in an Asian Context?", in: KEIGLAD (ed.), *Comparative Legal Education from Asian Perspective*, op. cit. (note 2 above), p. 12.

[4] The concept of "civil law" has different meanings depending on the context in which it is used, reflecting the historical development of the term. (a) As an English translation of the original term, "ius civile" in Roman law stood for the law of a state, which provided for the citizens so as to distinguish it from "ius gentium" (law of nations), which were applied to all nations, and from "ius naturale" (law of nature), which were applied to all human beings on the basis of human nature. (b) With the formation of common law concept in England, which were transmitted to Commonwealth countries, "civil law" features the legal systems developed by those countries in the European continent that have received Roman law, and were subsequently received by the European colonies and the developing countries in Latin America, Africa, and Asia. (c) In the further development of the legal system, "civil law" has been used to mean the general private law, which provides for the general principles and rules of private rights, distinguished from commercial law as the specific private law, and from criminal law and other public laws, which provide for the public powers of government organizations. In this Part, the term "civil law" shall be used in the sense of the general private law (above (c)) unless specifically indicated otherwise (e.g., p. 61).

been new developments in the larger history of the Asian region. The reason why civil law, as related to the general private law is "the real school of the political education", is that the individual citizen can learn how to assert his/her own primitive rights in the humblest relations of private life, which will subsequently be applied in the public relations of political life among the citizenry, and then in international relations among nations[5]. It implies that the importance of legal education concerning civil law becomes more significant in the developing stages of a country where fostering the consciousness of the rights and the attitude of citizens toward law, order, and legal culpability is indispensable to establish a functioning legal system and to promote the rule of law.

The knowledge of the law to be obtained through the legal education process must be the most viable measure to correct "unreasonableness" in private transactions as well as in the treatment of citizens by the government. Furthermore, solid knowledge of private law provides the very standard contents of law by stipulating the subject, object, transformation, and effect of the basic rights of citizens consisting of the rights concerning property, those toward the other person, and those in the personality of their own. This is the reason why civil law -- in the context of general private law -- has been playing a crucial role in the development processes of legal frameworks within Asian countries since the end of the 19th century where the concept of right of private citizens has been new in the history of those countries.

Civil law includes the law of persons, the law of property rights, and the law of transformation of property rights if we follow the "Institutiones" system such as in France and other countries which received the French civil code. It consists of the general part, the law of obligation or claim rights, the law of real rights, the law of family relations, and the law of succession if we follow the "Pandekten" system, such as in Germany and other countries, that received the German civil code. Both of them belong to the "Civil Law" system in the sense of the European continental law. They correspond to the separate fields of law such as proper-

---

[5] Jhering (translated by Lalor), op. cit. (n. 1), pp. 99–100.

ty law, contract law, tort law, and other non-contractual obligations law, family law, and succession law in the "Common Law" system developed in England, which was introduced into Malaysia, Singapore and other Commonwealth Nations, Hong Kong SAR, and Myanmar. This means that we can commonly talk about "civil law" in the sense of the general private law not only within the "Civil Law" (the European continental law) jurisdiction but also in the "Common Law" jurisdiction.

In this Part, the mechanisms of civil law education in Japan, Thailand, Cambodia, and Myanmar will be introduced to identify the specific role of civil law in the development process of legal education programs in Asian countries. This Chapter will focus on civil law education in Japan.

The process of legal education in Japan has been divided into two stages.[6] In the first stage, the main focus of legal education programs shall be put in the way of the *interpretation of law*. In the second stage, the focus of attention seems to shift to the way of the *finding of fact*. Before the introduction of a new law school system in 2004, the first stage was included in undergraduate programs in the university (mainly at the faculty of law) and the second stage was arranged in the programs at the Legal Training and Research Institute (the LTRI hereafter)[7] for the passers of the bar examination[8]. However, after the introduction of the law school system -- which is situated between the legal education in the undergraduate programs and that of the LTRI, -- the interpretation programs are combined with the factfinding programs because legal education at a law school aims to train professionals according to the educational philosophy of the law school. Namely, "building a bridge between theoretical education and practical education".[9]

---

[6] Matsuo, op. cit. (note 3 above), pp. 8–9.

[7] The LTRI (see 4.1 below) is administered by the Supreme Court.

[8] It is called "shiho-shiken" (the National Legal Examination). See 3.4 below.

[9] The Justice System Reform Council, *Recommendations of the Justice System Reform Council: For a Justice System to Support Japan in the 21st Century*, June 12, 2001, Chapter III, Part 2, 2 (1) b.

In this Chapter, the civil law education in both stages will be analyzed for the comparative study and improvement of legal education.

2. At University (1): Undergraduate Level

2.1 Curriculum

The treatment of civil law in the undergraduate curriculum in the university varies depending on the policies and conditions of each university. In the case of Keio University, Faculty of Law, the courses which treat the civil law subjects (civil law courses) consist of the following Units: [1] General Part I; [2] General Part II; [3] Real Rights I; [4] Real Rights II; [5]Claim Rights, Special Part I; [6] Claim Rights, Special Part II; [7] Claim Rights, General Part I; [8] Claim Rights, General Part II; [9] Family Law I, and [10]Family Law II. There are other specific courses concerned with civil law such as [11] Legal Person; [12] Cases on Civil Law; [13] Seminar on Civil Law I; [14] Seminar on Civil Law II; [15] Seminar on Civil Law III and [16] Seminar on Civil Law IV, etc.[10] For example, [1] General Part I consists of the following 15 Sub-Categories.

1	Law and Legal Science, Interpretation of Law
2	Law as a Legal System and Placing the Civil Law in the Legal System
3	Civil Law as a System of Private Rights and Personality Rights, Real Rights, Claim Rights, and Rights in Family Relations
4	New Rights Recognized in the Civil Law such as Right of Publicity
5	Birth and Death of Natural Person
6	Disappearance of Natural Person and Legal Capacity of Foreigner)
7	Legal Person and Its Legal Capacity
8	Acquisition of Rights by Legal Person, and Legal Personality of Foreign Legal Person
9	Association and Foundation without Legal Personality, and Partnership

---

[10] Each Unit consists of 15 Sub-Categories including examination, normally with one class lasting 90 minutes per week. However, the number of Sub-Categories of one Unit and the length of one of the Sub-Categories differ among universities. For instance, in the University of Tokyo, Faculty of Law, one unit consists of 13 Sub-Categories, the teaching time of each lasting 105 minutes.

10	Corporeal and Incorporeal Thing, and Immovable and Movable Property
11	Major and Subordinate Thing, Principal Thing and Fruits, and Special Things such as Used for Family Ritual, Public Property, Land Beneath the Sea, etc.
12	Juridical Actions, and Legal Capacities Necessary for Juridical Actions, Rescission and Confirmation of Juridical Actions for the Reason of Limited Capacity of Minor
13	Rescission and Confirmation of Juridical Actions for the Reason of Limited Capacity of Adult Ward, Person under Curatorship, and Person under Assistance
14	Validity of Judicial Actions Made with Concealed True Intention, Fictitious Manifestation of Intention
15	Examination

It is followed by [2] General Part II, which includes another set of 15 Sub-Categories.

1	Validity of Judicial Actions Made under Mistake and Mistake in Motivation
2	Validity of Judicial Actions Made under Fraud
3	Validity of Judicial Actions Made under Duress
4	Freedom of Contract and Other Juridical Actions, and Its Regulation by Consumer Contract Law
5	Conditions and Terms of Juridical Actions
6	Requirements for Valid Contract and Other juridical Actions
7	Juridical Actions through Agency
8	Juridical Actions through Agency without Authority
9	Apparent Agency
10	The Roles of Prescription and Limitation Period
11	Invocation, Renewal and Suspension of Prescription and Limitation Period
12	Application of Limitation Period
13	Acquisition by Prescription Period and Registration
14	General Principles of Good Faith, Prohibition of Abuse of Rights and Conformity with the Public Interest Concerning the Exercise of Private Rights
15	Examination

If the students complete each course, for example, [1] General Part I above, and pass the examination, 2 credit points are given to them. In order to graduate in the Faculty of Law, the students need to obtain 136 credit points in total including 16 points for foreign languages, 8 points for natural sciences, 8 for humanities, 8 for social sciences, and 88 for legal sciences. It means the civil law courses, which account for nearly 40% of the necessary credit points among legal subjects and around one-fourth of the total credit points necessary for graduation are recognized as the core program in the undergraduate legal education.

2.2 Teaching Method

Teaching methods vary depending on the preference of each lecturer. However, most of the civil law courses are lecture-based lessons[11], although teachers also ask students questions when they think it appropriate to confirm the understanding of students and lead discussions for deepening the understanding of the relevant topics. The lecturer explains the content of civil law not on a clause by clause basis in accordance with the order of provisions, but by rearranging the order of provisions from the logical point of view and focusing on the important topics from the theoretical and practical viewpoint. For instance, in the lecture of General Part I and II (see 2.1, [1] and [2] above), the order of the lecture is rearranged as starting from the introduction to civil law (see 2.1 [1] General Part I, sub-category 1) to 4) above), followed by the subject of rights (ibid., slot 5) to 9) above), the object of rights (ibid., slot 10) to 11) above), the transformation of rights (ibid., slot 12) to 13) and General Part II, slot 1) to 13), and the exercise of rights (General Part II, slot 14).

In the classes of Cases on Civil Law and Seminar on Civil Law, (see 2.1 [12] and [13] to [16] above), the case-based analysis by using precedents and the presentation by students are also frequently used.

Most of the teachers use textbooks in the class, which will be appointed in the syllabus in advance. Some teachers use electronic devices, and distribute résumés and/or the related materials in the class or in advance (sometimes provided from the database for the class by way of the internet) or just before the class starts. Teachers use the blackboard or whiteboard in order to note the key terms, and explain the outline of the case by describing the relationships between the plaintiff and the defendant and other related persons.

---

[11] Kahei Rokumoto, "Legal Education", in: Daniel H. Foote (ed.), *Law in Japan: A Turning Point*, University of Washington Press, pp. 194–197.

2.3 Examination and Evaluation

The examination is included in each unit and normally held at the end of each term (semester). It asks the participants how to solve a simple case by applying the relevant provision(s) of law through its interpretation. The length of the examination varies from 50 minutes to 120 minutes depending on the lecturer and the university.

For example, in General Part II (see 2.1 [2] above) the following questions were asked in the term-end examination for the autumn semester in January 2019. Students were asked to answer them in 50 minutes.

Read the following [Fact] and answer [Question] (1), (2), (3) and (4).
Full score 100 is allocated to [Question] (1), (2), (3) and (4), at 20, 10, 30, and 40, respectively.

[Fact]
1. On January 30, 2018, Y borrowed JPY 5 million from X for operating the business. The term of repayment was fixed on July 30, 2018. In order to secure the repayment which Y owed to X, Y concluded a contract with X in the name of "P", Y's father, to establish a hypothec on a piece of land "α", which P owns without the consent of P. Y signed as P and put P's seal on the contractual document. Based on this contract, the right of hypothec of X was registered on the land α.
2. Y did not repay the money to X by the due date. On December 1, 2018, X asked Y to repay the money, but Y did not and told to X that Y failed to manage the business and did not have any repayment fund.
3. On December 20, 2018, P died due to the deterioration of his chronic disease. P's property was succeeded by P's wife, Q, and his son Y, by half according to the statutory inheritance. There were no successors of P except for Q and Y, and P did not leave a will.

[Question]

(1) Under the conditions of [Fact] 1, can a contract for establishing a hypothec on Land α be recognized as concluded between X and P?

(2) Under the conditions of [Fact] 1 and 2, when X has applied the court to execute the hypothec on Land α, what counter-claim can P make against X's application?

(3) Under the conditions of [Fact] 1, 2 and 3, when X has applied the court to execute the hypothec on Land α, what counter-claim can Q and Y make against X's application?

(4) In addition to [Fact] 1, if, as an additional fact, Y had been authorized by P to manage P's apartment house and asked by P to keep P's seal and the certificate to prove the identity of that seal (additional fact), under the conditions of [Fact] 2, when X has applied the court to execute the hypothec on Land α, and P would not recognize X's application, what claim can X make against P? And what counter-claim can P make against X?

[Question] (1) and (2) asks the validity of a contract concluded by Y with X in the name of "P" even though Y was not authorized by P to conclude the contract as an agent of P. This is the problem of juridical action by Y, the agent without authority (the unauthorized agent) in the name of the principal, P. [Question] (1) asks whether the formation of the contract to establish a hypothec on whether the landαowned by P can be recognized even if Y signed the contractual document not as «Y, the agent of P» as it is stipulated in Art. 99 (1) Japanese Civil Code (JCC hereafter), but just as «P». It asks the conditions for the anomalous formation of the contract by the agency[12]. [Question] (2) aims to confirm that the principal P has a right to recognize or refuse to recognize the contract[13] concluded by Y without authority. Based on these questions, [Question] (3) asks the result of the fact that Principal P died and the unauthorized agency Y and P's wife, Q,

---

[12] Grand Trial Court [Supreme Court under the former Constitution] Judgment 1920 June 5, Minroku 26–812.

[13] Art. 113 and 116 JCC.

succeeded P's right to recognize or refuse to recognize the contract. It treats the case in which the status of the principal P merged into that of the unauthorized agent Y and another successor, Q. There is no explicit provision to treat this case but there is a case law, which recognized that the unauthorized agent Y might still exercise the right to refuse the contract succeeded from P if Q also refuses to recognize the contract, because Y and Q must exercise the right to refuse the contract jointly[14]. [Question] (4) asks another question under the different condition from that of [Question] (3), whether the principal P should be responsible for the juridical action made by the agent, Y, if agent Y acted beyond the power authorized by the principal, P. Students are asked about the applicability of the concerned provision[15] to the case by the interpretation of that provision under [Fact] 1, 2 and the additional fact given in [Question] 4.

3. At University (2): Postgraduate Level

3.1 Legal Education at the Postgraduate Level

There are two kinds of programs in legal education at the postgraduate level. One is the program mainly aimed at fostering legal researchers[16] that commences with the Masters of Law (LL.M.) course, which is followed by the Doctors of Law (LL.D.) course[17].

---

[14] Supreme Court Judgment 1993 January 21, Minshu 47–1–265. Then Y shall be responsible for the invalidity of the contract and must compensate X for the damages (Art. 117 JCC). If a successor of P was only the unauthorized agent Y, Y's refusal to recognize the contract should be recognized as against the good faith principle provided in Article 1 (2) JCC (Grand Trial Court Judgment 1942 February 25, Minshu 21–164), and the contract shall become valid (Supreme Court Judgment 1965 June 18, Minshu 19–4–986).

[15] Art. 110 JCC.

[16] Such as law teachers who will become law professors, researchers at the governmental or non-governmental level or in private research institutions.

[17] It seems to correspond to the S.J.D. program at the US law school or the Ph.D. course in the other countries.

Another is the Juris Doctor (J.D.) program to foster legal practitioners[18] which the law schools[19] have provided since 2004 as a result of the Justice System Reform[20]. Some students who completed the J.D. course enter into the LL.D. course at the graduate school of law[21] to become a legal researcher[22]. Most of the national universities that have a J.D. course include it within the graduate schools of law[23], while in the private universities, the law school is organized independently from the graduate school of law.

In some law schools, the new LL.M. program taught in English has been established.[24]

3.3 J.D. Program in Law School
3.3.1 Curriculum

The standard curriculum of law school is arranged for three-year programs. However, it can be reduced to two-year programs for students who are recognized as having already mastered a sufficient, basic knowledge of law[25].

In the case of Keio University Law School, in order to complete the law school programs, students need to acquire more than 69 credit points from the required subjects and more than 31 credit points from the elective subjects, so

---

[18] Such as judges, prosecutors, lawyers, etc.

[19] There are 39 law schools as of January 2019, although 74 law schools were established since 2004.

[20] See note 9 and corresponding text above.

[21] Graduate school of law which can award a degree of LL.D. is different from law school which can award a degree of J.D., though it is also postgraduate level.

[22] They can bypass the LL.M. course when they acquire the J.D. certificate.

[23] One exception is Osaka University which has the law school independent from the graduate school of law.

[24] For example, Keio University Law School launched the *LL.M. in Global Legal Practice* in April 2017 (see <http://www.ls.keio.ac.jp/en/llm/>), and Graduate School of Law, Waseda University offers the *LL.M. in Asian Economic Integration and Law* since April 2018 (see <https://www.waseda.jp/folaw/glaw/en/about_llm/>).

[25] The entrance examination for law school is divided into the three-year course and the two-year course.

that 100 credit points in total must be taken at least.

In the first year program, the civil law courses consist of: [1] Civil Law I (General Theory, 2 credits); [2] Civil Law II (Contract Law, 2 credits); [3] Civil Law III (Property Law, 2 credits); [4] Civil Law IV (Civil Liability, 1 credit); [5] Civil Law V (Secured Transactions, 2 credits), and [6] Civil Law VI (Family Law, 1 credit) in the spring semester.

In the second year, students must take [6] Comprehensive Civil Law I (2 credits) in the spring semester and [7] Comprehensive Civil Law II (2 credits) in the autumn semester as required subjects. They are the practical exercises of applying relevant provisions of the Civil Code and those of the special provisions of the civil law to the cases arranged by teachers on the basis of major case laws and legal theories concerning civil law. Students can learn a variety of techniques of the interpretation of the law by using practical materials. In the autumn semester, students must also take the course of Requisite Facts Theory (Yoken-Jijitsu-Ron, 2 credits). It is the theory used to identify the crucial facts corresponding to a certain legal requirement provided by the substantive law to create a certain legal effect, that is, the transformation of rights. These facts are called "yoken-jijitsu" (requisite facts) in Japanese legal education. The theory of requisite facts may be able to bridge between the legal education in the university and the legal practice in the court procedure[26]. In order to identify the requisite facts for each requirement of substantive law, both the interpretation of the provision of such substantive law and fact finding from the facts given in each case is necessary. Thus, it is one of the characteristic subjects in the law school programs, which is located between the faculty of law and the Judicial Training Institute.

In the third year, [8] Comprehensive Civil and Civil Procedure Law I (2 credits) and [9] Comprehensive Civil and Civil Procedure Law II (2 credits) must be taken by students to finalize the law school programs. They include not only the

---

[26] See Souichirou Kozuka, "'Closing the Gap' between Legal Education and Courtroom Practice in Japan: Yoken-Jijitsu Teaching and the Role of the Judiciary", in: Andrew J. Harding, Jiaxiang Hu and Maartje de Visser (eds.), *Legal Education in Asia: From Imitation to Innovation*, Brill/ Nijhoff, 2017, pp. 157–175.

exercise of the interpretation of civil law provisions but also the training in fact finding by using the practical materials arranged from the actual records of civil cases. They can be a bridge between the legal education at law school and that at the LTRI in which the passers of the National Legal Examination are trained to become legal professionals.[27]

3.3.2 Teaching Method

In the law school, the maximum number of students in each class is from around 40 to 50. Here, teachers frequently ask students questions concerned on the course materials. Especially in the above-mentioned [6] Comprehensive Civil Law I, [7] Comprehensive Civil Law II, [8] Comprehensive Civil and Civil Procedure Law I, and [9] Comprehensive Civil and Civil Procedure Law II, the so-called Socratic Method is undertaken by using the case-based materials which are provided to students in advance. The following is a sample of a part of the materials used in [7] Comprehensive Civil Law II[28].

2018 Comprehensive Civil Law II [Sub-Category 12: Joint Hypothec and Subrogation]
I Facts
1. In order to procure financing for its business, Company A took out a loan for 100 million yen on September 30, 2016 from Bank Y, with a repayment date of September 29, 2018.
2. In taking out this loan, Company A listed its property α (valued at 50 million yen) as a collateral on this loan, and established for Bank Y the first rank joint revolving mortgage for a maximum of 200 million yen on property α. Bank Y also has the first rank joint revolving mortgage for a maximum of 200 million yen established on property β (valued at 50 million yen), which is

---

[27] See Section 4 below.
[28] It is a material distributed for the Sub-Category 12 among the 13 Sub-Categories of Comprehensive Civil Law II in 2018.

owned by Z, who manages Company A.

II Questions

[Question 1] Answer the question below on the premise that in addition to [Fact] 1 and 2 above, there is [Fact] 3, below.

3. In borrowing 40 million yen from Company X on December 1, 2017, Company A established for Company X the second rank mortgage on property α, registering such on the same day as the loan.

Company A repaid 50 million yen of the aforementioned loan to Bank Y, though it was not able to repay the remaining amount by the due date of September 29, 2017, thus, Bank Y declared that it will exercise its first rank revolving mortgage on property α, receiving a dividend of 50 million yen from its sale. In this transaction, is Company X able to exercise its right to property β in subrogation to Bank Y?

[Question 2] Answer the question below on the premise that in addition to [Fact] 1 and 2 above, there is another [Fact] 3', below.

3'. In receiving 40 million yen from Company X on December 1, 2017, Z established for Company X the second rank mortgage on property β, registering such on the same day as the loan.

Company A repaid 50 million yen of the aforementioned loan to Bank Y, though it was not able to repay the remaining amount by the due date of September 29, 2018, thus, Bank Y declared that it would exercise its first rank revolving mortgage on property β, receiving a dividend of 50 million yen from its sale. In this transaction, is Company X able to exercise its right to property α in subrogation to Bank Y?

[Question 3] Answer the question below on the premise that in addition to [Fact] 3' of the above [Question 2], there are other [Fact] 4 and 5 as shown below.

4. Company A repaid 50 million yen of the aforementioned loan on April 1, 2018, and requested that Bank Y give up its first rank revolving mortgage to property α. Bank Y received the strong request from Z, the manager of Company A, and because residual property β is owned by Z, Bank Y complied with this request and gave up its first rank revolving mortgage to property α.
5. However, because Company A did not repay the remainder of the loan by the due date of September 29, 2018, Bank Y requested to exercise the first rank revolving mortgage on property β, and created a divided chart showing the dividend of 50 million yen from the sale paid to Bank Y.

What can Company X assert in relation to these actions? Assume that when Bank Y's first rank revolving mortgage on property β was established, there was a special agreement between Bank Y and Z, stating "Z will not assert any exemptions from responsibility in the case of modification or cancellations to collateral or other guarantee by Bank Y".

[Question 4] What would happen to the legal relationship in [Question 2], if there were a joint guarantee made by Z for the loan of 100 million yen, which Company A borrowed from Bank Y, as well as the establishment of a first rank-revolving mortgage on property β owned by Z? Consider that property α is owned by Company Q, a business partner of Company A, and that Company Q established the first rank revolving mortgage on property α for Bank Y.

[Question 5] In [Question 2] above, Z established the first rank revolving mortgage on his/her property β for Company Y from which Company A borrowed the money, and Credit Guarantee Association W became a guarantor for the loan given to Company A from Bank Y, and Credit Guarantee Association W made a special agreement with Z that when Credit Guarantee Association W repaid the loan in subrogation to Bank Y, it could stand in subrogation to Bank Y on all revolving mortgages established for Bank Y on property β, and may exercise all revolving mortgages on property β.

Company A repaid 50 million yen of the aforementioned loan from Bank Y but because it did not repay the remainder by the due date of September 29, 2018, Credit Guarantee Association W asked to execute the first rank revolving mortgage on property β in subrogation to Bank Y. Can Credit Guarantee Association W receive the entire dividend from the sale of 50 million yen? Can Company X lodge an objection to that?

III References

Supreme Court Judgment 1969 July 3, Minshu 23-8-1297.
Supreme Court Judgment 1992 November 6, Minshu 46-8-2625.
Supreme Court Judgment 1978 July 4, Minshu 32-5-785.
Grand Trial Court Judgment 1936 December 9, Minshu 15-2172.
Supreme Court Judgment 1995 June 23, Minshu 49-6-1737.
Supreme Court Judgment 1991 September 3, Minshu 45-7-1121.
Supreme Court Judgment 1986 November 27, Minshu 40-7-1205.
Sendai High Court Judgment 2004 July 14, Hanrei-jiho 1883-69.
Supreme Court Judgment 1984 May 29, Minshu 38-7-885.

This is one of the materials used in the Comprehensive Civil Law II for the autumn semester in the second-year programs. It questions the fair treatment of the providers of collateral (A, Z) and a guarantor (W) for the debtor (A, Z), and the creditors (X, Y) in various patterns. Teachers ask students questions starting from [Question 1] to [Question 5] by dividing them into smaller inquiries such as the confirmation of the basic knowledge of concerned provisions (Art. 392(2), 499, 500, 501(3)[4], 504(2) JCC) and precedents and asking for the results with reasoning based on the interpretation.

3.3.3 Examination and Evaluation

Examinations are held in the middle and at the end of each semester. Evaluation is based on the aggregate scores of [1] the participation in the class, [2] the result of the mid-term examination, and [3] the result of the final examination at the end of the term. For instance, in the case of Comprehensive Civil Law I and II ([6] and [7] in 3.2.1 above), the evaluation is based on the total scores of [1] 20% for the participation to the class, [2] 20% for the mid-term examination, and [3] 40% for the final examination.

The following is a sample of the final examination for Comprehensive Civil Law II[29].

Read the following [Fact], and answer the [Question 1] and [Question 2] below. Irrespective of the dates provided in [Fact] and [Question], answer the questions by applying the Civil Code amended in June 2017. The score is allocated to [Question 1] and [Question 2] at 2:1.

[Fact]
1. A owned a piece of land α (residential land, 200 m²) in Hachioji, Tokyo. A died on April 5, 1996, and B and C, the son and daughter of A, succeeded A's property. A had no successors other than B and C.
2. On April 20, 1996, B made a document of partition of heritage property to the effect that the land α shall be attributed to B, and registered the change of the title of the land α from A to B. On the partition document, B placed his seal and that of C, which C entrusted to B with the certificate of C's seal in accordance with B's request that he needed it to complete the succession procedure.
3. On 3 June 1996, B made a construction contract with the construction company D, that D would construct a Building β (a house with a shop) on

---

[29] It was held on January 25, 2019 s a part of the materials distributed for the 12th slot of Comprehensive Civil Law II in 2018.

the land α at the price of JPY 30,000,000. On October 10, 1996, D completed the construction of the Building β, and B paid the money as promised in exchange of taking the possession of the Building β, and registered it in the name of B.

4. B did not consult with C about the construction of the Building β. However, C did not make any claim on that construction. The taxes on the land α and the Building β have been paid for by B since 1996 until now.

5. On February 1, 2016, B lent the Building β to E for 5 years. B and E agreed that the amount of rent was JPY 400,000 per month, which shall be paid to B before the beginning of every month, and the amount of deposit money was JPY 2,000,000. On the same day, E paid the rent for February and the deposit money, and took the possession of the building β.

6. On April 1, 2017, B very urgently needed the money for his business, so that he transferred the claim right against E for the rent of Building β to F for the period of 25 months starting from May 2017 ending in May 2019 at the price of JPY 9,000,000. B gave notice of this to E by way of the content certificate mail, which was delivered to E on April 2, 2017.

7. On March 20, 2018, B sold the land α and Building β to E at the price of JPY 30,000,000. On April 1, 2018, E paid the purchase money as promised to B and B cooperated with E to register the change the title of land α and Building β from B to E.

[Question 1]

(1) Answer the following question on the premise of [Fact] 1 and 2:
In May 1996, C noticed that the title of the land α was changed from A to B. What can C claim against B for changing the title registered in the name of B to the title of the joint ownership of B and C?

(2) Answer the following question on the premise of [Fact] 1, 2 and 3:
During the lawsuit between B and C as mentioned above (1), B built Building β without the consent of C. Then, can C claim against B to remove Building β and pay the compensation money that was equivalent to the rent fee of the

land α, assumed to be JPY 100,000 per month?

(3) Answer the following question on the premise of [Fact] 1, 2, 3, 4, 5 and 7, and assuming that the procedures as mentioned (1) and (2) above had not been taken:

In April 2018, C claimed against E that the title of land α registered in the name of E should be changed to the title of the joint ownership of E and C. Can E make any counter-claim to refuse C's claim based on the prescription and other legal grounds?

(4) Answer the following question on the premise of [Fact] 1, 2, 3, 4, 5, 6 and 7, and assuming that the procedures as mentioned (1), (2), and (3) above had not been taken:

On April 10, 2018, F asked E to pay the rent fee for April 2018, which was included in the claim right that had been transferred from B to E in [Fact] 6. What counter-claim can E make to refuse F's claim?

[Fact]

8. On September 25, 2018, E needed the money for her business very urgently, so she borrowed JPY 15,000,000 from G and established the right of hypothec on the land α and Building β for G, and registered them in the registration book of land α and Building β. At that time, the price of the land α was JPY 20,000,000 and that of Building β was JPY 10,000,000.

9. On November 14, 2018, E became bankrupt due to E's business conditions having deteriorated rapidly. At that time, E's creditors were G, H (the amount of the claim was JPY 5,000,000), and I (the amount of the claim was JPY 15,000,000).

10. On November 15, 2018, E was asked by H very strongly to repay the money, so that E transferred the land α and Building β to H as a substitute performance of E's debt.

11. On November 30, 2018, H transferred the land α and Building β to J at the price of JPY 15,000,000 and registered the change of the title from H to J.

[Question 2]

Answer the following questions on the premise of [Fact] 1, 2, 3, 4, 5, 7, 8, 9, 10 and 11:

(1) Can I make an application to the court for the cancellation of the substitute performance by transferring the land α and Building β from E to H, and then return the land α and Building β from J which was transferred from H to secure the fund for paying E's debt against I? What counter-claim can J make against I's claim?

(2) What claim can I make against J on the premise of the following fact instead of [Fact] 10 above?

10. On the November 15, 2018, E sold the land α and Building β to H at the total price of JPY 30,000,000, and E repaid her debt to H (JPY 5,000,000) and that to G (JPY 15,000,000), and completed the procedure for the cancellation of the registration of the hypothec for G. Then, H sold the land α and Building β to J at the price of JPY 30,000,000 as prescribed in [Fact] 11 above.

[Question 1] is divided into sub-questions (1) and (4). Sub-questions (1) and (2) ask the legal effect of the share of joint ownership in the land α which was succeeded by C from A. Sub-question (3) asks whether E can assert that B had acquired C's share of ownership in the land α by the prescription as provided in Art. 162 (1) JCC, which requires «the will to own the property». E may claim that the analogical application of Art. 94 (2) JCC, which provides that the invalidity of fictitious juridical action cannot be asserted against a third party because C had left the incorrect title in the registration book for a long time. E may also claim that C must be regarded as having implicitly waived the share of ownership in the land α and B had acquired it in accordance with Art. 255 JCC. Sub-question (4) asks whether E can refuse to pay the rent from April 2018 because E, the lessee of Building β, had acquired ownership of that building which included the status of the lessor, and the lease contract ceased to exist because the status of lessor merged into the former lessee, even though the right to collect rent had been transferred to F until May 2019[30].

In [Question 2], Sub-question (1) asks whether I can assert the right to cancel the fraudulent juridical action between E and H and claim against J for the return of the land α and building β in accordance with Art. 424–3 (1) JCC, which requires the debtor (E)'s will to harm the creditor (I) in conspiracy with the other party (H), and Art. 425–5 (1) JCC, which requires the mala fide of the transferee (J). If I's claim against J is recognized, then J shall be able to exercise H's claim against E to return the purchase money within the amount which J had paid to H (Art. 425–4 [1] JCC).

Sub-question (2) asks the treatment of the case where G's right of hypothec and its registration had been extinguished by the payment of the debt. In that case, I's right to cancel the fraudulent juridical action between E and H and claim against J for the return of the land α and Building β shall be transformed into the claim for the price redemption for the value of the land α and Building β against J who was mala fide of the fraudulent transaction between E and H[31]. J shall be able to exercise H's claim against E to return the purchase money within the amount which J had paid to H (Art. 425–4 [1] JCC).

3.4 National Legal Examination

By completing the J.D. course, students are qualified as a J.D. and acquire eligibility to take the National Legal Examination (NLE)[32]. The NLE is held

---

[30] Supreme Court Decision, 4 September 2012, Kinyu-shoji-hanrei 1400–16.

[31] Supreme Court Decision, 19 July 1988, Hanrei-jiho 1299–70.

[32] In addition to the J.D., the passers of Preliminary Qualification Examination (yobi-shiken, PQE hereafter) are also eligible to take the National Legal Examination. It means that passers of the PQE can bypass the law school process and save the cost of expensive fees at a time of 2 or 3 years. The PQE consists of: (i) Short Answer Questions (Constitutional Law, Administrative Law, Civil Law, Commercial Law, Civil Procedure Law, Criminal Law, and Criminal Procedure Law, each for 30 points, and Liberal Arts for 60 points); (ii) Essay Writing Examination (Constitutional Law, Administrative Law, Civil Law, Commercial Law, Civil Procedure Law, Criminal Law, Criminal Procedure Law, Comprehensive Private Law, and Comprehensive Criminal Law, each for 50 points), and (iii) Oral Examination. The number

for four days in May[33]. It is the paper (written) examination covering the major fields of law: [1] Private Law Subjects (Question I for Civil Law, Question II for Commercial Law, and Question III for Civil Procedure Law; each question for 2 hours); [2] Public Law Subjects (Question I for Constitutional Law, Question II for Administrative Law); [3] Criminal Law Subjects (Question I for Criminal Law, and Question II for Criminal Procedure Law; each for 2 hours), and [4] Selective Subjects (one to be chosen from the following 8 subjects from Insolvency Law, Tax Law, Intellectual Property Law, Labor Law, Environmental Law, Economic Law, International Public Law, and International Private Law; for 3 hours). They are followed by [5] Short Answer Test on Constitutional Law (20 questions for 50 minutes), Civil Law (36 questions for 75 minutes), and Criminal Law (20 questions for 50 minutes)[34].

Civil law-related questions are [1] Question I in Private Law Subjects (for 2 hours), and [5] 36 out of 76 questions in Short Answer Test (75 minutes). The following is Question I in Private Law Subjects in 2018[35].

2018 Private Law Subjects Question I

Full score 100 is allocated to Question 1, 2, 3 at 40:35:25.

Read the following sentences and answer the following questions 1, 2, and 3 as below.

I Facts

1. A was engaged in a personal business for which he bought fruits and veg-

---

of passers of the PQE of 2018 was 433 out of 11,136 who took the examination. The passing rate was about 3.9%.

[33] In 2018, it was held on May 16th (Selective Subjects, Public Law Subjects), 17th (Privat Law Subjects), 19th (Criminal Law Subjects), and 22nd (Short Answer Test).

[34] The contents of subjects and the number of questions are based on the National Legal Examination in 2018.

[35] For the English translation of the Question I, I would like to express my gratitude to Ms. Erika Takahashi for her kind support.

etables from producers and sold them to retailers and food suppliers using a truck (hereinafter referred to as "Truck α").

2. On September 10, 2017, A and B entered into a contract under which A shall purchase 5 kg of mushroom from B for JPY 500,000 (hereinafter referred to as "Sale and Purchase Contract"). Under the Sale and Purchase Contract, it was stated that the delivery of mushroom should be made simultaneously upon its payment on the night of September 21 in a warehouse owned by B (hereinafter referred to as "Warehouse β") near B's apple orchard.

3. From around 11:00 to 14:00 on September 21, B harvested mushroom for the purpose of delivery under the Sale and Purchase Contract with C, whom B used to hire every year during the autumn harvest season, delivered the harvested mushroom into the Warehouse β, and completed packaging 5 kg of mushroom by 16:00, in accordance with the terms and conditions of the Sale and Purchase Contract. Upon its completion, B immediately contacted A through the telephone to inform A that the mushroom was ready to be delivered. A answered B that A shall receive them at the Warehouse β at around 20:00 on the day, which was accepted by B.

4. At around 18:00 on September 21, A was about to leave his home to deliver mushroom, however, he found that the Truck α, which A had parked in front of his house was missing. Soon A called B to tell him that there would be some delays on the receipt of his mushroom due to the loss of Truck α, and B agreed to wait for a while. Although A looked for the Truck α, finally it did not appear at all. Then, at around 20:00, A called B again and told B that he could not get to the warehouse for the delivery on the scheduled day and said that he would call B once again the next morning to talk about the rescheduling details.

5. B, upon A's notice via telephone, told C, who had been preparing for the delivery in the Warehouse β, that he may get off work. Since there had been a spate of robberies carried out across the neighboring area that people also knew via police warnings, B also directed C to make sure to lock the Ware-

house β firmly than they used to, as the warehouse kept valuable products to be delivered to customers. The Warehouse β, which usually only had an easy simple lock, was then double-locked by C with strong keys under the instruction of B.

6. At around 7:00 on September 22nd, A called B to tell him that an alternative vehicle was hired and A was willing to receive mushroom at the Warehouse β at around 10:00. B was at home letting C work on morning tasks in the Warehouse β, so A would stop by B's to pick him up and leave for the Warehouse β together.

7. A and B arrived at the Warehouse β at about 10:00. A brought JPY 500,000 to pay B for the mushrooms. However, they found the door of the Warehouse β left opened and unlocked, and harvested products that should have been kept inside the warehouse were gone.

8. Upon police investigation, it was identified that C forgot about the instruction given by B at the night of September 21st to double-lock the Warehouse β (see [Fact] 5). At around 7:00, C entered the Warehouse β to take some harvesting tools out, and left locking the door only with the simple easy key they used to apply. While C left the Warehouse β and before A and B arrived there, someone seemed to have broken into the warehouse and taken mushrooms, apples, and all other products away.

9. After a while, B requested A to pay JPY 500,000 for the Sale and Purchase Contract, however, A responded that A would refuse to make the payment until the completion of the delivery of 5 kg mushroom. B claimed that A should make the payment because B had once prepared mushrooms accordingly.

[Question 1]
Assuming the [Fact] 1 to [Fact]14, explain the reasons whether A's claim for payment based on the contract of sale is justifiable.

II Facts

In addition to [Fact] to [Fact] 9 as above, there were also [Fact] 10 to [Fact] 14 below:

10. A obtained the Truck α under the following circumstances. On November 9, 2015, A and D entered into a sale and purchase agreement for A's purchase of a used truck, the Truck α, from its owner D, to which Article 5 Clause 1 of the Road Transport Vehicle Act (the relevant article is mentioned below) shall apply, for JPY 300 million. Under the agreement, it was set forth as follows:

(1) A shall make payment of JPY 600,000 in cash upon delivery of the Truck α, and for 60 months thereafter, A shall pay JPY 40,000 every month to the bank account as designated by D;

(2) The ownership of the Truck α shall be withheld for retention by D until the completion of A's payment in accordance with (1) above, and the automobile registration title shall be transferred from D to A upon completion of all payment obligation by A;

(3) In the event that A failed to make any payment subject to the schedules stated as (1) above, A shall necessarily lose the benefit of time and D may immediately claim for return of the Truck α;

(4) A, upon delivery of the Truck α, may possess and use the vehicle, provided however that A shall keep the Truck α with the care of a good manager and may not make any alteration on the vehicle until the completion of all payment obligation;

(5) In the event that D has returned the Truck α from A in case of (3) above, D may sell the Truck α to a used-car distributor and appropriate the sales amount received therefrom to the satisfaction of D's claim against A's payment obligation;

(6) If any excess amount of money remained after the above sale of Truck α for D's satisfaction, D shall pay such excess amount to A.

On the same day, A made the advance payment of JPY 600,000 and D delivered the Truck α to A.

11. On and after December 2015, A has made a payment of JPY 40,000 every month without any delays to D's designated bank account.

12. After the loss of the Truck α (see Facts 4), A, although hired a car and kept doing his business for a while, eventually decided to close his business and move back to his home town. On December 22, 2017, A moved out of the rented house where he had lived in. A submitted notice of the closure of business to clients, including B, but did not inform them of his new address.

13. On February 20, 2018, E found the Truck α dumped in the middle of his land, the Land γ (forest). Then he came to know that the Truck α was registered under the name of D.

14. On March 10, E told D about the dumped Truck α on the Land γ and requested D for its removal. However, D refused and responded, (I) "I should not be in the position to remove the Truck α because I signed 'the sale and purchase agreement with reservation right to ownership' by and between A, and therefore A should be in the position to remove the vehicle," and (II) "I should not be requested to remove the vehicle merely because of the fact that I still reserve the registration title." E asked D about A's whereabouts, but D said he did not know. Moreover, according to D, D and A had not been in contact with each other since the payment of JPY 40,000 had been duly performed each month to D's bank account without any delays, although D received a notice from A on September 22, 2017 referring to the loss of the Truck α and the submission of the loss report to the police. At this point, E still could not identify A's whereabouts.

[Question 2]

Assuming [Fact] 1 to [Fact] 14, answer the following (1) and (2).

(1) As to the claim for removal from E of [Fact] 14, is D's underlined statement in [Fact] 14 (a) justifiable? Explain with reasons.

(2) If D's underlined statement in [Fact] 14 (a) is justifiable, can E's request

for the removal be approved? Explain with reasons, assuming D's underlined statement in [Fact] 14 (b).

[Reference]
Road Transport Vehicle Act (Law No. 185, 1951)
Article 15 (1) Acquisition and loss of ownership to the registered automobiles cannot be asserted to a third party without its registration.
(2) ... [Omitted.]

III Facts
In addition to [Fact] 1 to [Fact] 14, there were also [Fact] 15 to [Fact] 20.

15. C, whose wife died a few years ago, passed away due to a prolonged chronic disease.

16. C left assets of JPY 12,000,000, JPY 6,000,000, and JPY 2,000,000 each as time deposits. C had three children, F, G, and H. H had been ruled for disinheritance in 2015 as a result of C's petition at the family court.

17. When they gathered at the pre-funeral ceremony on January 21, 2018, they found out that C had JPY 3,000,000 debts to B, due on January 31, 2018.

18. F, upon strong request from B to make repayment for C's debts, paid JPY 3,000,000 to B on January 31.

19. On March 1, 2018, they found C's autographed will in a due form as of January 1, 2018 (herein after referred to as "Will"), and the probation process was proceeded on May 7.

20. It was stated in the Will as follows: "(1) Assets I leave are the time deposits of JPY 12,000,000, JPY 6,000,000 and JPY 2,000,000; (2) for F, who always cared me far from home, I leave JPY 12,000,000, which is greater amount than those for G; (3) for G, I leave JPY 6,000,000 time deposits, and (4) for H, I would not change my intention of disinheritance because he still needs some reflection but I leave JPY 2,000,000 time deposits as he recently got married, which is the only thing I leave for H."

[Question 3]

Assuming [Fact] 1 to [Fact] 20, answer the following questions.

How much amount of money can F request G to pay, based on the fact that F paid all debts of JPY 3,000,000 that C had owed B? Explain, with reasons, the interpretation of the Will. For clarification, you do not need to take into consideration on any interests and damages caused by delay.

[Question] 1 asks about the interpretation of the rules on the risk allocation in the case of non-performance of a contract of sale, which cannot be attributed to both the parties (Art. 536 (1), 567 (1) JCC).

[Question 2] asks about the responsibility of the owner (A) who sold the property (a Truck α in this case) to the purchaser (D) with the agreement that ownership of the property and the title in the registration book shall be retained by the seller (A) until the full payment of the purchase money is completed, even though the purchaser (D) can use the property.

[Question 3] asks about the interpretation of the Will which stipulates only the distribution of the remaining assets (monetary claim for bank account), but nothing was mentioned about the debt.

As for the balance of fields in the questions, [Question 1] is concerned with the law of obligation, [Question 2] with the law of property, and [Question 3] with the law of succession.

The result is announced around the middle of September every year. In September 2018, the number of passers of the NLE was 1,525 (375 of whom were women) out of 5,238 who took the examination. The passing rate was 29.1 % and the percentage of women and successful applicants was 24.6%. The latest score of the passers was 805 and the best score was 1197.79[36].

---

[36] See the Home Page of the Ministry of Legal Affairs <http://www.moj.go.jp/content/001269384.pdf>.

4. At the Legal Training and Research Institute

4.1 Teaching Program

The passers of the NLE are eligible to enter into the Legal Training and Research Institute (LTRI)[37]. The legal education in the LTRI is the final stage of the legal education program for legal professions in Japan. The total period of training was originally two years, but it was shortened to one year and a half from 1999 onwards, and further shortened to one year from 2006 onwards. The training starts from the end of November. The major focus of the program is put on practical training, mainly at court, prosecutors' offices, lawyers' offices, and the LTRI itself. The teaching program of the LTRI is a combination of the internship curriculum called "field practical training" for 10 months and lecture-based classroom instruction called "collective training" for 2 months.

The field practical training is divided into the required field training and the selective field training. The required field training is conducted in a district court (for 2 months on civil litigation training and for 2 months on criminal litigation training), a district prosecutors office (for 2 months on prosecution training), and a lawyer's office (for 2 months on defense activity). After that, the selective field training (for 2 months) shall be arranged by courts, prosecutors' offices, or bar associations in accordance with the interests of the trainees.

The collective training is held at the LTRI for 2 months by dividing the trainees into small classes. The curriculum is divided into five subjects: [1] civil litigation, [2] civil defense, [3] criminal litigation, [4] criminal defense, and [5] prosecution. The focus is placed on the practical documentation of the decision, the prosecution, and the defense. The materials are based on the actual cases so that the theory and the practice of fact-finding are most important components of the curriculum. However, civil law-related programs are included as a part of the major components both in the field training and in the collective training periods.

---

[37] As for the current activities of the LTRI, see <http://www.courts.go.jp/english/institute_01/index.html>.

4.2 Examination and Evaluation

At the end of the training programs, the trainees have to pass the final examination. It consists of those five subjects as civil litigation, civil defense, criminal litigation. criminal defense, and prosecution. In 2017, 16 trainees failed the examination to finalize the legal education process[38].

5. Conclusion

As can clearly be seen from all of the above, the key features of civil law education in Japan can be summarized as: it starts from the undergraduate level then continues through the law school curriculum, and ends in the LTRI program by gradually shifting the attention from the interpretation of the law to the identification of the crucial facts in each case.

Civil law education in Japan, however, is still undergoing development and will need continuous reform so as to fulfill its ultimate role as "the real school of the political education of the people"[39]. The central point seems to be the reform of the comprehensive legal education process by reshaping it so that there is a more streamlined linkage of the undergraduate level, the law school level, the LTRI level, and finally, the wider dissemination of basic legal concepts for students under the high school level, and moreover the ordinary citizen. This linkage must be the key to make civil law a more "inclusive institution"[40], which is the prerequisite for civil law education to be "the political education of the people".

Special emphasis can be placed on the reform of law school processes, which are situated between the legal education at the undergraduate level and that at the

---

[38] See the Home Page of the Court <http://www.courts.go.jp/saikosai/sihokensyujo/kousi_kekka_71/index.html>.

[39] See footnote 1 above.

[40] As for the ideal of a legal system as "inclusive institution", see Sustainable Development Goal 16 <https://sustainabledevelopment.un.org/sdg16>.

LTRI. Students in law schools tend to focus more narrowly on the preparation for passing the NLE rather than on deepening their ability to interpret the law and extend their intellectual horizons toward acquiring new knowledge of the legal practices that are developing within the context of globalization[41]. The cost of expensive fees and tight schedules in law schools urge students to minimize their attention to the technical memory of the patterns required to answer the typical questions rather than to maximize their ability to solve the questions which are neither provided by law, nor stipulated in precedents. However, one may argue that this maximization is best left to practicing legal professionals with real-world experience and that students of law should focus on creating the most solid intellectual and pragmatic foundation possible. Either way, we should seek to encourage the creation of legal professionals with a desire to develop beyond the narrow confines of what is patterned in a streotyped way as per their initial trainings.

In this problematic context, it seems to be important to consider again how to teach civil law in such a way that students can learn how to find the relevant facts from the parties' arguments and how to interpret the most concerned provisions of substantive law by always linking them in a systematic framework of the most fundamental legal thought originated in private law.

The promotion of comparative study of teaching civil law will prove that there are various patterns of the linkage between civil law education at undergraduate level and postgraduate level in universities and that in professional training organizations, and the education of civil law for citizens. It must be the key to make civil law more inclusive so that it can be "the real school of the political education of the people".

---

[41] Noboru Kashiwagi, "Creation of Japanese law schools and their current development", in: Stacey Steele and Kathryn Taylor (eds.), *Legal Education in Asia: Globalization, change and contexts*, Routledge, 2010, pp. 192–194.

Chapter 2

TEACHING CIVIL LAW IN THAILAND:

A Case Study of Thammasat University

Munin Pongsapan*
Junavit Chalidabhongse**
Viravat Chantachote***

(Thammasat University)

1. Introduction

The Association of South East Asian Nations (ASEAN) Economic Community (AEC), set to commence in 2015, has presented Thammasat University with an opportunity to take a leading role once more in devising educational innovation to meet social, political, and economic challenges it has brought to Thailand. From its founding, the University has been a main player in the legal education system that began formally when the Law School of the Ministry of Justice was established in 1897, a major step forward for the country, which was in urgent need of a modern legal system to end Western powers' consular jurisdiction and to escape colonization. The curriculum and styles of instruction were overwhelmingly influenced by English jurisprudence, but this early dominance of Thai legal education contrasted with the government's policy of adopting European codification as the country's legal model.

---

* Assistant Professor, Faculty of Law, Thammasat University.
** Lecturer of Law, Faculty of Law, Thammasat University.
*** Adjunct Assistant Professor, Faculty of Law, Thammasat University.

Not until the founding of Thammasat University in 1934 did legal education shift from English to French orientation. Monopolizing Thai legal education for more than 35 years, Thammasat University provided the template for subsequently established Thai law schools. Its curriculum was even adopted by the Institute of Legal Education of the Thai Bar, established in 1948, mainly to provide vocational legal training in the same fashion as English Inns of Court. However, in a stark diversion from its original purpose, the Institute seems to have repeated what had already happened at law school: it emphasized expounding judicial application of legal rules rather than producing practical lawyers. The absence of a government agency to regulate legal education in Thailand meant that the Thai Bar effectively directed its development by exercising regulatory authority over qualifications of prospective judges and public prosecutors. Strict academic requirements for law graduates who wish to be barristers, judges, and public prosecutors seem to leave no room for innovation. It is a true challenge for Thai law schools to overtake legal education's global development and successfully to a changing society.

2. Thammasat University's Monopoly on Legal Education

The Siamese Revolution of 1932 marked a crucial turning point in 20th-century Thai history. The architect of the revolution Pridi Banomyong, along with a group of young military commanders and civilians, successfully forced King Prachadhipok to adopt a new political regime: constitutional monarchy. The revolutionaries announced an ambitious plan to make education available to all citizens, ending higher education's monopoly by Chulalongkorn University, the country's first university, which had admitted fewer than 100 students a year.

Thammasat University's establishment as an open university in 1934 was the revolutionaries' main strategy for promoting democracy and the rule of law and for renewing legal education in Thailand. In 1933, the government abolished the Law School of the Ministry of Justice and established the Faculty of Law and

Political Science at Chulalongkorn University to assume responsibility for providing legal education.[1] Nevertheless, in 1934, on Pridi's initiative, Thammasat University[2] was founded, and it took over Chulalongkorn University's Faculty of Law and Political Science.[3] In its first academic year, Thammasat University admitted more than 7000 students. Pridi became the University's first President and exerted profound influence over its management and administration of education.[4] Thammasat University's curriculum of legal studies was considerably remodeled to accord with the civil law system, especially with French law.[5] As a result, English common law's influence in Thailand faded, despite many Thammasat law professors being judges educated in England or students of English law. French law eventually replaced English law as the predominant foreign jurisprudence in Thailand. By 1987, France was the most popular destination for higher legal education among Thammasat law academics.

Until 1971, Thammasat University was virtually the only Thai university offering law degrees[6] and had only one undergraduate degree, titled Thammasat Bundit, that focused on legal studies. Compulsory undergraduate courses consisted of Introduction to Law, Administration of Courts, Constitutional Law, Electoral Law, Administrative Law, Criminal Law, Civil and Commercial Law,

---

[1] Prasit Kowilaikul, 'การศึกษากฎหมายในคณะนิติศาสตร์ จุฬาลงกรณ์มหาวิทยาลัย (Legal Education in Chulalongkorn University Faculty of Law)' in *100 ปี โรงเรียนกฎหมาย* (A Hundred Years of the Thai Law School) (Institute of Legal Education of The Thai Bar 1999) 130.

[2] The original name of Thammasat University (มหาวิทยาลัยธรรมศาสตร์) is the University of Moral and Political Science (มหาวิทยาลัยวิชาธรรมศาสตร์และการเมือง). The name was changed by the military government after a *coup d'état* in 1947.

[3] Thammasat University Act B.E.1934, Section 5.

[4] Sawaengsak, *French Influence* 136. See also Charnvit Kasetsiri, 'ปรีดี พนมยงค์กับมหาวิทยาลัยธรรมศาสตร์และการเมือง (Pridi Banomyong and the University of Moral and Political Sciences)' in Thamrongsak Petchlertanan (ed) *ปรีดี ป๋วย กับธรรมศาสตร์และการเมือง* (Pridi and Puey and the University of Moral and Political Sciences) (Thammasat University Archive 2006) 10–30.

[5] Thammasat University, *แนวทางการศึกษาชั้นปริญญาตรี โท และเอก ของ มหาวิทยาลัยวิชาธรรมศาสตร์และการเมือง* (Bachelor Master and Doctoral Programmes of Thammasat University) (Sri Krung 1934) 1–69.

[6] Ramkhamhaeng University was established in 1971 with a law degree offered, and in 1972 Chulalongkorn University successfully established a law faculty.

Public International Law, Private International Law, International Criminal Law, Civil Procedure Law, Criminal Procedure Law, Bankruptcy Law, Evidence Law, Economic Theories, Economics, Public Finance Law, and Law of Government Organization. The university also offered postgraduate degrees in law, political science, economics, and international relations.[7] The integrated undergraduate degree program became popular among young progressive Thais and was successful in producing well-rounded men and women to serve the government. However, Thammasat University's popularity and success later proved a threat to the military government that came into power in 1947. To weaken its academic strength, the government took control of the university's administration and reformed the curriculum. Four faculties, the Faculty of Law, of Commerce and Accountancy, of Political Science, and of Economics, were founded, each operating individual undergraduate and postgraduate programs. Thus did the integrated undergraduate degree come to an end.

The curriculum reform of 1949 significantly increased the number of compulsory courses and laid foundations for later curriculums. The undergraduate program was structured around four academic years. From years one to three, students enrolled in nine to ten compulsory law courses and in the final undergraduate year, five compulsory courses.[8] In 1962, the Faculty of Liberal Arts was

---

[7] Thammasat University Act B.E. 2476.

[8] The courses offered in year one are: (1) Introduction to Law, (2) Administrative Law, (3) Economics, (4) Constitutional Law and Electoral Law, (5) Public International Law, (6) Legal History, (7) Criminal Law I, (8) Law on Persons, and (9) Property Law. The courses offered in year two are: (1) Criminal Law II, (2) Juridical Acts and Contract Law, (3) Obligations, Tort, and Unjust Enrichment, (4) Sales, Exchanges, and Gifts, (5) Securities Law, (6) Loans and Deposit, etc., (7) Leases and Hire Purchase, etc., (8) Family Law, (9) Private International Law, and (10) Land Law and Law on Natural Resources. The courses offered in year three are: (1) Criminal Law III, (2) Bills of Notes and Insurance Law, (3) Company Law, (4) Law on Agency, (5) Law on Succession, (6) Administration of Courts, (7) Criminal Procedure Law, (8) Civil Procedure Law and Bankruptcy Law, and (9) Law on Evidence. The courses offered in year four are: (1) Comprehensive Criminal Law, (2) Comprehensive Civil Law, (3) Comprehensive Criminal Procedure Law, (4) Comprehensive Civil Procedure Law, and (5) Judiciary Act, Public Prosecutor Act, and Lawyer Act.

founded at Thammasat University, which shortly afterwards required all students from any faculty to spend their first 2 years studying general courses offered by the newly established faculty. However, this requirement was sharply criticized for forcing law students to waste their time on non-law courses. In 1966, the university decided to reduce general studies' length to one year. During their first year, students would devote their time to liberal arts and begin studying law in their second year. Some minor changes were introduced, but the structure of the law undergraduate curriculum remains largely intact.[9] In terms of credit points, Thammasat University's 4-year undergraduate program in law is intense. Completing the degree requires students to earn 30 credits from general courses during the first year, 92 credits from compulsory law courses, and 24 credits from elective courses. Courses are usually worth three credits, each accounting for one instructional hour a week. For a three-credit course, the lecturer is therefore required to teach 3 hours per week for 15 to 16 weeks.

As the country's oldest continuously operating law faculty, Thammasat University's Faculty of Law has become a model for subsequently established Thai law schools. In particular, its undergraduate curriculum became the blueprint for others, and the Thai Bar recognized it as the standard Bachelor of Law qualification for those who wished to become a barrister. Any LL.B. degree accredited by the Thai Bar must resemble the Thammasat model.[10] Therefore, the similarity of law undergraduate curriculums in Thailand is not surprising. In their first year, Thai law students focus on general courses before being required to take an excessive number of law courses for another 3 years.

Despite being the pioneer of legal education in Thailand, Thammasat University seems to have lost its leadership in educational innovation. Even though to respond to social, economic, and educational changes, many new elective courses have been added to its Bachelor of Law curriculum, its structure and compul-

---

[9] Kietkajorn Vachanasvasti, 'การศึกษากฎหมายในมหาวิทยาลัยธรรมศาสตร์' (Legal Education in Thammasat University) in 100 ปี โรงเรียนกฎหมาย (A Hundred Years of the Thai Law School) (Institute of Legal Education of The Thai Bar 1999) 145.

[10] Regulations of the Thai Bar B.E. 2507, Article 5.

sory courses remain nearly the same. Until recently, no major innovations had been introduced. Thammasat University transformed from an innovative leader into a follower of new, prominent players in legal education's development: the Thai Bar, the Institute of Legal Education of the Thai Bar, and the Judicial Committee.

3. The Dominant Role of the Thai Bar, the Institute of Legal Education of the Thai Bar, and the Judicial Committee in Reshaping Legal Education in Thailand

As an organization, the Thai Bar was founded 17 years after establishment of the Law School of the Ministry of Justice. However, the "barrister qualification" can be traced to the Law School's early days when students who passed the Law School's final examinations would become barristers. They could then begin their legal careers. Even though no regulation of the legal profession existed, judicial positions were usually filled by those who held legal qualifications, either domestic or foreign. When it was established in 1914, the Thai Bar intended to administer legal education and exercise regulatory controls of lawyers' ethics. In fact, the Thai Bar's involvement in administration of legal education was limited to law school admission. The Law School of the Ministry of Justice had its own management, which had full control of its academic and administrative affairs.[11] However, the management team was normally composed of senior judges who were usually concurrent members of the Council of the Thai Bar. The Council, as the bar's governing body, has always been dominated by the judiciary. The President of the Supreme Court is the ex officio President of the Council of the Thai Bar.

The Thai Bar began to play a more active role in legal education after it

---

[11] Thai Bar, *80 ปี เนติบัณฑิตยสภา 1 มกราคม 2538* (80th Anniversary of the Thai Bar, 1 January 1995) (Amarin Printing 1995) 106.

established its educational arm, the Institute of Legal Education, in 1948. The Institute was originally intended to provide practical training for law graduates, mainly from Thammasat University, the successor of the Law School of the Ministry of Justice, and to administer bar examinations. This move met with protest from the university's students, who were, before 1952, automatically qualified as barristers upon graduation.[12] The Institute of Legal Education's establishment ensured that all Thai barristers had passed a one-year training program and bar examinations. However, in a stark diversion from its original purpose, the Institute's one-year training program turned into a repetition of what had already happened at law school. Most courses in the undergraduate program are taught again at the Institute by lecturers, most of whom are senior judges, with emphasis on expounding judicial application of legal rules. After one year of studying substantive law in the first semester and procedural law in the second semester, students must take examinations divided into four parts: civil law, criminal law, civil procedure, and criminal procedure. Substantive law parts are tested after the first semester, and procedural law after the second. In short, in Thailand, bar examinations mainly test theoretical knowledge acquired at law school and understanding of the Supreme Court judges' application of legal rules.

With the focus on theoretical knowledge rather than practical experience, being a barrister in Thailand is not a permit to practice law. Instead, it merely qualifies the holder for the judge and public prosecutor's examinations. Law graduates who wish to practice law, especially to represent clients in court, need a lawyer license issued by a separate professional body, the Lawyers Council. To obtain a lawyer license, a law graduate needs to have a year of apprenticeship and pass a written examination on practical skills. To be a legal consultant, no specific qualification is required. Even a law student can give legal advice. The Lawyer Act only prohibits anyone without a lawyer license from involvement in civil and criminal procedures.[13]

---

[12] Luang Saranaiprasas, *Development of Legal Education* 105.

[13] Lawyer Act B.E. 2528, Section 33.

Because the Thai Bar's curriculum and examination format have become fixed and nearly unchanging, Thai law schools are reluctant to depart from their accredited undergraduate programs. Any major change in curriculum risks losing the Thai Bar's recognition. Even at Thammasat University Faculty of Law, which produced the Thai Bar's accreditation standard, attempts to introduce major reforms to the Bachelor of Law curriculum, for example, reduction of study from 4 to 3 years and creation of the 5-year-bachelor-plus-master of law program, failed. The main reason was faculty members' concern that the Thai Bar and the Judicial Committee would not accept the changes.[14]

Despite having no direct role in legal education, the Judicial Committee's regulatory controls on judges' recruitment have profoundly impacted the direction of its development. Given that many Thais perceive the judicial as the most respected, most secure, and best paid legal career and that most law students dream of a judicial career, any Judicial Committee move in relation to prospective judges' academic qualification is watched closely by university educators. Judges are selected mainly by written examinations. An interview is also conducted, but failure at that stage is rare. A judge's entire career is largely determined by his or her performance in the written and oral examinations. A candidate younger than others of the same class[15] and ranking first in judge examinations will become the President of the Supreme Court if he or she behaves well and is mentally and physically in good health. The rank of judges of the same class must strictly accord with their examination performance.[16] Some see this selection system as the most appropriate for a country that has long strug-

---

[14] The Judicial Committee is the governing body of the Court of Justice, the country's main judicial system that deals with all kind of disputes, except constitutional and administrative cases that fall under the Constitutional Court and the administrative courts' jurisdictions. The Judicial Committee is ex-officio chaired by the President of the Supreme Court and comprised of 12 other senior judges elected by their peers and two non-judge members selected by the Senate. The Committee has charge of regulating recruitment, promotion, and punishment of judges.

[15] The minimum age for being a judge is 25 years old.

[16] Judicial Administration of the Court of Justice Act B.E.2543, Section 31.

gled against corruption.

Thirty years previously, the academic requirement for a judge was mainly a bachelor's degree in law and the bar qualification. Some practical experience was also required, but candidates and even the selection committee itself did not take this seriously because candidates were mainly tested on their theoretical knowledge of various law subjects taught at the Institute of Legal Education of the Thai Bar. The Court of Justice subsequently realized that they needed judges with specialized knowledge of law, and so created a special selection track. Besides normal requirements, this new track asked for a domestic master of law degree from at least a 2-year program. This new opportunity led to increased popularity of domestic master of law programs. Some years later, the Judicial Committee had to respond to the growing demand for judges who were proficient in English and who had mastered foreign laws by launching another selection track for those who held a bachelor's degree in law from a program of study that lasted at least 3 years or held one or two master's degrees in law, with at least 2 years of total study, from a foreign country. This special track's invention saw a sharp increase in the number of law graduates who went abroad to pursue two master of law degrees because doing so was the least competitive compared the other two tracks, and, during the early years, candidates' success rate was more than 90 percent.

Creation of the two special selection tracks was initially seen as a stimulus to legal education's development. Later, however, it proved rather a barrier to innovation. On the surface, it seems a good idea to have judges who specialize in new areas of law, such as intellectual property, international commercial law, environmental law, and tax law, or those who have mastered foreign laws. And this would also arouse law students' interest in emerging legal disciplines and encourage law schools to open new, specialized programs of study. In fact, what distinguishes foreign-degree, domestic-master-of-law, and bachelor-of-law tracks is the number of English language examination questions.

Those who hold a master's degree in law are not tested specifically on their specialized legal knowledge. Candidates for all three main tracks are tested on their theoretical knowledge of the same core subjects of law: civil and commercial law, criminal law, civil procedure, criminal procedure, law of evidence, and the English language. Applicants of the foreign-degree track are required to choose one more question on administration of courts of justice, law concerning municipal courts and their procedure, constitutional law, law concerning juvenile and family courts and their procedure, intellectual property law, tax law, labor law, bankruptcy law, international commercial law, or consumer protection procedure; applicants for the bachelor-of-law and domestic master-of-law tracks have more compulsory questions on the subjects previously mentioned.[17]

Two dividing lines between the three main types of judge examinations are the number of questions on compulsory law subjects and on the English language. Applicants for the bachelor-of-law track have 28 questions, including one question on the language, each of which counts 10 points. The number of questions for applicants of the domestic master-of-law track decreases to 17, including two compulsory questions on the English language. They can, however, choose one more question on language instead of on a law subject. In total, the language test comprises up to 30 of 170 points. By comparison, applicants for the foreign-degree track can benefit most from their English proficiency because its three compulsory English questions account for 60 of 170 points. This English language test concerns translation of legal passages from Thai to English and *vice versa* and analysis of a problem-solving question. In all three tracks, candidates must earn 50 percent of total points to pass the written examination. The oral examination, although scored, is rather ceremonial. Rarely does a candidate who passes the written examination fail the interview.

True, the foreign-degree track encourages hundreds of law graduates to study abroad each year, especially in English-speaking countries or in postgraduate programs taught in English. Unfortunately, what they learn from foreign legal systems is largely irrelevant to judges' examinations that focus more on

---

[17] See Judicial Committee's Regulations on the Application, Selection, and Examination of Judge-Trainees Act B.E. 2558, Sections 11, 25, and 28.

their English writing skills. This situation can be seen as a wasted opportunity to recruit a genuine expert on foreign law or on a specialized area of law. An even more undesirable outcome is that the system creates hunger for degrees rather than for knowledge. However, the most controversial outcome is the concern, held by many, about inequality between the poor and the rich who can afford two foreign master of law degrees.

The domestic master of law selection examination is also highly controversial and has been producing detrimental effects on administration and development of postgraduate programs in law. The existence of this examination system significantly increases the number of students in master of law programs in many Thai law schools. Despite recognition of different specialized programs, the Judicial Committee imposes a minimum academic requirement that the applicant must pass certain basic courses, for example, civil and commercial law, criminal law, and procedural law. This makes students focus their attention on passing required law courses rather than on building genuine interest in a particular area of law. It is normal for law schools to divide their master of law program into various specialized areas. At Thammasat University Faculty of Law, the master of law program splits into eight specialized programs: civil law, commercial law, criminal law, public law, international law, tax law, international commercial law, and environmental law. Each specialized program requires students to take five core courses and to choose three elective courses. A long list of available elective courses for each specialized program is offered, but most students choose courses enabling them to apply for judge examinations. As a result, each specialized program's elective courses are mostly ignored by its own students. Attempts to limit students' choices of elective courses to those offered by their specialized program have always failed since many feared that this would result in a significant drop in the number of applicants.

Regardless of differences in educational backgrounds, all applicants of the same selection track have the same questions on the same subjects of law. Therefore, it is reasonable to believe that the Judicial Committee's regulations on judge examinations do not encourage diversification and specialization in legal education and actually discourage any introduction of innovation to the accredited degree program. Understandably, law schools are reluctant to change their master of law curriculum for fear of losing accreditation from the Judicial Committee and most of their prospective students who wish to be a judge or a public prosecutor.[18]

4. Law Degree Programs Entirely in English: Innovative Experiments

With Thailand's ever increasing levels of global economic interdependence propelled by international trade and investment, English is becoming the common language adopted to communicate internationally. English has played an important role in assisting ASEAN Member States to fulfill their AEC aspirations. The prospect of Thailand's domestic business landscape shifting toward a regional or international orientation based on the AEC raises concerns that language may be a trade barrier for Thai business lawyers. For Thai legal practitioners preparing to catch the ASEAN wave, quality legal education grounded in international business law and English may be the best asset available. More than 15 years ago, Chulalongkorn University Faculty of Law successfully launched a master of law program in business law, taught fully in English, in collaboration with a number of foreign law schools. In 2009, Thammasat University Faculty of Law followed suit; the 2-year Master of Laws Program in Business Law (English Program) was established.

To run a postgraduate program taught in English, administrators have faced two major challenges: the number of applicants and compatibility with academic requirements of the judge and public prosecutor examinations. A high number of Thai law graduates go abroad each year to pursue legal education at the postgraduate level. It is challenging to persuade prospective students to enter a 2-year

---

[18] Selections systems for public prosecutors resemble those of the judiciary.

domestic postgraduate program taught in English when, for the same amount of time, they can complete two master of law degrees abroad and may subsequently be eligible for foreign-degree judge examinations. In 2015, the number of students in Chulalongkorn and Thammasat Universities' English-taught master of law programs *combined* was less than 25 percent of the number of students who went abroad for postgraduate degrees.[19] Administering the curriculum is even more challenging, that is, avoiding the effect of the Judicial Committee's academic requirements for judge examinations. Even though the business law program was originally designed to prepare students to become practitioners in law firms rather than judges or public prosecutors, most students prefer to have all career opportunities available to them, including eligibility for these two most popular legal careers. This forces the law school to distort its curriculum to serve the popular need and to be compatible with the Judicial Committee's academic requirements. For example, Thammasat University's English-taught Master of Laws Program in Business Law requires students to pass eight law courses, four compulsory and four elective, before they can enroll for a dissertation. Two non-business law courses, criminal law, and procedural law, are included as available courses since they are among subjects that the Judicial Committee requires of applicants for the domestic master of law track for judge examinations. Each year, the majority of the class enrolled in these two elective courses. Their popularity, however, came at the expense of some interesting elective business law courses that did not enroll enough students to open.

Since the ASEAN Economic Community became an imminent reality, there has been a pressing need for Thai lawyers to practice Thai law in English locally, regionally, and internationally. Thailand's two existing English-taught master of law programs are helpful, but do not satisfy the growing demand. Thammasat University Faculty of Law spent at least 2 years preparing a proper response.

---

[19] In 2015, Chulongkorn University admitted fewer than 10 students to its English-taught Master of Law Program in Business Law, while Thammasat University's similar program had around 30 students. In the same year, the estimated number of law graduates who went abroad for postgraduate degrees was 200.

In 2014, it launched a new 4-year undergraduate program titled the Bachelor of Laws Program in Business Law (International Program), aiming mainly to fulfill lawyers' needs to cope with increasingly complex commercial disputes in rapidly growing economies, especially in Asia, and to practice in English-speaking environments. This program is Thailand's only bachelor of law program entirely in English.[20] In what must be seen as one of the most innovative experiments in Thai legal education, Thai law is, for the first time, the subject of learning in a foreign-language environment at the undergraduate level. This presents an immense challenge for the legal education system in a country where English is not an official language and where English publication on its law is rare.

Since this new undergraduate program aims to produce legal practitioners for private entities and regional and international organizations, rather than judges and public prosecutors, program administrators can largely avoid pressure from students' strong desire for judicial careers. The program's main target is students who go to domestic and overseas schools that teach in English. These students have relatively high English proficiency and more interest in business than in public careers including that of judges and public prosecutors. In 2014 and 2015, the majority of admitted students graduated from English language high schools, and, according to an internal survey, the majority preferred to be legal consultants and business owners. Despite this, the most frequently asked question from prospective students' parents is whether the Thai Bar and the Judicial Committee have accredited the program. Making the program compatible with academic requirements of judge and public prosecutor examinations seems inevitable. However, unlike master of law programs, the Thai Bar and the Judicial Committee do not look into specific details of law courses offered in the program. In fact, they examine the program holistically, using existing recognized bachelor of law programs as a frame of reference.[21] This allows program administrators flexibility in designing and operating the undergraduate curriculum.

---

[20] For more information about the program, please visit http://interllb.law.tu.ac.th/.

[21] See Regulations of the Thai Bar B.E. 2507, Section 56.

As administrators of Thammasat University's Bachelor of Laws Program in Business Law (International Program), the authors have observed the program's development from its beginning. Although it was launched only in August 2014, the course environment is already thriving, thanks to a huge collaborative effort between the Faculty of Law at Thammasat University and a number of foreign institutions. It is the first program of its kind in Thailand, the only international undergraduate program in law in the country, teaching Thai law in English at the undergraduate level. The authors are satisfied with the program's development and offer its self-evaluation in four areas.

First, we already see significant improvement in our students' abilities to interpret Thai law in English, even during their first year. Becoming familiar with Thai law in English, while at the same time understanding correct terminology in Thai, is challenging. However, our students are rising to this challenge and taking advantage of opportunities offered by lectures and tutorials in English, together with additional classes to ensure they have the correct Thai terminology. They are already demonstrating progress in their skills and clearly have the potential to excel in whatever avenue they choose to pursue. Secondly, the authors are satisfied that our students are already taking advantage of all extra-curricular activities open to them as members of the student community at Thammasat University. Even though in some ways, it feels like our students have just arrived, they have quickly become heavily involved in all kinds of activities, including various sporting events, the Asian Law Student Association (ALSA), the Pro Bono Club in collaboration with the National University of Singapore's Pro Bono Group, and a number of international moot court competitions. The program encourages students to engage in these activities, not just to expand their experience, but also to help them develop highly valued skills, whatever their careers. Thirdly, we are so fortunate as to have been visited by renowned guest lecturers from academic institutions all over the world, who have given presentations on a wide range of topics. These guest lectures are a useful resource for students, providing broader perspectives and inspiring global views. Finally, the program is in advanced discussions relating to exchange schemes with a large number of internationally renowned foreign academic institutions. An excellent opportunity, these schemes will allow students to spend one year, in most cases, the fourth, overseas, reading law in, for example, the United Kingdom, the United States, or elsewhere. We have also received exchange students from foreign law schools—a welcome addition to the program's already international atmosphere.

5. Teaching Civil Law at Thammasat University

For the undergraduate level, most civil law courses, for example, contract law, obligations law, tort law, property law, family law, and succession law, are compulsory; that is, all students must enroll in them. For a civil law course, class size is relatively large, ranging from 100 to 400 students depending on how many sections the course has. Thus, the civil law course is normally lecture-based. Discussions occur, but do not usually take much time. At the beginning of the semester, students receive a course syllabus and a reading list to prepare them for lectures. In the Thai-language LL.B. program, students are assigned and recommended to read Thai-language texts and materials. Although instructors frequently include English-language materials, they are not main texts, and only a few students read the foreign materials. In the English-language LL.B. program, instructors cannot require students to study materials in Thai. Most recommended texts and materials are in English. Due to a limited amount of English-language materials on civil law, in practice, students also consult abundant Thai-language materials.

Assessment modes for compulsory civil law courses are one final examination that requires students to write essays on five questions, mostly problem-based, within 3 hours. However, in the English-taught LL.B. program, in addition to the final, students have a mid-term examination or assignment.

For elective courses, class size is relatively small, usually 20 to 50 students. A small class allows the instructor to employ a seminar-based method. The degree of interaction between instructors and students and among students themselves is relatively high. Modes of assessment can vary, and normal practice includes instructors encouraging students to be more critical of materials. They should be able to evaluate theories and ideas critically and to communicate their ideas through individual essays, reports, group assignments, presentations, and independent research.

For the postgraduate level, teaching and assessment formats resemble those of an elective civil law course. The instructor does not expect students to apply rules to hypothetical situations as they do at the undergraduate level. Instead, the instructor encourages them to analyze theories and ideas critically and to communicate their critical analysis effectively.

6. Conclusion

Teaching compulsory civil law courses in Thailand relies mainly on a lecture-style of teaching with the exception of small-class-size elective courses on civil law. Materials used in compulsory courses are mainly Thai publications. Rarely does the instructor recommend foreign-language texts and materials. In the English-language LL.B program, the instructor has more opportunities to refer to English-language materials despite their relative scarcity in Thai law. Students in the English-language LL.B program are more interactive than in the Thai-language program, and this explains why a lecture-style of teaching is more popular and common in the Thai-language program.

Chapter 3

HOW CIVIL LAW IS TAUGHT AT UNIVERSITY OF YANGON

Khin Phone Myint Kyu*
(University of Yangon)

1. Introduction

At University of Yangon, the Department of Law has two main programs: undergraduate and postgraduate. In the undergraduate program, we only offer the LL B degree. But in the postgraduate programs, we offer LL M and Ph D degrees as part of the regular program. In the LL M course we have four specializations: Civil Law, International Law, Maritime Law, and Commercial Law. In the Human Resource Development program, we offer four diploma degree courses (DBL, DIL, DML, and DIPL) and an MA (Business Law) Degree. The diploma is a part-time course. Any graduate is allowed to attend these diplomas. However, they have to appear for the entrance exam. These are one year diplomas (2 semesters). The MA (Business Law) is a full-time course of 2 years (4 semesters). It is necessary to have a graduate diploma in Business Law and to clear an entrance examination in order to enroll for the MA. Each semester lasts four months.

---

* Professor, Department of Law, University of Yangon, Myanmar.

2. Undergraduate Program (LLB)

The LLB course is a five-year full-time course offered by the Department of Law at the University of Yangon. Every undergraduate program at the University of Yangon is one of the center of excellence in Myanmar. A student who gets high marks in matriculation is eligible to attend the University of Yangon. In order to attend the University of Yangon, an applicant must have 65 marks in English and at least a total of 425 out of 600. If a student has earned an English distinction and over 490 total marks, he or she can get 100,000 Myanmar Kyats (about 75 US$) for each month during his or her whole academic year as a scholarship honored by the government. One hundred students are admitted as outstanding students in each academic year.

2.1 Modes of Teaching

Most of the subjects in the LLB course are taught in English, but some are in Myanmar and some in a mix of Myanmar and English, depending on the nature of the subjects. There are two kinds of subjects: compulsory and elective. All students have to attend classes for compulsory subjects, which are taught in a large classroom. Elective subjects are taught in a small classroom. For both compulsory and elective subjects, teaching notes of the lecture are distributed to students in advance so that they can read and participate in class discussion and consult teachers regarding any difficulties with the material. Furthermore, the teacher provides guidelines to students for studying the related Statutory Laws and Law Reports so that they understand the subjects thoroughly and are more effective at solving the problems set by teachers. Moreover, teachers allocate assignments to students in the form of an essay and/or individual or group presentation. Tutorial teachers supervise the students and teach them how to organize and present their essay and discuss with them while they take their tutorials.

2.2 Teaching Time

Compulsory subjects are taught thrice a week for lecture class and twice a week for tutorial class. Elective subjects are taught twice a week for lecture class and twice a week for tutorial class. The duration of each class is 50 minutes.

2.3 Structure of LLB Course

Since the LLB course is a five-year program, each year's facts will be presented as follows:

2.3.1 First Year

In the first year, students must take 12 subjects for two semesters. Four of which are major subjects. Introduction to the Study of Law I and History of State and Law are taught in the first semester and Introduction to the Study of Law II and Jurisprudence are taught in the second semester.

There are four credit points for each subject. Therefore, there are 16 credit points for major subjects in the first year. However these subjects do not cover the civil law field. These basic subjects are designed for law students to understand what is law?, how do the students study law and ruling?, What are the ethics of legal profession?, How does the State evolve?, and so on.

First year students do not have to choose a law elective. However, they can choose one minor elective offered by a different social science department. The remaining three are foundation subjects such as Myanmar, English, and Aspects of Myanmar.

2.3.2 Second Year

In the second year, students must take 12 subjects for two semesters. Among these are three compulsory subjects per semester. These include Myanmar Customary Law I, Law of Contract, and Labor Law in the first semester and Myanmar Customary Law II, Law of Tort, and Land Law in the second semester. Second year students are required to choose one elective from two subjects such as Law Relating to Sale of Goods and Principles of Legal Professions in the first semester and Negotiable Instruments Act and Law of Banking in the second semester.

There are four credit points for each compulsory subject, equaling to a total of 24 for all. For elective subjects, three credit points are earned, and thus, there are six credit points of elective subjects. All these subjects are related to the civil law field. Altogether, there are 30 credit points' subjects relevant to the civil law field in second year.

The remaining two are foundation subjects (English) and one elective, which is offered by a different social science department, as a minor subject.

2.3.3 Third Year

In the third year, students must take 12 subjects in each semester. Three compulsory ones are taught in both semesters. Therefore, there are six compulsory subjects: Criminal Law, Public International Law, Business Law I, Criminal Procedure Code, Human Rights Law, and Business Law II.

Since four credit points are earned for each subject, the total is 24. However, Criminal Law, Public International Law, Criminal Procedure Code, and Human Rights Law subjects are not relevant to the civil law field; hence, there are only eight credits of third year compulsory courses that are related to the civil law field.

For each semester, students can choose one of two electives: Conflict of Laws or Special Criminal Laws (for 1st Semester) and Law of Insurance or Law of Treaties (For 2nd Semester). Credit points for elective subjects are three, and a total of six for both semesters. Among these electives only two subjects are related to the civil law field. Therefore, considering credit points for the civil law field depend on the student. The remaining two are foundation subjects (English) and one elective offered by a different social department.

2.3.4 Fourth Year

In the fourth year, students must take 12 subjects for two semesters. All of which are law subjects. The four subjects, i.e., Constitutional Law, Civil Procedure Code I, Revenue Law I, and Law of International Institutions I are core ones for the first semester. Administrative Law, Civil Procedure Code II, Revenue

Law II, and Law of International Institutions II are the core ones for the second semester.

There are four credit points for each core subject, and thus the total credit points are 32. However, credit points of subjects like Constitutional Law, Law of International Institutions I & II and Administrative Law cannot be counted in the civil law field. Therefore, there are 16 credit points of compulsory subjects in the civil law field.

In the fourth year, students can choose two electives for each semester. The elective include: Environmental Law, International Economic Law, and Child Law of Myanmar (for 1st Semester) and Law of the Sea, Transport Law and Intellectual Property Law (for 2nd Semester). Besides Transport Law and Intellectual Property Law, these electives are not related to the civil law field. The credit points for each elective subject are three, and thus the total credits for electives are 12 . Credit points for the civil law field depend on the students' choice.

2.3.5 Fifth Year

In the fifth year, students must take 10 subjects for two semesters. Law of Evidence I, Shipping Law I, and Military Law are the core ones for the first semester and Law of Evidence II, Shipping Law II, and Civil Litigation are the core ones for the second semester. Law of Evidence I and II are related to Procedural Law, and thus, this subject is considered part of the civil law field. Shipping Law I & II and Military Law cannot be considered in the civil law field. Hence, there are 12 core course credit points for the civil law field.

Students can choose two subjects from Comparative Law, Criminology and International Humanitarian Law as elective subjects for the first semester and two subjects from Constitutions of ASEAN Countries, Law of Commercial Arbitration, and International Air and Space Law for the second semester. In this year there is a distinct variation in counting the credit points for the civil law field i.e., it depends on the two electives because they can choose two elective subjects for the first semester and second semester as follows:-

First semester -

1. Comparative Law and Criminology; or
2. Comparative Law and International Humanitarian Law; or
3. Criminology and International Humanitarian Law.

Second semester -
1. Constitutions of ASEAN Countries and Law of Commercial Arbitration; or
2. Constitutions of ASEAN Countries and International Air and Space Law; or
3. Law of Commercial Arbitration and International Air and Space Law.

In the Comparative Law subject, we not only teach comparison between three major legal systems (civil law system, common law system, and socialist law system) but also a comparison between domestic laws of different countries such as property law, contract law, tort law, family law, and related laws in the private law field. This subject is therefore considered part of the civil law field. Moreover, the Law of Commercial Arbitration is related to the civil law field, while the rest are not. Therefore, credit points for the civil law field as electives depend on the students' choice.

2.4 Assessment of LLB Courses

Assessment is based on examination and class work through attendance, tutorial tests, and paper presentation. There is one paper presentation, six tutorial tests for each subject, and an examination in each semester. Marks distribution is 80/20, i.e., 80 is for the examination and 20 is for class work. With regard to this assessment system, there is no difference between core and elective subjects.

The examination pattern includes: eight questions, out of which students have to attempt any six. These questions include problem solving, essay type, and suggestions. In order to answer such questions students must refer to not only statutory law, rules, regulations, principle of law, and theories of law but also commentary from eminent authors and the decision of the court of law.

The passing score is 50 out of 100. Results of the compulsory and elective courses are counted toward the GPA. When marks are converted to grades, the passing scores 50 to 64 are equal to grade 3, 65 to 74 are equal to grade 4, and 75 to 100 are equal to grade 5. Grade 5 is distinction. If the student gets a CGPA of

4.0 in the fifth year, he or she is eligible to attend the LL M course. If the student gets a CGPA of 5.0 in the fifth year, he or she will graduate with LL B credit.

3. Postgraduate Program

We also offer Postgraduate Programs at the University of Yangon. These include LL M, M Res, Ph D under the regular stream and diploma and MA in Business Law under the HRD Program.

Under the regular stream, only those with suitable qualification can enroll in the LL M, M Res, and Ph D courses. For the LL M course, a student graduated in LL B with a qualified score is eligible to attend the LL M course. Similarly, when an LL M student earns a 4.5 CGPA in his LL M course, he or she can join the M Res program. Starting from 2018-2019 academic year, we do not offer the M Res degree.

There are two ways to apply for a Ph D. First, anyone with an M Res can apply for a Ph D. Second, any government staff of other Ministries who holds an LL M degree and Law Teaching staff at different universities, holding an LL M can apply as a Ph D candidate.

M Res holders do not need to attempt the Ph D Preliminarily Entrance Written Examination, however they will be interviewed by the Ph D Steering Committee. LL M holders are required to attempt the Ph D Preliminary Entrance Examination and if they clear it they will have a viva.

Any graduate can join under the HRD program. There are four diplomas in the HRD program: DBL, DIL, DML, and DIPL. These are offered as early morning part-time courses from 7:00 am to 9:00 am. Although any graduate can attend these diplomas, they must first attempt the entrance exam. These are one year diplomas (two semesters).

Moreover, our department offers an MA in Business Law under the HRD program. This is a full-time course that lasts two years (four semesters). In order to attend this, it is necessary to have earned a graduate diploma in Business Law and clear an entrance examination.

3.1 LL.M Course

The LL M program is a two-year full-time course. LL M students can take one specialization between Civil Law Specialization, International Law Specialization, Maritime Law Specialization, and Commercial Law Specialization. All subjects in each specialization are taught in English. Forty students are admitted per year.

3.1.1 Modes of Teaching

Before starting the lecture, subject teachers provide a lesson plan as well as a list of references facilitating the students to prepare in advance. Teachers explain and discuss the lessons with students. After this lecture, teachers assign topics or problems as assignments and ask students to prepare Power Point presentations as well as submit their papers. Students research from books, laws, rules, regulations, and law reports that have been listed in the references given by the teachers. After studying from the necessary material, they need to participate in class discussion. Each and every student is expected to participate in class work. Students need to write their assignments and make presentations in English. Being law students, their opinions and legal perspectives are of utmost importance and must be included in their writing. After they have finished their assignments, they have to submit them to the respective lecturer and seminar teacher. Moreover, they need to do a paper reading and a PowerPoint presentation in front of the seminar teacher. Furthermore, students must take a tutorial test. These activities are also a type of assessment and part of the exam.

3.1.2 Teaching Times

In the LL M course, the subjects are taught four times per week and two seminar times per week. The duration of each is 50 minutes.

3.1.3 Structure of the LLM course

As the LLM course takes two years to complete, the students have to attend four semesters. The course offers the opportunity to specialize in four different areas and students can select one specialization. During their first three semesters, they need to be taught their master level course relating to their respective specialization. They are taught the following subjects:

(a) Civil Law Specialization

Civil Law in this specialization implies the domestic laws. In this specialization, there are 12 compulsory subjects for three semesters. These are Criminal Law, Law of Business Organizations, Myanmar Customary Law, Constitutional Law I, Criminal Procedure, Civil Litigation, Family Laws, Constitutional Law II, Special Criminal Laws, Law of Evidence, Labor Law, and Land Law. Among these only seven subjects i.e., Law of Business Organization, Myanmar Customary Law, Civil Litigation, Family Laws, Law of Evidence, Labor Law, and Land Law are related to the civil law field. In the final semester, students have to undertake their own research. The title of their thesis must be in the field of Civil Law Specialization. At the end of the semester students submit their thesis and defend it.

Students earn four credits for each subject, therefore there are 48 credit points in total. Out of 48 credit points, only 28 are related to the civil law field.

(b) International Law Specialization

Public International Law I, International Economic Law, International Law of Armed Conflict, Law of Treaties, Public International Law II, Law of International Trade, International Humanitarian Law, International Environmental Law, Law of International Institutions, International Air and Space Law, Law of the Sea, and Intellectual Property Law are the compulsory subjects for three semesters. In the final semester, students have to submit and defend their thesis.

There are 48 credit points for three semesters. Not all subjects are related to the civil law field, besides the Law of International Trade and Intellectual Property Law. Therefore only eight credit points can be counted as part of the civil law field.

(c) Maritime Law Specialization

For the first three semesters, students have to learn Marine Insurance I, Carriage of Goods by Sea I, Maritime Law I, Law of the Sea I, Marine Insurance II, Carriage of Goods by Sea II, Maritime Law II, Law of the Sea II, Marine Insurance III, Carriage of Goods by Sea III, Maritime Law III, and Law of the Sea III. In the final semester, students have to submit and defend their thesis.

There are 48 credit points. Six subjects (Marine Insurance I, II, and III and Carriage of Goods by Sea I, II, and III) are related to the private law field. Therefore, only 24 credit points can be counted as related to the civil law field.

(d) Commercial Law Specialization

In this specialization, Law of Business Organizations, International Economic Law, Investment Laws and Law of Arbitration, Law of Taxation, Transport Laws, Private International Law, Law of Employment, Banking and Finance Law, General Insurance, Law of International Trade, Environmental Law, and Intellectual Property Law are compulsory subjects in the first three semesters. In the final semester, students have to submit and defend their thesis.

There are 48 total credit points. Most of the subjects other than International Economic Law and Environmental Law are related to the civil law field. Thus, 40 credit points can be counted as related to the civil law field.

3.1.4 Assessment of LL M Course

During the first three semesters, assessment is based on examination and class work, including tutorial tests and paper presentation. There is one paper presentation, six tutorial tests for each subject, and an examination in each semester. Marks distribution is 70/30. That is, 70 is for the examination and 30 is for class work.

Examination pattern includes: six questions, out of which students have to attempt any four. These questions include problem solving, essay type, and suggestions. In order to answer such questions, the students must refer to not only statutory law, rules, regulations, principle of law, and theories of law but also commentary from eminent authors and the decision of the court of law.

The passing score is 65 out of 100. If the marks are converted to grades, the passing score 65 to 74 is equal to grade 4 and 75 to 100 is equal to grade 5. Grade 5 is distinction. If the student CGPA is 4.5 in LL M, he or she is eligible to attend the M Res course.

3.2 M Res Course

This is a one year program for those who wish to complete their research in the field of law. LL M holders who are qualified to do research can be admitted to this course. During this period, the student is required to complete his or her research and present as well as discuss the thesis with his or her supervisor, and finally defend it.

Assessment of M Res Course

Students are required to give a regular presentation and a credit presentation. Credit points are to be counted based on the student's presentation and research findings. After the two presentations, the final defense is held. In the final defense, the department invites two external examiners who are experts in their respective field. With the approval of those experts, students can earn their M Res.

3.3 Ph D Course

Since 1999, the Department of Law has offered a Ph D, which has consistently been in high demand. The duration of the doctoral course is five years. The first year is a preliminary qualifying year, which includes methodological and theoretical study. In this year, students are taught the four different areas of law (civil law, international law, maritime law, and commercial law). Among these subjects it is very difficult to distinguish which subject is related to the civil law field because it depends on the choice of topic in the relevant subject. Students are required to take an exam, which consist of six questions and students can answer any four. The question types are problem solving and essay.

The passing score is 65 out of 100. The remaining four years are devoted to completing research for the final dissertation. Candidates are required to complete regular and credit presentations each year. In the fourth year, there is also an open defense and final defense in addition to the regular and credit presentations. In the final defense, the department invites an external expert and a referee to assess the thesis.

4. HRD Course

Graduate diploma courses have been offered by the Department of Law, University of Yangon, under the University's HRD Program since 2004. There are four part-time diplomas. Any graduate can attend these diplomas. However, they have to attempt an entrance exam. These diploma courses last one year (2 semesters).

Another program is the M A in Business Law. It is a full-time course and lasts 2 years (4 semesters). In order to gain entry into the program, a student must have a graduate diploma in Business Law and should clear an entrance examination. Each semester lasts four months.

4.1 Diploma Course
4.1.1 Diploma in Business Law

There are eight subjects each student must learn: Law of Contract, Law of Business Organizations, Investment and other Related Laws, Law of Employment, Banking and Intellectual Property Laws, Law of Insurance, Transport Law, and Law of Taxation and Commercial Arbitration. Lecture notes are already distributed to the students before the class.

The subjects are taught thrice a week and discussions are conducted twice in each semester with two tutorials per semester.

There are 32 total credit points in this program. All these subjects are within the field of civil law. They are assessed based on the two tutorial tests and the exam in each semester. In the exam, there are eight questions and students must answer any six. The passing score is 65. Nearly 600 students per year are admitted to this program.

4.1.2 Diploma in International Law Course

There are eight subjects in the DIL course: General Principles of International Law I, International Trade Law I, Law of Treaties and International Institutions in semester I and General Principles of International Law II, International Trade Law II, International Human Rights Law and International Humanitarian Law, and Environmental Law. With the exception of International Trade Law I and II, the subjects are not related to civil law. Thus there are only eight credit points that can be counted as civil law.

The teaching methods, teaching times, and type of assessment are the same as the DBL course.

4.1.3 Diploma in Maritime Law Course

There are eight subjects in the DML course: Marine Insurance I & II, Carriage of Goods by Sea I & II, Maritime Law I & II, and Law of the Sea I & II for two semesters. Among these subjects Marine Insurance I & II and Carriage of Goods by Sea I & II are related to the private law field. Therefore, 16 credit points are counted as civil law.

The teaching methods, teaching times, and type of assessment are the same as the DBL course.

4.1.4 Diploma in Intellectual Property Law Course

There are eight subjects in the DIPL course: Intellectual Property Rights, Copyrights I, Trademark I, and Patent in the first semester and Non Traditional Intellectual Property Rights, Copyrights II, Trademark II, and Industrial Design in the second semester. These subjects are all considered as part of the private law field. There are 32 total credit points in this course.

The teaching methods, teaching times, and type of assessment are the same as for the DBL.

4.2 Master of Arts in Business Law (MA Business Law)

In the MA program, there are four semesters. The subjects that are offered for the first two semesters are Law of Contract, International Economic Law, General Principles of Private International Law and Business Transaction, and ASEAN Integration in the first semester and Human Rights, Business and Environment, Investment and Related Laws, Litigation and Commercial Arbitration, and Law of Employment in the second semester. In the second year they learn Intellectual Property Law, International Sale of Goods, Transport Laws, and General Insurance and Banking Law.

During these semesters, the teacher gives lecture and assignment topics for written papers. Furthermore, the lecturer recommends books, laws, rules and regulations, and the court's decisions.

There are four lecture times and two seminar times per week. Each lasts for 50 minutes.

There are 44 credit points for the civil law field. They are assessed based on the assignments, PowerPoint presentations, attendance, tutorial tests, and the exam. About 20 students are admitted per year. During the last semester, the students are required to submit a thesis. The procedure for this last semester is the same as with the LLM Course.

5. Conclusion

To receive the LL B degree the student must earn a total of 156 credit points for law subjects. Out of 156 at least 66 credit points for core courses are counted toward the civil law field. Depending on the student's elective course choices, the credit points can be counted as zero, or nine, or 18, and so on. For example, in the 3rd year if the student chooses Special Criminal Law and Law of Treaties his or her credit points for electives will be zero.

To earn the LL M degree the credit points for the civil law field depends on the specialization.

Specialization	Credit points
1. Civil Law	28

2. International Law   8
3. Maritime Law   24
4. Commercial Law   40.

Credit points for the diploma course for the civil law field are as follows:

1. DBL   32
2. DIL   8
3. DML   16
4. DIPL   32.

In the MA (Business Law) course, there are 44 credit points for the civil law field.

Chapter 4

A PRACTICAL EXAMPLE OF TEACHING AND APPLYING CIVIL LAW IN CAMBODIA:

A Law School's Perspective

Kong Phallack*
Mao Kimpav**

(Paññāsāstra University)

Introduction

This paper illustrates the practical experience of legal education in the Faculty of Law and Public Affairs at Paññāsāstra University of Cambodia (PUC-FLPA). Therefore no citations and bibliographies appear. Part one describes law courses and civil law are taught. Part two outlines the method of using cases and applying Cambodian law to common cases developed for comparative legal study between Japan and Mekong region countries Cambodia, Lao PDR, Myanmar, Thailand, and Vietnam.

1. Law Programs and Teaching Civil Law at PUC-FLPA

PUC-FLPA offers a bachelor program (LL.B.), three masters programs (LL.

---

* Dean and a professor of law at the Faculty of Law and Public Affairs, Paññāsāstra University of Cambodia.
** Manager of Law Programs, Faculty of Law and Public Affairs, Paññāsāstra University of Cambodia.

M. in international human rights law, international business law, and intellectual property law) and two doctoral programs (a professional program (LL.D.) and a research program (Ph.D.). All programs are taught in English by professors and lecturers graduated from overseas universities and practitioners, including lawyers, judges, prosecutors, bailiffs, notaries, arbitrators, and government officers.

PUC-FLPA adopts a credit system. Each course spans 48 hours and earns three credits. The LL.B requires 130 credits (43 courses), the LL.M 54 credits, and the LL.D and PhD 54 credits (18 courses).

Taught in the LL.B program, civil law features four courses: contracts and torts), real rights and claims, family law, and succession. Each is 48 contact hours and earns three credits. Civil law is not offered in the current LL.M programs. The doctoral program offers one civil law course to prepare students for research in the discipline.

FLPA has developed a standard syllabus in line with the university's academic guidelines and the National Qualification Framework of the Ministry of Education, Youth, and Sports. The Japan International Cooperation Agency prepares all civil law teaching materials. Faculty prepare handouts and must use the standard course syllabus, recommended materials, teaching methods, and assessment methods developed by PUC-FLPA. PUC-FLPA welcomes faculty suggestions for materials.

2. Teaching Methodolgy: Cases And Analysis Applying Cambodidan Law

2.1 Teaching Using Cases

Teaching by case prevails throughout PUC-FLPA. Faculty develop hypothetical cases to test students' application of law. Group discussion observes the IRAC Method (issues, rules, application, and conclusion). While teaching law via case study, the author applied techniques such as client consultation (students role play as lawyer and client) and group discussion. Faculty read the cases and questions for students before breaking them into groups to discuss assigned cases. Students select one colleague to report the results of their group discussions, which include identifying statutes and articles relevant to the case and answer questions about their conclusions. Students whose opinions differ from their groups' are asked to share. Faculty comment on students' reports.

2.2 Selected Laws Used In Hypothetical Cases And Case Analysis

The following laws were selected for their relevance to the common topics cases: the Civil Code (hereafter, CCC), the Law on the Application of the Civil Code, Decree 38 on Contracts and Torts, the Law on Commercial Enterprises, the Law on Non-Governmental Organizations and Associations, the Law on Commercial Rules and Register, and Labor Law. Other laws could be relevant to the common topics, but they are excluded here for brevity. The following depiction is not intended to represent any single standard of legal interpretation in Cambodia. It merely shows statute is applied to the hypothetical cases:

2.2.1 Groups of Persons as Subjects of Rights
[Case 1] Legal Personality of MT (Part 3, Chapter 1, 2.2)
[Question 1] The nature of MT; requirements for becoming a legal person; differences and distinguishing criteria between partnerships and associations

Application of Cambodian Law

Under Article 8 of the Cambodian Law on Commercial Enterprises, MT is a general partnership. That is, a contractual relation between two or more persons who combine property, knowledge, or activities to conduct business in common with a view to profit. Per Article 12 of the Law on Commercial Enterprises, a general partnership acquires a legal personality when it registers under the Law on Commercial Rules and Register. A general partnership has a legal personality separate from that of each partner.

In short, partnerships are commercial entities created to earn a profit, and associations are created for non-profit-making purposes. Partnerships must register with the Ministry of Commerce to obtain a legal personality. Associations must register with the Ministry of Interior to acquire a legal personality (LANGO, Article, 9–10)

[Question 2] Claims of creditors D, E, F and G against MT for its remaining assets

Application of Cambodian Law

D can make a claim against MT according to lease provisions in the CCC.

E can make a claim against MT according to provisions of loan for consumption in the CCC.

F can make a claim against MT according to provisions of sale in the CCC.

G can make a claim against MT according to provisions of contractors contract in the CCC.

The remaining assets of MT are 10 pieces of carpet and a claim for US$2,000 against H. According to the Law on Commercial Enterprises, general partners are jointly and severally liable for obligations of the partnership. A third party can seek enforcement of obligations against partnership MT and general partnership assets before seeking enforcement against partners (Article 42).

[Question 3] Individual responsibility of members of MT for its debt

Application of Cambodian Law

According to the Law on Commercial Enterprises, each general partner (A, B, C) shares in the profits and losses of the general partnership (Article 23). Furthermore, Article 24 of the Law on Commercial Enterprises states the proportion of the interest of each general partner in the assets, profits, and losses is equal unless otherwise provided by contract. Therefore, A, B, and C are individually responsible for MT's debt. However, A third party shall seek enforcement of obligations against a partnership and general partnership assets before seeking enforcement against partners (A, B, C) (Article 42).

2.2.2 Transformation of Property Rights: Acquisitions of Immovable Property

[Case 2] Double Transactions of Immovable Property (Part 3, Chapter 1, 2.3)
[Question] Claim of first purchaser B against second purchaser C and vice versa

Application of Cambodian Law

C makes a claim against B based on the contract between A and C. That contract is a sale contract (Article 516, Formation of Sale Contract) and must take the form of a notarized document concerning transfer of ownership of immovable property (Article 336).

However, B can rebut A on the basis that B had acquired contractual ownership of the land from A before C concluded the contract with A. Based on Article 5 of the CCC, it is difficult for B to get the land registered unless C acts in bad faith.

2.2.3 Contractual Liabilities

[Case 3] Debtor's Liability for Non Performance of Contract (Part 3, Chapter 1, 2.4)
[Question 1] Debtor's liability for impossibility that occurred after conclusion of contract (impossibility after contract) due to natural disaster

Application of Cambodian Law

B can file claim for delivery of the oranges under Articles 384(1) (Duty of obligor to perform) and 385 of the CCC (right to demand performance of obligation). B can terminate the contract under Articles 407 (termination for non-performance) and 408(1-c) of the CCC (material breach of contract). B can claim damages from A based on Articles 398(1) (requirement of damages) and 545 of the CCC (right of buyer to demand damages).

A can defend against B's claim on the basis of impossibility of performance under Articles 415 (extinction of obligation in case of impossibility of performance) and 416(1) of the CCC when the subject matter of the contract is destroyed (burden of risk in a contract to transfer title to specific property). A can refuse to pay damages based on Article 398(1) of the CCC because non-performance is not his fault (requirement of damages).

[Question 2] Debtor's liability for impossibility that occurred before conclusion of contract (initial impossibility) due to natural disaster

Application of Cambodian Law

B can file claim for the delivery of oranges under Articles 384(1) (duty of obligor to perform) and 385 of the CCC (right to demand performance of obligations). B can terminate the contract under Articles 407 (termination for non-performance) and 408(1-c) of the CCC (material breach of contract). B can claim damages from A based on Articles 398(1) (requirement of damages) and 545 of the CCC (right of buyer to demand damages). Article 355(2) of the CCC (initial impossibility) is also relevant because the typhoon was an obvious event known to A.

A can rebut B's claim on the basis of impossibility of performance under Articles 392 (impossibility of performance) and 415 (extinction of obligation in case of impossibility of performance), and 416(1) of the CCC when the subject matter of the contract is destroyed (burden of risk in a contract to transfer title to specific property). A can refuse to pay damages based on Article 398(1) of the CCC because the non-performance is not his fault (requirement of damages).

[Question 3] Debtor's liability for delayed performance of contractual obligation due to natural disaster

Application of Cambodian Law

A can rebut B's claim on the basis of impossibility of performance under Articles 392 (impossibility of performance), 415 (extinction of obligation in case of impossibility of performance) and 416(1) of the CCC when the subject matter of the contract is destroyed (burden of risk in a contract to transfer title to specific property). A can refuse to pay damages based on Article 398 (1) of the CCC because the non-performance is not his fault (requirement of damages).

B can file claim for delivery of the oranges under Articles 384(1) (Duty of obligor to perform) and 385 of the CCC (right to demand performance of obligation. B can terminate the contract under Articles 407 (termination for non-performance and 408(1-c) of the CCC (material breach of contract). B can claim damages from A based on Articles 398(1) (requirement of damages) and 545 (right of buyer to demand damages) and 355(2) of the CCC (Initial impossibility) because the typhoon is obvious and A knew of it.

2.2.4 Non-contractual Liabilities, Succession, Status of Fetus

[Case 4] Claim for Compensation for Damages Caused by Traffic Accident (Part3, Chapter 1, 2.5)

[Question 1] Claim for compensation by victim A (injured by the accident), B (A's wife who died from the accident), and D (a fetus who was delivered after the accident)

Application of Cambodian Law

A and D can file claim against C for the following:
(1) compensation under Articles 743, 744, and 761 (damage for bodily harm) of the CCC,
(2) compensation for damages under Articles 1145 (cause of initiate of succession), 1149 (persons eligible for succession), 1156 (successors of first rank), 1161 (succession by spouse), and 1162 (share in succession in case of succession by spouse) caused to B and inherited by A and D. B's claim for compensation consists of loss of income to be earned during her life, calculated on the basis of her annual income of US$60,000 and average of workable years (Articles 743 and 744 of the CCC).

[Question 2] Claim for compensation by victim D who suffers aftereffects of the accident

Application of Cambodian Law

D can claim compensation for expenses necessary to live in a wheelchair and lost future income calculated by reduced working ability and average life expectancy under Articles 743, 744, and 761 (damage for bodily harm) of the CCC.

[Question 3] Claim for compensation by A against C when the fetus could not be delivered due to the accident

Application of Cambodian Law

The fetus cannot acquire rights if it was not born according the Cambodian Civil Code because a natural person acquires legal capacity upon birth and loses it upon death (Article 8 of the CCC). However, A can file claim for mental anguish caused by C's tortious action under Articles 743 and 744 of the CCC. This claim may be based on analogous application of Article 760 of the CCC (damage for wrongful death).

Conclusion

This description and explanation of how civil law is taught and laws are applied to the referenced hypothetical cases should be regarded as the sharing of experience and not the position of Cambodia's legal education and legal interpretation. Other law schools and legal scholars may have different views and ways to analyze and apply the law.

PART II
INTRODUCTION TO LEGAL SYSTEMS IN ASIAN COUNTRIES

Chapter 1

GROUP LITIGATION (CLASS ACTION) IN JAPAN

Toshitaka Kudo*
(Keio University)

1. Prologue: Defining "Group Litigation" and "Class Action"

In one sense, "class action" and "group litigation" indicate a lawsuit filed by a group or class of people as a multiparty action. The legal nature of this proceeding is just a bundle of ordinary individual lawsuits to which general rules of civil procedure apply. As a basic rule, a party seeking a substantive individual right has standing (due qualification) to file a lawsuit; a final judgment is binding only between parties.

In another sense, those terms indicate a lawsuit subject to special procedural rules, particularly concerning standing and *res judicata*. A plaintiff satisfying special standing requirements may file a lawsuit on behalf of a group or class of absent parties, who will be bound by a final judgment eventually. In this sense, a class action the U.S. federal law[1] is the most well-known system worldwide.

---

* Associate Professor, Faculty of Law, Keio University. This article was reproduced with minor revisions from an oral presentation at the International Summer School 2018 at Hanoi Law University. I thank the staffs and faculties at HLU who dedicated themselves to the wonderful program. All cited URLs in this article have been visited on November 30, 2018.

[1] Fed. R. Civ. P, Rule 23.

Usages of "group litigation" and "class action" are not clearly distinguished. The lawsuit processed under a group litigation order (GLO)[2] in England and Wales is theoretically categorized as "group litigation" in the former sense, while some scholars refer it as an opt-out class action. On the other hand, "class action" is sometimes used in the former sense, especially when common law jurisdiction refers multiparty lawsuits in Continental law jurisdiction.

The bottom line is that no one made clear distinction between "group litigation" and "class action." Nevertheless, there seem to be subtle differences in usage of the two terms in Japan. In nuance, "group litigation" might be preferred in the former sense; "class action" in the latter. We use "group litigation" in the former sense and "class action" the latter, unless noted. Today, class action attracts more academic and practitioner attention globally, but in Japan group litigation often drives social and political movements beyond judicial dispute resolution. The following sections examine systems and actual cases in Japan.

2. Group Litigation in Japan

2.1 Overview

Since enactment of the current Constitution after WWII, Japan has seen a variety of group litigation cases. In many of those cases, a group of attorneys solicits possible claimants to file a lawsuit and represents them in court as grassroots social outreach, often pro-bono.

The most popular type of group litigation is personal injury despite immanent challenge to collective processing. Even if injuries are caused by the same or homogeneous factual ground, each victim's suffered damage differs significantly. Therefore, a practice called "categorized comprehensive damages" was generated to process group litigation efficiently. In this practice, plaintiffs voluntarily categorize themselves into several subgroups, depending on suffered damages.

---

[2] Civil Procedure Rules 2000, SI 221, Sch. 2, Rule 19.11.

Plaintiffs in the same subgroups seek the same amount of damages regardless of their specific injuries or diseases.[3] For example, in hepatitis C cases mentioned below, plaintiffs are categorized to three subgroups: successors of a victim dead from chronic hepatitis C, victims suffering chronic hepatitis, and asymptomatic carriers of the hepatitis C virus.

Another common practice in personal injury group litigation is to sue the state as a co-defendant allegedly owing secondary liability. This practice is believed to attract public attention and political involvement. Again, in hepatitis C cases, pharmaceutical companies that manufactured blood derivatives contaminated by hepatitis C virus were sued as defendants owing primary tort liability. In addition, the state was sued as a co-defendant owing supplemental liability based on negligent delay in revoking approval of contaminated derivatives.

Following sections describe several actual group litigation cases. They are a small portion of various actual cases.

2.2 Examples of concluded milestone cases
(1) Coal workers' pneumoconiosis case

In 1985, coal workers who suffered pneumoconiosis (black lung disease) triggered by ingestion of coal particulates and heirs of coal workers who died from the disease filed a lawsuit claiming damages against coal mine companies and the Japanese government. Because those 169 workers worked for coal mines in the Chikuho area of Kyushu, a major source of energy for Japan until the 1970s, this case is customary called the "Chikuho pneumoconiosis lawsuit."[4] Most defendant companies settled the case and paid damages to the plaintiffs, but one defendant company and the state fought all the way to the final appellate

---

[3] Sup. Ct. judgment on December. 16, 1981 (35–10 Minshu 1369) affirmed such practice in finding damages (This case is unusual, because the Court justified blanket finding of damages, responding the group litigation plaintiffs' criticism on it.).
[http://www.courts.go.jp/app/hanrei_en/detail?id=66]

[4] Fukuoka Bar Association Chikuho Division's website summarizes outline of the case at [http://www.chikuho.org/jirei/jinbai.html] (in Japanese).

instance. The final judgment by the Supreme Court in 2004 held the remaining defendants liable.[5] In particular, the judgment of state liability is regarded as a landmark because it found the state liable under doctrine of "negligent omission of administrative control" for the first time.[6]

(2) Hepatitis C cases

The lawsuits were filed by people who were administered blood-clotting agents during operations or childbirth between 1971 and 1990, and allegedly were infected with human hepatitis C virus (HCV) contamination in the administered products. Since 2002, the plaintiffs sought damages against pharmaceutical companies and the government in five district courts (Tokyo, Osaka, Fukuoka, Sendai, Nagoya). The first-instance judgments were rendered between 2006 and 2007, but each district gave different rulings on the period for which defendants were liable and types of products. Although all of these judgments were appealed, the Osaka high court proposed settlement negotiation in September 2007. After difficult negotiation at the working level and fierce political debate in the Diet, the prime minister accepted state liability for all plaintiffs regardless of timing and types of agents administered to them. In January 2008, the Diet immediately passed a special law that established a system to pay compensation to victims of the HCV contaminated products.[7] As a consequence, all pending lawsuits were settled. Under the new system, a victim who seeks compensation must file a lawsuit and obtain necessary fact-finding by the court. Upon the court's positive finding, the plaintiff can file a claim to the special fund, which

---

[5] Sup. Ct. judgment on Apr. 27, 2004 (58-4 Minshu 1032) [http://www.courts.go.jp/app/hanrei_en/detail?id=696]

[6] Supreme Court judgment in Chloroquine drug-harm case (Sup. Ct. judgment on Jun. 23, 1995 (49-6 Minshu 1600)) recognized the theory, but the court did not find liability of the State in the case. [http://www.courts.go.jp/app/hanrei_en/detail?id=221]

[7] Act on Special Measures concerning the Payment of Benefits to Relieve the Victims of Hepatitis C Virus Infections Caused by Specific Fibrinogen Products and Specific Coagulation Factor IX Blood Products" (Law No.2, 2009).

was raised by the state and the pharmaceutical companies.

2.3 Examples of pending high-profile cases
(1) Isahaya bay tide gate cases

(a) Background: Isahaya Bay reclamation project

Isahaya Bay is part of the Ariake Sea in northwestern Kyushu. The Ariake Sea is characterized by a large tidal range and wide tidelands. The state implemented the Isahaya Bay reclamation project with the objectives of improving disaster-prevention and creating superior agricultural land. The "Tide Levee" was established as part of that project. It is a levee approximately 7km in length established to divide Isahaya Bay and create reclaimed land and a retention basin on its interior. Sluice gates installed on this levee allow control of the water level of the interior freshwater retention basin.

(b) Fishermen's suit demanding opening of the gates

In December 2010, the Fukuoka High Court ruled in favor of a suit brought by a group of fishermen from Isahaya Bay who claimed the fishing industry had suffered as a result of the Tide Levee and who sought the opening of the sluice gates by the state (the 2010 Fukuoka High Court Decision).

The fishermen applied for indirect compulsory execution of the 2010 Fukuoka High Court Decision, and the court issued an order for indirect compulsory execution. The state appealed, but the Supreme Court rejected this appeal in January 2015.[8] Accordingly, the state was obliged to pay JPY450,000 per day in indirect compulsory performance until it opened the sluice gates (later this indirect compulsory performance payment increased to JPY900,000 per day when an application from the fisherman to increase this amount was granted).

The state filed an action to oppose execution with regard to the 2010 Fukuoka High Court Decision, seeking disapproval of compulsory execution. The judgment at the first instance denied the state's application, but it was overturned at the second instance (Fukuoka High Court judgment on July 30, 2018: hereinafter

---

[8] Sup. Ct. decision on Jan. 22, 2015 (249 Shumin 43).

the 2018 Fukuoka High Court Decision), which ordered a stay of the indirect compulsory execution. The group of fishermen has made a final appeal seeking to resume the execution; the case is still pending at the Supreme Court.

(c) Farmers' suit demanding an injunction against opening the gates

Meanwhile, a group of farmers who farm the reclaimed land to the interior of the Tide Levee had applied for a provisional disposition, seeking an injunction preventing the state from opening the sluice gates. In November 2011 the Nagasaki District Court gave a provisional disposition ordering an injunction against opening the gates; the state appealed, but the Supreme Court dismissed its appeal in January 2015.[9] Accordingly, the state was obliged to pay JPY490,000 per day in indirect compulsory performance, until it performed its obligation not to open the gates.

In April 2017, the Nagasaki District Court ruled in the first instance to allow the farmers' application for an injunction preventing the state from opening the gates. The state did not appeal, aiming to settle with the fishermen without opening the gates by establishing a fund for them. Although the fishermen's group, which had not been party to this case, applied for intervention as an independent party and appealed against the decision in the first instance, the court of second instance dismissed this application to intervene. The fishermen's group has made a final appeal against this judgment, and a ruling from the Supreme Court is pending.

(d) The state's dilemma, and three-party settlement negotiations

Because court proceedings relating to the fishermen and farmers proceeded separately and the Supreme Court rendered conflicting judgments in relation to those respective proceedings, the state has found itself facing a dilemma whereby it is required to make indirect compulsory execution payments whether it opens the gates or not. The Fukuoka High Court (which heard the action to oppose execution, described above (b)) and the Nagasaki District Court (which heard the suit for an injunction against opening the gates, described above in (c))

---

[9] Sup. Ct. decision on Jan. 22, 2015 (249 Shumin 67).

recommended a three-party settlement among the fishermen, farmers, and state; negotiations were being held, but they did not reach a settlement, and so the suits reached judgment. As a consequence of the 2018 Fukuoka High Court Decision, at present the state has no obligation to make indirect compulsory execution payments for not opening the gates, but the triparty dispute has yet to reach final solution.

(2) Fukushima nuclear accident evacuees' cases
(a) Background: compensation for nuclear damage

Many people residing in Japan were affected by the accident at the Fukushima Daiichi Nuclear Powerplant, triggered by the huge earthquake and tsunami on March 11, 2011. Individuals and corporations that suffered damages caused by the nuclear accident can seek compensation in three routes: filing a claim directly to the owner and operator of the plant, alternative dispute resolution, and litigation.

(i) Direct filing

Following provisional payments started after a month after the accident, the plant owner Tokyo Electric Power Company (TEPCO) launched the formal compensation scheme in September 2011. Filing can be made by completing a detailed form provided by TEPCO. A specialized unit within TEPCO processes the lodged claims, complying with general standards published by the Dispute Reconciliation Committee for Nuclear Damage Compensation, which is described below. If a claimant and TEPCO agree on compensation, it will be paid immediately upon signing agreement. As of November 22, 2018, TEPCO had received approximately 2.8 million filings, of which it had settled 2.6 million. A cumulative total of paid compensation is exceeding JPY 8 trillion.[10]

(ii) Alternative dispute resolution (ADR)

Claimants who cannot reach agreement with TEPCO or are disinclined to file a claim directly to TEPCO can refer the dispute to mediation provided by

---

[10] TEPCO website [http://www.tepco.co.jp/fukushima_hq/compensation/results/index-j.html] (in Japanese)

the Nuclear Damage Dispute Resolution Center (NDDRC).[11] The NDDRC was established in August 2011 as a subsidiary of the administrative committee in charge of mediation under the Nuclear Damage Compensation Act,[12] namely, the Dispute Reconciliation Committee for Nuclear Damage Compensation organized under the Ministry of Education, Cultural, Sports, Science and Technology.

The mediation scheme is operated by part-time mediators and full-time investigators. Mediators appointed to individual cases by the NDDRC process the mediation individually or as a panel, depending on complexity of a case. The investigators, all of whom are term-appointment attorneys, support the mediators by gathering facts, researching legal matters, and refining issues. Mediators can persuade parties to settle by themselves or issue recommended terms of settlement when no agreement is reached. Because evaluation of nuclear damage is highly technical and many people suffered homogeneous damages under similar circumstance, the NDDRC created a series of "general standards" for common categories of damages to ensure equal treatment. In recommending terms of settlement, the mediators must comply with the general standards, which legally are just unbinding internal guidelines. As of November 22, 2018, the NDDRC had received approximately 24,000 filings, of which it had settled 18, with 1,199 cases now pending. The rest of the flied cases had been mostly withdrawn or terminated without reaching agreement.[13]

(iii) litigation

Litigation is the last resort open to all: those who are disinclined to file either the direct claim or the ADR; those who are dissatisfied with amounts of compensation (actually or potentially) proposed at the direct claim or the ADR; those who want to use litigation to express their anger and denounce culpability of TEPCO and the state in public. If as claimant's motivation is either of former

---

[11] Theoretically, a claimant can choose other private ADR services, however such choice is not practical due to mediator's or arbitrator's lack of expertise for nuclear damage.

[12] Nuclear Damage Compensation Act, Art. 18.

[13] NDDRC website [http://www.mext.go.jp/a_menu/genshi_baisho/jiko_baisho/detail/1329118.htm]

two, s/he can just file an ordinary individual lawsuit. In fact, substantial numbers of group litigations have been filed.

(b) Group litigation cases

Most group litigation cases seeking compensation for the 3/11 nuclear accident have several common features. Plaintiffs are generally individuals who evacuated after the nuclear accident. Some lived in mandatory evacuation zones and others evacuated voluntarily. The majority of plaintiffs seek compensation exceeding standards established by the Reconciliation Committee based on various legal grounds such as general provision of tort in Article 709 of the Civil Code, the alleged individual rights guaranteed in Article 25 (wholesome and cultured living) and Article 13 (pursuing of happiness and developing personalities) of the Constitution, etc. As of November 2018, over 30 group litigation lawsuits comprising more than 10,000 plaintiffs are pending across the nation. Judgments of the first instance have been rendered in seven district courts. In four cases, both TEPCO and the state were held liable; in one case only TEPCO by negating state liability. In two other cases, the state was not designated as a defendant. Over 3,600 plaintiffs prevailed with JPY2.7 billion awarded. All these judgments have been appealed. In addition to the above-mentioned cases, one exceptional lawsuit claims liability of the reactor manufactures: GE, Hitachi, and Toshiba. As of November 2018, the case was pending at the Supreme Court after dismissal judgments at the first and appellate instances.

(3) HPV vaccine cases

(a) Background: controversies over HPV vaccination

The World Health Organization recommends human papillomavirus (HPV) vaccination to prevent HPV-related diseases such as cervical cancer. HPV vaccines are approved and available in over 100 countries. Over 50 countries, mainly European and North/South American, have adopted HPV vaccine in their national immunization program.

At present, Japan is among these countries. HPV vaccine Cervarix manufactured by GlaxoSmithKline obtained governmental approval in November 2009;

Gardasil by MSD (Merck) in July 2011. Since December 2011, the approved HPV vaccine has been provided at no cost to Japanese girls ages 12–16 by public funding. In April 2013, HPV was added to the list of recommended routine vaccinations specified in Immunization Act.

However, unconfirmed unusual post-vaccination neurological symptoms were reported. In worst cases, teenage girls suffered from numbness allegedly due to their HPV immunization. In March 2013, victims suffering serious symptoms established an organization to promote prohibition of the immunization and more public relief for the side-effect victims. Responding to media pressure and public attentions, MHLW suspended its proactive recommendations for the vaccine in June 2013, only two months after enactment.[14]

According to MHLW's evaluation of research conducted after the suspension, it is highly probable the reported post-vaccination symptoms were not causally associated with HPV vaccination but were psychosomatic responses. Nevertheless, the MHLW insisted on further studies before resuming the governmental recommendation.[15]

In any event, approval of the HPV vaccines itself has never been under review. In addition, the Immunization Act provides a compensation scheme for a routine vaccination recipient suffering health damage caused by the vaccination including one for HPV vaccination.

(b) Group litigation cases

Groups of HPV vaccination recipients suffering adverse neurological symptoms filed lawsuits against the two manufactures and the state. The first groups filed lawsuits at four district courts (Tokyo, Nagoya, Osaka and Fukuoka) in July 2016, followed by the second groups in December 2016. The 119 plaintiffs insist HPV vaccines have not proved useful in preventing cervical cancer but incur serious side effects more often than other routine vaccines. All cases are still pend-

---

[14] [https://www.mhlw.go.jp/bunya/kenkou/kekkaku-kansenshou28/pdf/kankoku_h25_6_01.pdf]

[15] [https://www.mhlw.go.jp/bunya/kenkou/kekkaku-kansenshou28/dl/tp160316_01.pdf]

ing at the first instances.

3. Special Procedural Measures for Consumer Protection

Japan had no class action system for a long time. However, in the area of consumer protection, new procedural measures were created during the past two decades. One is for injunctive action, the other for monetary compensation. These new statutes do grant standing not to individual consumers but to consumer organizations. Therefore, the systems are often called *Shohisya Dantai Soshou* ("consumer group litigation"), and the latter one *Shohisya Shugou Soshou* ("consumer collective action") or "Japanese class action," distinguishing from the former one.

3.1 Action for injunctive relief
(1) Background

Prior to the legislation in Japan, a tide came from Europe. In 1993, a Council Directive on unfair terms in consumer contracts (Unfair Terms Directive)[16] recommended measures to prevent unfair contractual clauses. In 1998, a Directive of the European Parliament and of the Council on injunctions for the protection of consumers' interests[17] mandated member states to establish injunctive actions by qualified consumer organizations. Following the directives, each member state designed systems for injunctive relief by their national law.

In Japan, responding the Opinion Paper of the Judicial Reform Council released in 2002, the Economy Welfare Bureau, an affiliate of the Cabinet, begun a study for a group action for consumers in 2004. Getting through discussion at the committee and the Diet, a special rule for injunctive action was added to the

---

[16] Council Directive 93/13/EEC, OJ L 95, 21.4.1993, p. 29–34.

[17] Directive 98/27/EC of the European Parliament and of the Council of 19 May 1998 on injunctions for the protection of consumers' interests, OJ L 166, 11.6.1998, p. 51–55.

Consumer Contract Act (CCA) in 2006 and enacted in 2007. In drafting a bill, national laws in Europe, especially Germany, were referenced intensively.

(2) Standing

Only a qualified consumer organization (QCO) can file the injunctive action against an enterprise allegedly violating consumer protection law. Neither a governmental agency nor an individual consumer has standing. To qualify, a consumer organization needs to be certified by the government. Substantive requirements and procedural rules for certification are specified in CCA.[18] On the statutory text, the prime minister has authority to certify, but the Consumer Affairs Agency is in charge. As of July 2018, 19 organizations were certified.

(3) Subject matters

Either of the following unfair activity by the defendant enterprise constitutes a subject of injunction:[19]

(i) Inappropriate solicitation or contractual clauses prohibited under CCA

(ii) Violation of Act against Unjustifiable Premiums and Misleading Representations

(iii) Violation of Act on Specified Commercial Transactions (regulation on door-to-door sales etc.)

(iv) Violation of Food Labeling Act

(4) Pre-action requirement

Prior to filing the lawsuit, a QCO must send a written demand to stop violation to an alleged violator (enterprise). In addition, violation has been continuing over 1 week even after the demand; or the violator expressly refused the demand.[20]

---

[18] CCA Art. 13–14.

[19] CCA Art. 12; Violation of Act against Unjustifiable Premiums and Misleading Representations Art. 30(1); Violation of Act on Specified Commercial Transactions (regulation on door-to-door sales etc.) Art. 58–18 to 58–24; Food Labeling Act Art. 11.

[20] CCA Art. 41(1).

(5) Judgment

Upon finding the violation, the court issues a judgment granting injunctive relief, while monetary relief is not allowed.

(6) Statistics

As of December 2017, 48 actions were filed.[21] Because most cases were settled in or out of court, judgment was rendered in just a few cases.[22]

3.2 Action for recovery of monetary damages

(1) Background

Class actions and collective redress for consumer cases had been a topic of academic interest in the early 21st century.[23] In 2013, the EU Commission issued a Recommendation for collective redress mechanisms in member states for injunctions against and claims for damages caused by violations of EU rights.[24] The Recommendation pointed out consumer protection as one area where collective redress is valuable.[25]

In Japan, following research and discussions by study groups organized by the Cabinet Office and Consumer Agency, the Expert Committee for Consumers' Collective Redress organized by the Consumer Committee issued a final report in 2011. A two-stage system (mentioned in detail below (5)) of the new procedure

---

[21] [http://www.meti.go.jp/shingikai/shokeishin/pdf/004_03_00.pdf](in Japanese)

[22] [http://www.caa.go.jp/policies/policy/consumer_system/collective_litigation_system/about_system/case_examples_of_injunction/pdf/06sashitomejirei.pdf]

[23] For example, Christopher Hodges, The Reforms of Class and Representative Actions in European Legal Systems, A New Framework for Collective Redress in Europe (Hart, 2008).

[24] C(2013)3539/3, Commission Recommendation of 11 June 2013 on common principles for injunctive and compensatory collective redress mechanisms in the Member States concerning violations of rights granted under Union Law, OJ L 201, 26.6.2013, p. 60–65.

[25] In April 2018, the European Commission issued a proposal that aims to launch representative actions on behalf of consumers and introduce stronger sanctioning powers for member states' consumer authorities as part of the "New Deal for Consumers." COM(2018) 184 final; 2018/0089 (COD).

was modeled mainly from French and Brazilian laws. After long discussions on drafting, a proposed bill passed the Diet in 2013. The new law was named "Act on Special Measures Concerning Civil Court Proceedings for the Collective Redress for Property Damage Incurred by Consumers" (ACCA) became effective in 2016.[26]

(2) Standing

Only a QCO with special certification (specially qualified consumer organization: hereinafter SQCO) can file the lawsuit for the first stage.[27] To obtain special certification, a QCO has to meet additional requirement such as financial soundness, etc.[28] As of November 2018, there are 3 SQCOs.

(3) Subject matter

Individual consumers' claims must be related to a consumer contract and meet all requirements below ((a) to (d)).[29] The subject matter at the first stage is not individual claims themselves but conceptual common liability that a defendant enterprise owes to consumers. Therefore, SQCOs are granted special third-party standing.

(a) Seeking monetary relief

Defendant's monetary obligations to consumers shall arise from a consumer contract, such as: (i) Failure to perform the contract, (ii) Return of unjust enrichment or (iii) Damage caused by non-performance of the contract, fraud, etc.

(b) Numerosity

Damages shall be suffered by a substantial number of consumers. Because no specific number is written in the statute, the court decides the "substantial

---

[26] Law No. 96 of 2013.

[27] ACCA Art. 3.

[28] ACCA Art. 65.

[29] (a) to (c) are developed from statutory construction of ACCA Art. 2(iv). (d) is implied from Art.3(4). One can detect flavors similar to class certification requirement of US federal law (F.R. Civ. Pro R.23(b)).

number" case-by-case.

(c) Commonality

The common liability shall be based on common factual and legal grounds. In most consumer cases, individual claims were arisen under not exactly the same, but substantially same (or homogeneous), grounds because each consumer individually signed a contract with the enterprise.

(d) Predominance

Questions of law or fact common to consumers shall predominate over questions affecting only individual consumers.

(4) Scope of damages

Even though the requirements above (3) are satisfied, damages specified below shall not be sought:[30] (i) consequential damages, (ii) lost profits, (iii) personal injury damages, (iv) solatium (moral damages). In other words, only direct monetary damage arisen from the consumer contract is allowed.

(5) Structure of two-stage proceedings

(a) Classification of class action system in general

In general, structures of class action systems can be classified into three models: (i) opt-in, (ii) opt-out, (iii) two-stage. (i) Opt-out means that a class action judgment is binding to a non-party class member, unless s/he affirmatively excludes her/himself from the class. (ii) Opt-in means the judgment is NOT binding to a non-party class member unless s/he affirmatively includes her/himself in the class. (iii) Two-stage consists of a first stage to determine common issues for a class and a second stage to determine individual recoveries. The first-stage proceeding does not provide opportunity to opt-in or opt-out. Only at the second stage can a class member utilize a first-stage judgment prevailing for the class.[31]

---

[30] ACCA Art. 3(2).

[31] In broad sense, the two-stage can be included in the opt-in because a class member is not automatically bound by the first-stage judgment.

A judgment for the opponent is not binding to a class member.

The new Japanese system falls under the two-stage class action. The first stage is called a "declaratory judgment action on common obligation," which determines issues common to all individual consumers such as enterprise practices violating consumer law, its illegality, an causation to damage.

The second stage is called a "simplified determination proceeding," which determines existence of each consumer's claim, with judicial binding power. The consumer side can proceed to the second stage only if a plaintiff SQCO obtained final judgment or in-court settlement finding for consumers at the first stage. If not, the case is terminated.

(b) First stage: declaratory judgment action on common obligations

A legal nature of the first-stage proceeding is a declaratory judgment action litigated between a SQCO and a business enterprise allegedly violating consumer law. A subject matter of the first stage is "common obligation," the defendant's obligation to pay money compensation to consumers based on common factual and legal grounds.

Under general rules of civil procedure, the final judgment of the first stage is binding between the plaintiff SQCO and the defendant enterprise. Furthermore, ACCA stipulates special rules on res judicata;[32] (i) The first-stage judgment is binding also on other non-party SQCOs. (ii) If the plaintiff SQCO prevails in the first-stage judgment, individual consumers can utilize the judgment in the second-stage proceeding.

(c) Second stage: simplified determination proceeding

(i) Commencement of the second stage

The court issues a commencement order upon filing by the SQCO within one month from its prevailing judgment or in-court settlement at the first stage.[33] Simultaneous with the commencement order, a period for filing individual con-

---

[32] ACCA Art. 9.
[33] ACCA Art. 14–18.

sumers' claims and a period for approval or disapproval by court are specified.[34]

To guarantee individual consumers' opportunity to seek their claims, periods specified by court are posted in public notices in the Official Gazette.[35] In addition, the SQCO must inform known individual consumers in writing or digital media[36] and post a public notice by a reasonable method.[37]

(ii) Review of individual claims

To seek compensation by utilizing the outcome at the first stage, individual consumers must delegate the power regarding his/her claim to the SQCO.[38] Therefore, the only SQCO that filed the second stage can submit all delegated individual claims to the court within the designated period.[39]

Of course, the defendant in the first stage (business enterprise) has opportunity to argue individual claims submitted by the SQCO. Compared with ordinary civil litigation in court, the process to determine individuals' claims at the second stage is quite simplified due to judgment on common liability at the first stage and fair representation by the SQCO.

The enterprise which was defeated at the first stage must state its opinions of approval or disapproval regarding each submitted individual claim within the designated period.[40] Approved claims become enforceable with *res judicata*.[41] On the other hand, with respect to disapproved claims the SQCO has a choice of contesting or not. If the claim is contested, the court determines if it has merit, upon hearing and examining documentary evidence presented by parties (the SQCO and the enterprise).[42] The process of determination is called "simplified determination," much quicker and simpler than ordinary civil litigation.

---

[34] ACCA Art. 24(1).
[35] ACCA Art. 24(3).
[36] ACCA Art. 25.
[37] ACCA Art. 26.
[38] ACCA Art. 31.
[39] ACCA Art. 30.
[40] ACCA Art. 42.
[41] ACCA Art. 42(3)(5).
[42] ACCA Art. 44.

Against the determination, the party may file an objection to seek further review in court.[43]

(iii) Enforcement of determined individual claims

What if the enterprise does not pay the determined individual claims? In that case, the SQCO of the first-stage plaintiff can enforce all such claims on behalf of the claimants[44] via proceedings prescribed in the Civil Execution Act. If enforcement is successful entirely or partly, the SQCO makes distributions to individual consumers.

(6) Statistics and evaluation

As of November 2018, no single case has been filed in two years since the enactment. This situation is ironic; ACCA enacted with expectations turned out to be toothless from the outset.

Among shortcomings would be limited subject matters and collectible damages. Generally speaking, amounts of individual claims are small in consumer cases, but the ACCA further discourages consumers or consumer organizations by limiting the scope of damages narrowly. In addition, because tort claims are entirely excluded, contemporary mass torts such as information leaking, environmental pollution etc. never fall under the new system's jurisdiction.

Another shortcoming might be limited standing to file the action. Consumer organizations in Japan are doing their best, but it is undeniable that their human and financial resources are not necessarily sufficient compared with ones in foreign countries. In some countries, governmental agencies are granted standing to file lawsuits for consumer protection. However, such models did not incur interest from lawmakers, presumably because of long-standing support for deregulation and "small government."

---

[43] ACCA Art. 46.
[44] ACCA Art. 47(2).

(7) The class action menace?

One would like to ask why such a weakened ACCA was created in Japan. In the course of drafting ACCA, business circles lobbied against the legislation based on bitter experiences in U.S. class actions. Voices from the consumer side vanished into the din, which deemed class action a menace to business operations.

However, does only a class action contribute to abusive class action lawsuits and bellicose litigants in the United States?

The answer would be "No." A famous scholar comparing class actions in the world stated, "Importing class action law does not necessarily mean importing American-style litigation. The transplant is 'surgically controlled.' There is no reason to believe that the whole 'Yankee Package' would invade a foreign system through the window opened by the class action device."[45]

"Yankee Package" refers to unique features of the American civil judiciary, such as discovery, contingent fees, an entrepreneurial bar, the jury system, and punitive damages. In my opinion, this insight should be shared among Japanese business circles to make discussions for reform[46] sensible and productive.

4. Epilogue

For two decades, collective redress for consumer protection has been a topic of interest, especially in Europe and North/South America. In emerging countries, areas such as consumer protection and environmental protection are often set aside because legal development tends to focus on business and industrial growth. Nevertheless, such tendencies would change as a country's economy grows. I hope the Japanese experience will encourage Mekong Delta countries to hold productive legislative discussion, free from class action phobia.

---

[45] Antonio Gidi, Class Actions in Brazil. A Model for Civil Law Countries, 51 Am. J. of Comp. L. 311, 322–23 (2003).

[46] ACCA Supplementary Provisions Art. 5(2) mandates the government to review the new law after 3 years from the enactment.

Chapter 2

OVERVIEW OF
THE VIETNAMESE LEGAL SYSTEM

Phan Thi Lan Huong*
(Hanoi Law University)

1. The Influence Factors of the Legal System in Vietnam

The legal system differs from country to country because of differences in history, socio-political, and economic conditions. In other words, the nature of the legal system of a country depends on the nature of its social system established in law. Vietnam is a socialist country under the leadership of the Communist Party; therefore, the current legal system of Vietnam has its own history and tradition.

In general, Vietnamese legal ideologies were influenced by various legal ideologies and can be divided into four periods such as: feudal legal system, French colonialist, Soviet Union traditional legal system, and the legal system in the period of integration and globalization. However, this article only focuses on the legal system from 1975 to present because the current legal system of Vietnam has significantly changed since the introduction of Doi Moi (*renovation*) in 1986.[1]

---

* Deputy Head, International Cooperation; Professor, Department of Hanoi Law University.
[1] For more information, see: Dao Tri Uc, "Doing Legal Research in Asian Countries- Vietnam: Basic Information for Legal Research: A Case Study of Vietnam" (Institute of Developing Economies, 2003), http://www.ide.go.jp/English/Publish/Download/Als/pdf/23.pdf.

a) Political Influence–socialist ideology

The current legal system of Vietnam is based on the ideologies of the former Soviet Union. The Soviet's legal system is based on the civil law system combined with modifications from Marxist-Leninist ideology. Vietnam relied deeply on the support of the Soviet Union during the war and after reunification in 1975; therefore, the 1980 Constitution was drafted based on the constitution of the Soviet Union as a significant example for reference.

The 1980 Constitution was a mirror image of a Soviet Union style constitution. It explicitly stated, "The Socialist Republic of Vietnam is a state of proletarian dictatorship" (Art. 2). Further, it speaks of the "collective mastery" of the working class, the collective peasantry and the socialist intelligentsia (Art. 3). For the first time the Constitution contained a provision on the role of the Communist Party of Vietnam as the only political party (Art. 4). The party was only limited insofar as "its organizations [were to] operate within the framework of the Constitution" (Art. 4, Par. 3).[2]

"Most of the lawmakers and senior state officials in Vietnam were trained in the Soviet Union and Eastern European nations. The legal system and the role of law were used in the flexible way in order to maintain the autonomous role of the Communist Party."[3]

The legal system of Vietnam was formed gradually under the leadership of the Communist Party and the *democratic centralism principle*. The legal system is formed under the principle of socialist legality *(phap che xa hoi chu nghia)* and democratic centralism *(tap trung dan chu)*.

---

[2] *Constitutionalism in Southeast Asia* (Konrad-Adenauer-Stiftung, 2008), 337.

[3] Thi Lan Anh Tran, "Vietnam's Membership of the WTO: An Analysis of the Transformation of a Socialist Economy into an Open Economy with Special Reference to the TRIPS Regime and the Patent Law" (The University of Leeds, 2009), 153, http://etheses.whiterose.ac.uk/2688/1/uk_bl_ethos_509876.pdf.

These principles shape the nature of legislation in Vietnam. Although the National Assembly is with vested legislative power, executive organs have played an important role in legislation. Hence, sources of law and interpretation are different from rule of law in the state. "The legal ideologies that provide the foundation for the establishment and operation of Vietnamese legal institutions significantly differ from those of rule-of-law systems."[4] Under the democratic central principle, there is no separation of state power. All three state branches are involved in legislation. Hence, the concept of law refers to various types of legislation issued by competent agencies in written forms.

In addition, the Communist Party has played a leading role in all aspects; therefore, the legal system is under the influence of the Party's policies. Therefore, the law cannot conflict with the Party's policies. It becomes a condition of legal validity in Vietnam that is also different from other countries. Constitution 2013, article 4 defines the leading role of the Communist Party as follows: *"The Communist Party of Vietnam - the Vanguard of the working class, concurrently the vanguard of the laboring people and Vietnamese nation, faithfully representing the interests of the working class, laboring people and entire nation, and acting upon the Marxist-Leninist doctrine and Ho Chi Minh Thought, is the force leading the State and society."* The Communist Party takes a leading role in policy making on important national issues such as administrative reform and judicial reform.

The National Assembly is the highest representative body of the people and the highest state power body of the Socialist Republic of Vietnam. The National Assembly shall exercise constitutional and legislative powers, decide on important issues for the country, and conduct the supreme oversight over the activities of the State (Article 69, Constitution 2013). The government is the highest state administrative body and shall exercise the executive power. The government is

---

[4] Bui Thi Bich Lien, "Legal Interpretation and the Vietnamese Version of the Rule of Law," *National Taiwan University Law Review* 6 (2009): 323, http://www.law.ntu.edu.tw/ntulawreview/articles/6-1/11-Article-Bui%20Thi%20Bich%20Lien_p321-337.pdf.

responsible to the National Assembly and shall report on its work to the National Assembly, the Standing Committee of the National Assembly, and the President (Article 94, Constitution 2013). In addition, the Chief Justice of the Supreme People's Court is responsible and shall report on his or her work to the National Assembly (Article 105, Constitution 2013). Table 1.1 shows the structure of Vietnamese government system.

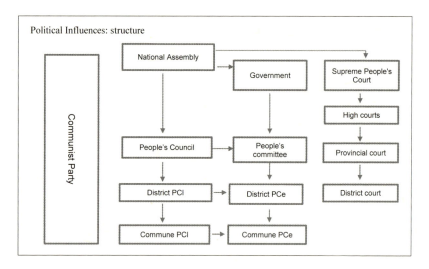

b) Socio-Economic Conditions

Socio-economic conditions have significantly affected the legal system. The legal system must respond to the changes in socio-economic conditions. The remarkable changes in socio-economic conditions in Vietnam have called for the following significant changes in the legal system:

– *Introducing the Doi Moi (renovation) policy in 1986*: *shifting from a centrally-planned economy to a market economy with a socialist orientation.* The legal system was considered an instrument for defining the role of the state and the market. Related to the *Doi Moi* policy, some significant changes in the legal system are summarized such as:

1) 1986 Land reform: Directly after introducing *Doi Moi,* the government decided to give Vietnamese farmers more rights on land and for the first time, the right to decide what to produce on their own. As a result, the agricultural output increased so much that within two years, Vietnam was transformed from a rice-importing to a rice-exporting nation.

2) 1990/91 Recognition of private ownership: For the first time, Vietnam officially recognized the lawful existence of non-state economic sectors by issuing the *Company Law* and the *Private Enterprise Law*.

3) 1995/96 Liberalization of foreign trade: The re-establishment of formal diplomatic relations with the USA constituted the starting point for an opening of international economic relations, allowing private enterprises to engage in import/export activities.

4) 1999 Right of business freedom: Clarification of entrepreneurs' basic rights to operate in all business areas as not explicitly forbidden by law.[5]

The 1992 Constitution replaced the 1980 Constitution with the focus mainly on an open market under a socialist oriented economy. The rule of law and the clear distribution of state functions (legislative, executive, and judicial functions) were mentioned as the target of legal reform in Vietnam.

– *Globalization: Vietnam became a member of the WTO in 2007*: In 1995, Vietnam aimed at bringing the national legal system up to the level required by the World Trade Organization (WTO) in order to become a member. Therefore, all legal sectors have been reformed based on the international trade rules. For example, Vietnam established the Administrative Court in 1996 and adopted the Law on Administrative Complaints and Denunciation in 1998 to meet a requirement of the WTO.

– *Achieving success as a Middle- Income Country:*[6] *Master reforming pro-*

---

[5] "Vietnamese Economic Reforms, Socialist versus Social Orientation - a Policy Debate" (German Development Cooperation, n.d.), 3, http://www2.gtz.de/wbf/4tDx9kw63gma/VN_economic_reforms_socialistvs_social_orientation.pdf.

[6] Reforms have transformed Vietnam from one of the world's poorest countries 25 years ago to a lower middle-income country (MIC) (2011 per capita income of US$1,260). The poverty

gram

The Communist Party issued Resolution No 48: Strategy for the Development and Improvement of Vietnam's Legal System to the Year 2010 and Direction for the Period up to 2020. This strategy calls for a modern transition to the rule of law and a market-based economy and lays out a strategy to develop Vietnam's laws as well as improve their application and execution by 2020.

In the process of building the state rule of law and democratic society, especially since it became a middle-income country, Vietnam introduced a Master Plan on Administrative Reform period 2011–2013 with the aim of building an effective, efficient, transparent, and strong administrative system from the central to the local level. Hence, the 1992 Constitution was amended in 2013 as a significant effort in the reform process.

Currently, Vietnam has carried out a review of all legal documents and has planned to promulgate new laws to ensure that legal documents comply with the 2013 Constitution.

c) Traditional Culture, Beliefs, and Religions

– Vietnam includes 54 ethnic groups which have different traditional cultures, beliefs, and religions. Buddhism is identified as the main religion in Vietnam and is influenced by Confucianism. The law making and law enforcement systems at present are crucially influenced by Confucianism and Buddhism.[7]

---

headcount fell from 58 percent in the early 1990s to around 10 percent by 2010. According to a new poverty line, which is more appropriate for Vietnam's status as a middle-income country, this rate was just about 20% in 2010. Five of Vietnam's ten Millennium Development Goal (MDG) targets have been attained, with two more likely to be met by 2015 (see: http://www.worldbank.org/en/results/2013/04/12/vietnam-achieving-success-as-a-middle-income-country)

[7] Tran, "Vietnam's Membership in the WTO: An Analysis of the Transformation of a Socialist Economy into an Open Economy with Special Reference to the TRIPS Regime and the Patent Law," 151.

"Vietnamese culture is said to be a rich fabric of Confucianism and Buddhism. Most notably, Confucian values brought in from China exerted a profound influence on the way of thinking and practices of a large population. They advocated traditional moral principles (such as virtue and sentiment versus rule and reason) and hierarchical practices. Legal rules were subordinated to moral and pragmatic expediencies."[8]

- *"Village customary regulations"* still exist in parallel to the *"law of state."* To some extent, village customary regulations have affected law enforcement in Vietnam.

"A well-known saying goes, *'the laws of the emperor give way to the customs of the village'*. The saying implies a sense of attitude and perception of the people toward (central) formal laws, and broadly a degree of hesitation and resistance to obedience of, and compliance with, law and use of formal dispute settlement (e.g., the court) in general. The "laws of the emperor," associated with the legal rules by foreign domination, over two thousand years have shaped attitudes, even in modern days."[9]

Many ethnic groups living in mountainous or remote areas still follow their village's rules, including child marriages or forcing marriages which are still acceptable in some villages. It is also a sizeable challenge for law enforcement in Vietnam.

d) International cooperation in legal reform

In the period of integration and globalization, Vietnam has received support from advanced countries such as the US, Japan, Denmark, Canada, and Ger-

---

[8] "Legal and Judicial Systems" (World Bank, n.d.), 87, http://siteresources.worldbank.org/INTVIETNAM/Resources/chuong5.pdf.
[9] Ibid.

many in implementing legal reforms. For example, JICA (Japan International Cooperation Agency) has assisted Vietnam in implementing legal reform by supporting the drafting of legal documents in civil and commercial areas as well as with human resource development[10]; USAID's STAR project helped Vietnam to rewrite or adopt 93 legal documents related to trade agreement[11].

"More recently, donors and entrepreneurs have advocated reforms to support the marketization of the economy, producing a diverse set of civil and common law influences from various sources including Sweden, the United States of America, Canada, Japan and Australia to name a few."[12]

Consequently, the current legal system in Vietnam has been impacted sig-

---

[10] "Technical Assistance Project for Legal and Judicial System Reform | Vietnam | Countries & Regions | JICA," accessed May 12, 2014, http://www.jica.go.jp/vietnam/english/activities/activity09.html.

[11] "USAID STAR Project Helped Propel Vietnam into the Global Economy | DAI Online Publications," accessed May 12, 2014, http://dai-global-developments.com/articles/usaid-star-project-helped-propel-vietnam-into-the-global-economy.html.

[12] Penelope Nicholson and Nguyen Hung Quang, "The Vietnamese Judiciary: The Politics of Appointment and Promotion," *Pacific Rim Law and Policy Journal Association*, 2005, 5, http://digital.law.washington.edu/dspace-law/bitstream/handle/1773.1/659/14PacRimLPolyJ001.pdf?sequence=1.2005, 5, http://digital.law.washington.edu/dspace-law/bitstream/handle/1773.1/659/14PacRimLPolyJ001.pdf?sequence=1.}","plainCitation":"Penelope Nicholson and Nguyen Hung Quang, "The Vietnamese Judiciary: The Politics of Appointment and Promotion," Pacific Rim Law and Policy Journal Association, 2005, 5, http://digital.law.washington.edu/dspace-law/bitstream/handle/1773.1/659/14PacRimLPolyJ001.pdf?sequence=1."},"citationItems":[{"id":1592,"uris":["http://zotero.org/users/572316/items/JDRBX9MQ"],"uri":["http://zotero.org/users/572316/items/JDRBX9MQ"],"itemData":{"id":1592,"type":"article-journal","title":"The Vietnamese Judiciary: The Politics of Appointment and Promotion","container-title":"Pacific Rim Law and Policy Journal Association","URL":"http://digital.law.washington.edu/dspace-law/bitstream/handle/1773.1/659/14PacRimLPolyJ001.pdf?sequence=1","author":[{"family":"Penelope Nicholson and Nguyen Hung Quang","given":""}],"issued":{"date-parts":[["2005"]]}},"locator":"5","label":"page"}],"schema":"https://github.com/citation-style-language/schema/raw/master/csl-citation.json"}

nificantly by the donor countries. The legal system is gradually changing and has some new features that are different from the period of a centrally-planned economy. The reforms of Vietnam in the new century relate more to the state of the rule of law than socialist legality (*phap che xa hoi chu nghia*).[13] The problem is how Vietnam uses legal models and reforming solutions of different legal traditions (civil law, common law, socialist law) to create a coherent legal system.[14]

2. Sources of Law

It is essential to answer the question: *what is law in Vietnam*? Law refers to legal normative documents issued by competent agencies as prescribed by laws. Article 2, Law on Promulgation of legal normative documents (hereinafter Law on Laws 2015) defines the concept of legislative documents as documents that contain legal regulations and the promulgation of which complies with regulations of law on authority, manner, and procedures provided for in this Law. In addition, Article 3, section 1 states that: "Normative regulations are general rules of conduct, commonly binding, and applied repeatedly to agencies, organizations, and individuals nationwide or within a certain administrative division, promulgated by the regulatory agencies and competent persons in this Law, and the implementation of which is ensured by the State."

The legal system includes many types of legal normative documents; therefore, it also forms a hierarchical legal validity. The Constitution is the highest legal authority. Law on Laws 2015, Article 5 defines principles in development and promulgation of legal documents as follows:

1. Ensure the constitutionality, legitimacy, and uniformity of legislative

---

[13] Albert Chen, *Constitutionalism in Asia in the Early Twenty-First Century* (Cambridge University Press, 2014), 202.

[14] Per Sevastik, *Legal Assistance to Developing Countries: Swedish Perspectives on the Rule of Law* (Martinus Nijhoff Publishers, 1997), 115.

documents in the legal system.
2. Comply with regulations of law on authority, manner, and procedures for formulating and promulgating legislative documents.
3. Ensure transparency of legislative documents.
4. Ensure the feasibility, frugality, effectiveness, promptness, accessibility, and practicality of legislative documents; integrate gender equality issues in legislative documents; ensure simplification of administrative procedures.
5. Ensure national defense and security, and environmental protection without obstruction of implementation of the international agreements to which the Socialist Republic of Vietnam is a signatory.
6. Ensure publicity and democracy in receipt of and response to opinions, complaints of agencies, organizations, and individuals during the process of formulating and promulgating legislative documents.

Legal normative documents include many types of documents with different legal variations.

According to these regulations, a court's precedent is not defined as laws because it is not a legal document. It is essential to note that the concept of a legal document defined as laws differs from the concept of a legal document that is applied to a specific case (such as a judgment of the court or an administrative decision).

Sources of law in Vietnam are defined as all fundamental/basic elements used by authorized entities for developing, promulgating, and interpreting laws as well as for application in dealing with specific case in practices.[15] Sources of law are divided into two major types: 1) The party's Policy, Economic Policies, and Legal Philosophy (*nguon noi dung*) are fundamental elements that shape the nature of the legal system (*refers to natural sources of law*); 2) General legal

---

[15] TS. Nguyễn Thị Hồi, *Về khái niệm nguồn của pháp luật*, Tạp chí Luật học, số 2/2008, 29, 30.

principles, the written legal documents, international treaties, customary regulations, and judicial decisions (*nguon hon hop*) are fundamental elements for the interpretation and application of laws in practice (*refers to statutory sources of law*).[16]

Legal documents are the main sources of law:
Vietnam has a *civil law system*; therefore, sources of law include mainly written laws. Law refers to various types of legislation as prescribed by Law on Laws 2015. The sources of law include the following documents (Article 4, Law on Laws 2015):

1. The Constitution.
2. Codes and Laws (hereinafter referred to as Laws), Resolutions of the National Assembly.
3. Ordinances, Resolutions of Standing Committee of the National Assembly; Joint Resolutions between the Standing Committee of the National Assembly and the Management Board of the Central Committee of the Vietnamese Fatherland Front.
4. Orders and Decisions of the President.
5. Decrees of the Government; Joint Resolutions between the Government and the Management Board of the Central Committee of the Vietnamese Fatherland Front.
6. Decisions of the Prime Minister.
7. Resolutions of the Judge Council of the People's Supreme Court.
8. Circulars of the executive judge of the People's Supreme Court; Circulars of the Chief Procurator of the Supreme People's Procuracy; Circulars of Ministers, Heads of ministerial agencies; Joint Circulars between the executive judge of the People's Supreme Court and the Chief Procurator

---

[16] Nguyen Thi Hoi, "Các Loại Nguồn Của Pháp Luật Việt Nam Hiện Nay," *Thông Tin Pháp Luật Dân Sự*, 2008, http://thongtinphapluatdansu.edu.vn/2008/09/09/1635/.

of the Supreme People's Procuracy; Joint Circulars between Ministers, Heads of ministerial agencies and the executive judge of the People's Supreme Court, the Chief Procurator of the Supreme People's Procuracy; Decisions of the State Auditor General.
9. Resolutions of the People's Councils of central-affiliated cities and provinces (hereinafter referred to as provinces).
10. Decisions of the People's Committees of provinces.
11. Legislative documents of local governments in administrative - economic units.
12. Resolutions of the People's Councils of districts, towns and cities within provinces (hereinafter referred to as districts).
13. Decisions of the People's Committees of districts.
14. Resolutions of the People's Councils of communes, wards and towns within districts (hereinafter referred to as communes).
15. Decisions of the People's Committees of communes.

The sources of law include legal documents which are formed with hierarchical legal validity in principle. The Constitution has the highest legal validity in the national legal system. All legal documents must be consistent with the Constitution and legal documents issued by the higher state organs. If a legal document issued by the lower state organ is inconsistent with the Constitution and legal document issued by the higher state organs, the higher state organ will hold the power to suspend it.

It is crucial to note that Vietnam is still struggling to develop a comprehensive and consistent legal system. The main issue of the legal system is its consistency.

Judicial precedents

Judicial precedents were not defined as a source of law prior to 2016. However, the precedents have been recognized as a source of law since 2016. The Civil Procedure Code 2015 (Article 45) states that: "Precedents shall be studied

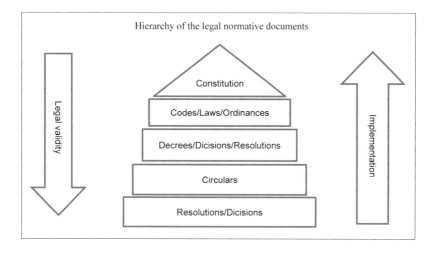

and applied in the resolution of civil cases after being selected by the Council of Judges of the Supreme People's Court and announced by the Chief Justice of the Supreme People's Court."

In addition, Resolution No. 03/2015/NQ-HDTP on the process for selecting, publishing, and adopting precedents states:[17] *"Precedents are arguments and rulings written on effective judgments or decisions (hereinafter referred to as judgment) of the courts that are selected by the Council of Justices of the Supreme People's Court and published by the Chief Justice of the Supreme People's Court in order for other courts to study and adopt them when deciding later cases."* (Article 1, Resolution No. 03/2015). Decision No. 220/QĐ-CA dated April 06, 2016 issued by the Chief Justice of the Supreme People's Court published the first 10 precedents. In 2017, 6 precedents were selected and published by Decision No. 299/QĐ-CA dated December 28, 2017. In 2018, there were 11 precedents published under Decision No. 199/QĐ-CA dated 17/10/2018. Up until now, there have been 27 precedents in total that have been selected, published, and adopted by the Council of Justices of the Supreme People's Court (CJSPC).

---

[17] Resolution No.03/2015/NQ-HDTP on Process for Selecting, publishing and adopting precedents, dated October 28, 2015

Notably, it is different from the common law in other countries in that only the precedents selected by the CJSPC are the source of the laws in Vietnam. Resolution No. 03/2015/NQ-HDTP also defines the criteria for selecting precedents, including: 1) Containing arguments to clarify the provisions of the law which have differing interpretations as well as analyze and explain legal issues or events and legal principles and guidelines to be followed in a specific situation, 2) Having normative value, 3) Ensuring the consistency of law in adjudication and the same settlement results from the two cases having the same facts or events (Article 2).

The precedents will be used to handle similar cases to ensure that the two cases have similar facts to one another and shall have the same settlement results. "If a precedent is used, all judgments of courts having precedential value, all similar facts specified in the precedent and all similar facts in the case to be solved and the legal opinion mentioned in the precedent must be cited, analyzed and specified in the judgment or the decision of the court; if the precedent is not adopted, they must provide an explanation in the judgment" (Article 8, section 2).

International treaties/Conventions

To be a source of law, international treaties/conventions must be ratified by Vietnam. International treaties/conventions become sources of law if they are applied directly or indirectly in dealing with a specific case in Vietnam. In general, Vietnam often interprets international treaties as domestic laws as a way of implementing international treaties in Vietnam. For example, the law on the anti-corruption of Vietnam in 2009 interprets the regulations of UNCAC.

Customary regulations

In principle, a customary regulation is not a source of law. However, customary regulations will be adopted as a source of law if they are used to deal with a specific case. Vietnam defines customary regulations as a source of law in some legal documents. Article 5 of the Civil Code 2015 defines the application of practices as follows:

1. Practices mean rules of conduct necessary to define rights and obligations of persons in specific civil relations, formed and repeated over a long time, recognized and applied generally in a region, race or a community or a civil field.
2. In cases where it is neither provided for by law nor agreed upon by the parties, practices may apply but they must not contravene the principles provided for in Article 3 of this Code.

In brief, sources of law in Vietnam mainly include legal documents issued by competent agencies as prescribed by the Law on Laws 2015. However, the legal system still has many problems such as its contradictory nature, loopholes, and overlaps due to the lack of an effective channel for constitutional review. The Government and Ministries hold the power to interpret laws adopted by the National Assembly and have played an important role in legislation. This mechanism ensures that the legal system responds quickly to socio-economic changes, but it also raises many challenges to the process of reforming the legal system in Vietnam.

3. The Court System

The court system of Vietnam is hierarchical including the Supreme People's Court, High Courts, Provincial People's Courts and District People's Courts. Constitution 2013, Article 102 provides that:

1. The people's courts are the judicial organ of the Socialist Republic of Vietnam, exercising the judicial power.
2. The people's courts comprise the Supreme People's Court and other courts established by law.
3. The people's courts are responsible for the protection of justice, human rights, citizen's rights, the socialist regime, interests of the State, and le-

gal rights and interests of organizations and individuals.

- The Supreme People's Court is the highest judicial organ of the Socialist Republic of Vietnam. The term of the President of the Supreme People's Court is consistent with the term of the National Assembly (5 years). The President of the Supreme People's Court is responsible for presenting his reports to the National Assembly and, when the latter is not in session, to its Standing Committee and to the State President. Vietnam has six types of courts namely the Administrative, Labor, Civil, Criminal, and Economic Courts; the Military Court is established for dealing with military crimes. The Supreme People's Court holds the power to re-adjudicate appealed cases that have been sent from the Provincial Court.
- The High Court is established in Hanoi, Da Nang, and Ho Chi Minh. The High Court conducts appellate trials of cases in which first-instance judgments or decisions of people's courts of provinces within their territorial jurisdiction which have not yet taken legal effect are appealed or protested against in accordance with the procedural law and conducts trial according to cassation or a reopening procedure of cases in which judgments or decisions of people's courts of provinces, centrally run cities, rural districts, urban districts, towns, provincial cities or the equivalent within their territorial jurisdiction which have taken legal effect are protested against in accordance with the procedural law (Article 29, Law on organization of people's court, 2014).
- The Provincial Courts are established in each province of Vietnam (currently Vietnam has 63 provincial courts). The provincial courts deal with appeals for District cases and other cases as prescribed by law.
- The District Courts are established in every virtually every district. The District Courts deal with civil, economic, labor, administrative, and criminal cases (first-instance cases). District Courts include one Chief Justice, one or two deputy Chief Justices, judges, jurors, and clerks.

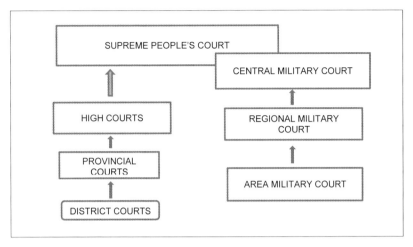

Vietnam has adopted a system of two-instance trials. If a party does not agree with the judgment of the first-instance court, she/he may appeal to the second-instance court for another trial. The decision of the second-instance court is the final decision and must be enforced. The jurisdiction of the court is determined by the territory, the level of the trial, and the nature of the case in question.

The Chief Justice of the Supreme People's Court exercises the power to submit to the National Assembly for approval of the appointment, relief from duty and dismissal of judges of the Supreme People's Court, and to propose that the President appoint, relieve from duty or dismiss Deputy Chief Justices of the Supreme People's Court and judges of other courts (Article 27, Section 7, Law on Organization of People's Court).

4. Legal Professionals

Laws on organization of the Court, Ordinance on Judges and Jurors, and the Law on Lawyers provide clear criteria for becoming judges, public prosecutors, and attorneys.

Judges

Article 67, Law on the organization of the Court 2014, defines the criteria for becoming a judge as follows.

1. Being a Vietnamese citizen who is loyal to the Fatherland and the Constitution of the Socialist Republic of Vietnam, has good ethical qualities, a firm political stance, courage and resolve to safeguard justice, and is incorrupt and honest.
2. Possessing a bachelor or higher degree in law.
3. Having been professionally trained in adjudication.
4. Having been engaged in practical legal work for a certain period of time.
5. Being physically fit to fulfill assigned duties.

In general, judges of people's courts include: Judges of the Supreme People's Court, High-level judges, Intermediate-level judges, and Primary-level judges. The National Assembly Standing Committee will decide the number of judges in the Supreme People's Court and the number of middle and lower-ranking judges according to the proposals made by the Supreme People's Court's Chief Judge.

Article 68 defines conditions for the appointment of primary-level, intermediate-level, and high-level judges as follows:

1. Having been engaged in legal work for at least 5 years;
2. Being capable of adjudicating cases and settling other matters under the jurisdiction of his/her court prescribed by the procedural law;
3. Having passed a primary-level judge selection examination.

The initial term of office of judges is 5 years. For judges who are reappointed or appointed to another judge rank, the subsequent term of office is 10 years (Article 74).

In general, a judge is a type of public official in Vietnam, so he/she has to work for a court from the beginning as the court's staff member and it may take time to become a judge. Hence, lawyers or the other legal practitioners are not transferred or nominated to become a judge if they do not take the examination to be public officials.

In 2017, the total number of staff members working for the court system in Vietnam was 14,725 people. There were 1870 judges who were appointed and reappointed in 2017 (1,131 newly appointed and 739 reappointed judges).[18]

Public prosecutors

Constitution of Vietnam, Article 107 defines that: The people's procuracies shall exercise the power to prosecution and control judicial activities. Procurators are persons who are appointed in accordance with the law to perform the function of exercising the power to prosecute and supervise judicial activities (Article 74, Law on Organization of People's Procuracies, 2014).

General criteria for procurators are defined under Article 75 as follows:

1. Being Vietnamese citizens who are loyal to the Fatherland and the Constitution of the Socialist Republic of Vietnam, have good ethical qualities, are incorrupt and honest, have a firm political stance and resolve to safeguard the socialist legislation.
2. Possessing a bachelor's or higher degree in law.
3. Having been professionally trained in prosecution.
4. Having been engaged in practical work for a certain period of time in accordance with this Law.
5. Being physically fit to fulfill assigned duties.

Ranks of procurators of the people's procuracies include: Procurators of the Supreme People's Procuracy, high-level procurators, intermediate-level procurators, and primary-level procurators.

---

[18] Report of Supreme People's Court on assessment of work implementation in 2017 and the main tasks of the courts in 2018 (draft), page 12.

Similar to the judges, a prosecutor often works for the Procuracy office as a staff member and he/she will be appointed as a prosecutor when they fully meet the criteria prescribed under Article 74.

The term of office of procurators is 5 years. For procurators who are reappointed or entitled to rank promotion, the subsequent term of office is 10 years (Article 82).

Currently, there are around 15,860 people who are working for procuracies from the central to the local level. The number of prosecutors at all levels is around 9,418 people.[19]

Lawyers

The Law on Lawyers of Vietnam defines that: "Lawyers are persons who fully meet the criteria and conditions for professional practice under the provisions of this Law and provide legal services at the request of individuals, agencies or organizations (hereinafter collectively referred to as clients)" (Article 2).

The Law on Lawyers was adopted in 2006, which provided working conditions of lawyers in Vietnam. This law was revised in 2012. Criteria of lawyers are defined by Article 10 (Law on Lawyers 2006) as follows:

- Vietnamese citizens;
- Demonstrate loyalty to the motherland and the Constitution of the Socialist Republic of Vietnam;
- Observe the Constitution and law;
- Have good moral qualities;
- Possess a law bachelor's degree;
- Have been trained in the legal profession;
- Have gone through the probation of the legal profession;
- Have good health for law practice.

In general, to practice law, lawyers must be licensed by the Bar Association if he/she meets the following conditions:

---

[19] Information shared by the staff of Statistic Division of the Supreme People's Procuracy

- A lawyer training course lasting 12 months which is certificated by the Vietnam Judicial Academy;
- A 12 month practical training at any law firm;
- They must pass the national exams and get the lawyer practicing certificate issued by the Ministry of Justice;
- The Bar Association of the area in which the lawyer practices issues a license to the member.

The Vietnamese Lawyers Association (Vietnamese Lawyers Federation) was established in 2009 as the National Bar Association which includes the Local Bar Association established at each province. Provincial Bar Associations are established after consideration from the Ministry of Justice and a decision by the People's Committee. The Ministry of Justice holds the power to regulate the legal profession of lawyers in Vietnam. The Ministry of Justice has a specialized department for the administration of Bar Associations.

The number of licensed lawyers in 2014 was around 6000–7000 and Vietnam aims to reach 15,000 lawyers by 2020. The ratio of lawyers to the population in Vietnam is just around 1/14,000 which is considered lower than other Asian countries.[20] In 2017, the number of lawyers had increased up to around 12,000 lawyers from 7,000 in 2014.[21] However, in reality, Vietnam still lacks lawyers who have the capacity to practice law in an international environment.

Since Vietnam became a member of the WTO, foreign law firms have been

---

[20] The ratio is 1/1,000 in Singapore, 1/1,526 in Thailand and 1/1,546 in Japan. Furthermore, lawyers in Vietnam are mainly stationed in Hanoi (1,630 lawyers) and in HCMC (2,880 lawyers) while other provinces and cities only have three to five lawyers each. See: "Vietnam's Lawyer-to-Population Ratio the Region's Lowest - Vietnam's Lawyer-to-Population Ratio the Region's Lowest - SaiGon Times Daily," accessed May 16, 2014, http://english.thesaigontimes.vn/31264/Vietnam%E2%80%99s-lawyer-to-population-ratio-the-region%E2%80%99s-lowest.html.

[21] Hoạt động hành nghề luật sư: Nâng cao tiêu chuẩn, siết chặt quản lý, http://hanoimoi.com.vn/Tin-tuc/Xa-hoi/875782/hoat-dong-hanh-nghe-luat-su-nang-cao-tieu-chuan-siet-chat-quan-ly(lawyers practicing in Vietnam: improving the standards and tightening management) accessed 26 October 2018.

established in Vietnam which provide advice on Vietnamese legislation and regulations. Foreign law firms can operate in Vietnam as a branch of a foreign lawyers' organization, a subsidiary of a foreign lawyers' organization, a foreign law firm, or a partnership between a foreign lawyers' organization and a Vietnamese law partnership.

It is a known fact that judges, public prosecutors, and lawyers are provided only legal training in the beginning. Therefore, the Bachelor of Law degree is the most important criteria for a person who wants to become a judge, a prosecutor or a lawyer. Professional skill training has been a significant condition for appointment as a judge or prosecutor since 1998. [22] Consequently, a person who wants to become a judge, prosecutor or lawyer must study at the Vietnam Judicial Academy, the Court Academy, and the University of Procuracy.

In brief, the legal system of a country includes many elements. Studying the key factors of the legal system such as the legal ideology and its influencing factors, sources of laws, judicial system, and legal professionals is important for identifying the differences between the legal systems in each country.

---

[22] Decision No 34/1998 issued by Prime Minister dated February 10, 1998 on the establishment of the Vietnam Judicial Academy.

Chapter 3

USING CASE LAW IN LEGAL EDUCATION IN VIETNAM

Nguyen Ba Binh*
(Hanoi Law University)

1. The Need for Using Case Law in Legal Education in Vietnam

Although Vietnam does not belong to the common law system, case law is a topic which has attracted the attention of many lecturers and leaders of Vietnam's legal education institutions in recent years. Using case law in legal education in Vietnam is a necessary and pressing demand mainly for the following reasons:

Firstly, case law is already recognized as one of the sources of law in Vietnam. Therefore, law students must understand how case law works and how it is applied in practice. According to several important legal documents, such as the Law on the Organization of People's Courts of 2014[1], the Civil Code 2015[2], the Civil Procedures Code 2015[3], the Administrative Procedures Law of 2015[4] and

---

* *PhD (UNSW), Deputy Dean in Charge of Faculty of International Business and Trade Law, Hanoi Law University; Arbitrator at Vietnam International Arbitration Centre (VIAC), Vietnam.*

[1] Article 22.2(c).
[2] Article 6.
[3] Article 4.2, Article 45.3, Article 266.2(b), Article 313.4.
[4] Article 194.2(b), Article 242.4.

Resolution 03/2015/NQ-HĐTP[5], case law can be applied by courts to make decisions. The Chief Judge of Vietnam's Supreme Court has already issued four Decisions to publish 26 cases recognized as case law. In practice, Vietnam's courts have applied case law in trials. Therefore, case law is important and useful to graduates who work in fields related to not only international commercial law and international law but also domestic laws.

Second, using case law in legal education in Vietnam can help satisfy the objective demand of aligning education with practice through "learning in alignment with practice". In general, the training programs of legal education institutions currently focus only on theoretical issues rather than practical skills and the need for an improved labor force in society. Professional training is not an important element of training programs at legal education institutions in Vietnam;[6] these institutions mainly emphasize training in areas such as legal theories and regulations.[7] Although the institutions have been trying to improve their teaching methods, lecturing is still the major method used. With the popularity of the "one-way communication" approach in Vietnam's legal education, teachers often simply give lectures while students merely listen and take notes.[8] Law graduates generally are not practice-ready when leaving law schools.[9]

Third, the deep and wide international integration era has resulted in the requirement that Vietnam's legal training programs provide legal knowledge and practical skills to students related to not only domestic cases but also international cases and not only domestic laws but also foreign laws. At present, case law is not only an important source of the common law system but it is also being recognized in the legal systems of many other countries. Case law can also be creat-

---

[5] Resolution 03/2015/NQ-HĐTP of the Judge Council of Vietnam's Supreme Court, issued on October 19, 2015, on the Procedures on Choosing, Publishing and Applying Case Law.

[6] Ho, Ai Nhan, 'Legal Education in Vietnam: The History, Current Situation and Challenges' (2017) 26(1) *Legal Education Review*, tr.74.

[7] Ibid, tr.83.

[8] Ibid, tr.87.

[9] Ibid, tr.91.

ed and popularly applied by international dispute settlement organizations, such as the dispute settlement body of the World Trade Organization and international arbitration centers. Therefore, with case law playing such an important role in foreign countries and international dispute resolution organizations, it should be included in legal education in Vietnam.

2. The Current Situation of Using Case Law in Legal Education in Vietnam

Currently, Vietnam has over 60 legal education institutions. However, case law is rarely used in training programs at legal education institutions in Vietnam. In general, case law can be used in legal education in Vietnam in the following three ways: i) Teaching fundamental issues of case law as a discrete subject; ii) Teaching fundamental issues of case law as part of the content of several subjects; and iii) Using case method in teaching.

2.1 Teaching fundamental issues of case law as a discrete subject

In undergraduate education, only Hanoi Law University and Ho Chi Minh City Law University provide a discrete subject on case law. However, the teaching of this subject is still limited with respect to teaching topics and students. Hanoi Law University has a course on "Case Studies and Analyses" (2 credits), but it is only taught to students of the training program in International Trade and Business Law.[10] Ho Chi Minh City Law University has a course on "Case law in Vietnam's law system" (2 credits), but it is only a selective one. The subject on "Case Studies and Analyses" focuses on the following issues listed in the box below:

---

[10] There are currently four training programs at Hanoi Law University: i) Law, International Trade and Business Law, iii) Business Law, iv) English Language (Legal English).

> **Box 1. Detailed Contents of
> the Course on "Case Studies and Analyses"**
>
> **Topic 1. Some theory issues on Case law**
> 1.1. Case law concept
> 1.2. History and development of case law
> 1.3. The importance of case law in the common law system and in the civil law system
> 1.4. Conditions for a case's award becoming case law
> 1.5. Principles of applying case law
>
> **Topic 2. The court system of some countries of the common law system**
> 2.1. Court hierarchy of some countries of the common law system
> 2.2. Jurisdiction of courts in creating case law
> 2.3. Court's ways of analyzing previous court's awards
> 2.4. Methods of reasoning and argument
> 2.5. Storing and publishing case law
>
> **Topic 3. Case law in the common law system**
> 3.1. Principle of stare decisis
> 3.2. Ratio decidendi and obiter dictum
> 3.3. Distinguish cases
> 3.4. Overrule prior precedents
>
> **Topic 4. Case law in the civil law system and in Vietnam's law system**
> 4.1. Case law in the civil law system
> 4.2. Case law in Vietnam's law system
>
> **Topic 5. Practicing skills of case studies and analyses**
> 5.1. Basic steps of practicing skills of case studies and analyses
> 5.2. Practicing case studies and analyses
> 5.3. Practicing studies and analyses of case law of WTO
> 5.4. Practicing studies and analyses of case law related to international business

At the higher education level, most legal education institutions do not provide a discrete subject on the fundamental issues of case law. Hanoi Law University is an exceptional case due to its subject on "Case law and using case law in the rule of law state," but it is only a selective course and used in the Applied LLM program.[11]

---

[11] There are two LLM programs: i) Research program, ii) Applied program.

2.2 Teaching fundamental issues of case law as part of the content of several subjects

In the undergraduate program, case law is often introduced basically as a source of law or a case method at legal education institutions in Vietnam in different subjects, such as "State and Law Theory," "Comparative Law," "International Trade Law," "Public International Law," "Private International Law," "Legal reasoning and legal writing for law professionals."

In higher education, some legal education institutions provide subjects, for example, "Methods of Legal Analysis and Modern Legal Reasoning" at Hanoi Law University, which covers a part of introduction of case law.

2.3 Using case methods in teaching

In both the undergraduate programs and higher education, the case method has been used by lecturers for teaching different subjects. However, this is very limited. According to a survey report conducted with 112 law lecturers of different law schools within the Ministerial-Level Research Project entitled "Using case law in training legal and judicial staff in Vietnam today" in 2018, 68.8% of the interviewees said that case law is rarely used in teaching and 8% of interviewees said that they have never used case law in teaching.[12] Only in some subjects, such as "Legal reasoning and legal writing for law professionals" for undergraduates and "Methods of Legal Analysis and Modern Legal Reasoning" for students of the Applied LLM program at Hanoi Law University, the case method has been commonly used by lecturers. In some other subjects, including but not limited to, "Public International Law," "Private International Law," and "International Trade Law," case law has often been introduced in the learning materials or the course outline for the subjects. However, lecturers rarely use the case method in delivering lectures or seminars for these subjects. When using the case method, lecturers often cite case law in teaching or require students to

---

[12] "Using case law in training legal and judicial staffs in Vietnam today", Ministerial-Level Research Project of Vietnam's Ministry of Justice, chaired by Dr. Nguyen Ba Binh, 2018.

read cases and give their opinion on different issues raised by the lecturers.

3. Some Suggestions for Using Case Law in Legal Education in Vietnam

In order to use case law more effectively in legal education in Vietnam, it is necessary to consider the following major solutions:

First, legal education institutions should provide a discrete subject on the fundamental issues of case law for undergraduates as applied at the Hanoi Law University for students studying international trade law. Vietnam does not belong to the common law system as compared to other countries, consequently, not only people in general but also law students are unfamiliar with the concept of case law. Therefore, providing a discrete subject on the fundamental issues of case law can help students understand case law in general and apply case law in different subjects.

Second, similar to the countries which belong to the common law system, to teach and study case law effectively, one of the prerequisite conditions is the availability of casebooks. According to the survey report conducted with 400 people (3 groups: law students, law lecturers, and law practitioners) in the Ministerial-Level Research Project entitled "Using case law in training legal and judicial staff in Vietnam today" in 2018, over 70% respondents (the total interviewees and also in each group) said that the current learning materials cannot satisfy the needs of law students. Therefore, in the short-term, it is necessary for Vietnam's legal education institutions to write and publish casebooks and commentary books on case law.

Finally, Vietnam's legal education institutions must develop strategies to provide an adequate number of exceptional lecturers on case law. The quality of teaching depends largely on the quality of the lecturers. However, in Vietnam, which has not had a "culture of using case law" for a long time as in the countries belonging to the common law system, there are currently not many law lecturers who are proficient in case law and/or the case method. Therefore, in the short-term (within five years), when not many lecturers at legal education institutions are proficient in case law and case methods, the institutions should use both their own lecturers and visiting lecturers who are practicing law as lawyers or judges and are conversant in case law. In the long-term (over five years), the institutions need to attract more people who have graduated from foreign universities in countries that belong to the common law system to be lecturers or guest lecturers, especially for the discrete subject on the fundamental issues of case law. The institutions' lecturers also need to improve their knowledge on case law, teaching skills, and English language ability.

Chapter 4

GENERAL VIEW OF THE LEGAL SYSTEM IN VIETNAM

Nguyen Ngoc Dien*

(University of Economics and Law Vietnam National University in Ho Chi Minh City)

Introduction

The contemporary Vietnamese legal system is set up by way of the development of the soviet model, which is characterized by the prevalence of public law and the tutelary role played by the public authority in the social life scenario. A number of consequences have resulted from this structure. Among these consequences, on the one hand we can quote the originalities of the concept of sources of law, and on the other the position of law with respect to individual freedom.

Regarding the sources of law, the running system was characterized by the almost absolute domination of statutory law. It has indeed been taught for a long time that law is composed of the written rules elaborated by the competent state organs in accordance with strictly defined legal procedures[1]. Customs and habits exist naturally as an ordinary social phenomenon; they are practiced all the time in civil life and respected spontaneously by the people, however they have not

---

* Associate Professor–Vice rector, University of Economics and Law, Vietnam National University in Ho Chi Minh city.

[1] Nguyen Van Dong (2017), *Giáo trình lý luận chung về nhà nước và pháp luật (Manual of Introduction to State and Law)*, Chính trị Quốc gia Su That, Hà Nội, p. 165 to 170.

been recognized by the public authority as norms of conduct whose observation is guaranteed by public forces.

As for the content, the law was impregnated with the guiding idea, according to which organized society was a well-directed human community[2]. In light of this idea, it is generally acknowledged that subjective rights are nothing but a favor granted to citizens by the public authority. Thus, citizens only have the rights formally defined by laws and regulations. Moreover, for these rights to be effective, they must be sufficiently defined by regulations in terms of exercise modalities.

The integration of the country into the world political and economic life logically leads the way to, as well as it logically requires, deep change in human thinking toward liberalism and flexibism. This finally results in revamping the running system. In the domain of law, these movements are translated into efforts to adapt other legal cultures' achievements without considering the ideological divergence. Among these adaptations, the introduction of the new concept of sources of law and subjective rights are particularly remarkable. This results in a regard for civil law, in thorough revision of the legal regimes of property and contract within the framework of elaboration of the new Civil Code adopted in 2015. This further leads to the consolidation of the role of judge in the settlement of disputes in civil life.

1. New Concepts of Sources of Law

There is now a strong tendency in Vietnam to acknowledge the modes of creation of rules of law, which is similar to that in Western countries. Thus, cus-

---

[2] According to article 12 of the Constitution of 1980, "The State manages the society in accordance with law and constantly reinforces the socialist legislation. All State organs, associations, State's employees, associations' employees and citizens must observe the Constitution and regulations, must struggle against criminal actions and constitutional or legal infractions". These strong words transport the leader's will to set up the public authority's overall control of social life.

toms and judicial precedents join the legislation (statutory law) in the family of sources of positive law[3]. The written law–statutes–however remains the most important source among the modes of creating rules of law. The principle which governs the settlement of conflicts between the sources of law is that, on the one hand, statutory law occupies the preponderant place, and on the other, rules of other origins are applicable only in cases of insufficiency or ambiguity of the statutory law.

1.1. Statutory law

Definition. Statutory law might be defined as the written rule elaborated by a competent state organ in accordance with the Constitution and the Law on elaboration of statutory documents. Through the perspective of competency, a distinction is made between legislative statutes and executive statutes: the former is relevant to the parliament, while the latter is placed under the government's competence.

Enforcement of the law. The legislative statutes are necessarily promulgated by the state president.

Regarding time, statutory law is, in principle, enforced for the future. The non-retroactivity of law's effect is only repelled in case of its advantageous application in favor of the society as a whole or the concerned organizations and/or individuals. Moreover, the retroactive enforcement of statutory law is prohibited in case of newly created liability or more severe liability.

Constitutionality of statutory law. The statutory law must be in conformity with the Constitution. This principle is set up by the Constitution. However, unlike many Western laws, Vietnamese law does not confer the constitutional power to the judge. More precisely, the constitutional control of statutory law is actually ensured by the National Assembly in Vietnam.

---

[3] According to the article of the Civil Code of 2015, the customs and judicial precedent might be used as subsidiary sources of law for the purpose of settlement of disputes in case of silence or insufficiency of statutory law.

By way of consequence, the author of legislative statutes takes responsibility for the constitutionality of the statutes. The control of constitutionality of legislative statutes is normally performed as part of the elaboration of the related statutes: once revealed, the unconstitutional provisions are withdrawn from the draft before it is subjected to the vote for adoption. As for the legislative statutes already enforced and containing the provisions that are considered unconstitutional, it is necessary to proceed with revision or abolition of the related statutes.

The control of constitutionality of executive statutes is also placed under the authority of the national assembly. Although, in reality, the effective control is ensured by the government and the parliament only plays the role of a supreme supervisor. For its part, the government relies on the ministry of justice, which is considered the guardian of the legal system. In case of unconstitutionality acknowledged by the ministry of justice, the related executive statute should be abolished.

1.2. Customary law.

Definition. Customary law is formally defined in Vietnam. According to the current Civil Code Article 5 paragraph 1, customary law is a set of rules whose content is sufficiently clear for the determination of rights and obligations of a natural person or a legal entity in a determined civil relation. Moreover, the lawmakers require that a customary rule must be something that is done repeatedly for a long time and widely acknowledged in a region, an area, or a human community.

Place of customary law. In principle, customary law has the same authority as statutory law. However, it is only applied where there is no statutory rule applicable upon condition. Nevertheless, it is not contrary to the basic principles of civil law mentioned in Article 3 of the current Civil Code. In case of contrariety of customary law and statutory law, the latter prevails; however, there are customary rules that are constantly observed by the people, despite contrary statutes. The underage customary marriage is a typical example.

1.3. Case law.

Notion. Basing the legal system on statutory law, the Vietnamese current jurisdiction acknowledges that the judge is not competent to create rule, he is only allowed to say (interpret) the statutory law. In certain cases the judicial interpretation of statutory law is acknowledged to be case law.

Formation. However, the formation of case law in Vietnam is not carried out in the continental way. At the beginning of the process, a case is chosen and recommended by a provincial court or a superior court. If it is acknowledged by a competent organ of the supreme court as a potential case law, it will be published on the official review of the people's court for public commentary. The most applauded solution will be submitted to the so-called case law consulting committee for selection. The selected solution is finally submitted to the plenary assembly of the supreme court judges for adoption. The logical consequence of this complicated process is that case law in Vietnam is binding against all judges.

2. New Concept of Subjective Rights

2.1. Reasons of change

Provocation to sustainable development and social progress. Personally experienced by a society where everything is under the supervision of public authority, the country's leaders have realized that a centrally managed society is easy to manage, but it is sluggish, with constantly tired, timid, and passive members. An authoritatively administered society moves slowly and with difficulty and is above all devoid of the creative spirit. As a result, the country is constantly underdeveloped and marked by the generalization of poverty.

The liberalization of social life is therefore essential for the sustainable development of society. Further, the recognition of individual freedom conceived in the Western ideology could expose Vietnamese society to the risk of falling into disorder. There is an evident spring effect: being compressed for a long time, society tends to rebound to the maximum of its ability to move once released and risks falling into a chaotic state. In contrast, the Vietnamese have lived under the supervision and guidance of public authorities for centuries and they are not accustomed to autonomy. As a result, they risk being embarrassed by the freedom granted to them by the law and do not know how to exercise these rights.

By way of consequence, it is necessary to organize the adaptation of individual freedom to the political, social, and cultural context of Vietnam in a suitable way. More precisely, for Vietnam, there is a double question of promoting private freedom and controlling it so that it can be at the best service of the enjoyment of subjective rights and contribute to the social progression as well as the sustainable development of human society[4].

2.2. Illustration of the new concept of subjective rights: property rights

General view. Ownership is indeed acknowledged in the Vietnamese positive law as the most important property right. Similar to Western law, the Vietnamese current law confers upon the owner possible extensive prerogatives on his properties, except for respect of the state interests, national interests, public interests, and other people's rights and legitimate interests, as prescribed in Article 3 of the Civil Code of 2015.

Property rights on land. Similar to Chinese law, the Vietnamese law sets up the legal regime of immovable property on the fundamental principle, according to which land belongs exclusively to the people who, for the effective performance of their ownership on land, are represented by the State. In contrast, the State is engaged by the Constitution to proceed with the reasonable distribution of land to those in need. The land use right, initially set up by a Land Law enforced in 1987,

---

[4] According to article 15 of the Constitution of 2013: "1. The citizen's rights are unseparated from the citizen's duties; one must observe other's rights; the citizen is responsible for performance of his duties towards the State and the society; the exercise of human rights and citizen's rights must not harm the national interest and other people's legitimate rights and interests". Thus, the citizen's rights are acknowledged as a reward of the performance of the citizen's duties toward the nation, the society and the community.

has constantly been improved as a fundamental private right to land. Effective of the new Constitution of 2013, the new Land Law of 2013 acknowledges the land use right to be the almost ownership of land: the right holder is indeed entitled to use and transfer his rights in accordance with the civil law. Perhaps the only difference between land use right and ownership of land is that the former is subject to retaking without indemnity in case of non use[5]. The Civil Code of 2015, for its part, places the land use right among the so-called "property interests" within the framework of formal classification of assets (art 115). In regards to property law, land use right constitutes the elementary real estate; the immovable property law, as part of private property law, is set up around this institution.

2.3. Illustration of the new concept of subjective rights: freedom to contract

From credibility to judiciousness. Similar to most legal systems, the Vietnamese current contract law is set up on the basis of the idea that law intervenes in contractual relations, essentially for the purpose of defense of public order, social morality, and general interest. Thus, unless a set of mandatory rules are imposed for this purpose; the law leaves ample space to customs and habits and especially to agreement between the contracting parties.

Moreover, it is noted that in Eastern traditional thinking, credibility constitutes the moral basis of civil transactions developed in a well-organized society. Based on this, contractual relationships can be established and maintained without relying on a written contract containing many clauses that make clear, tight, detailed commitments. It is generally recognized that commitments clearly stated on paper are only necessary to tie up those who are dishonest or tricky.

However, an increase in the number of litigations related to contracts in contemporary social practice could help in reconsidering the above-mentioned prejudice. The causes of disputes might be various, but most scandals attracting

---

[5] In French law, the non use of land must not be sanctioned by the confiscation of the property: F. Terré, *Droit civil – Les biens*, Précis Dalloz, Paris, 2006, p. 306.

public attention are characterized by the fact that the litigious parties had been close friends or at least in a good relationship. The mutual faith and good feelings served as a solid platform whereon important transactions were carried out without long and intensive dealings. However, once a difference occurs the contracting parties find themselves in possession of a contract whose content is too sketchy, vague, and laconic to help determine an appropriate way for reasonably ending their contractual relationship. The judge is seized by way of consequence to settle the differences that cannot be resolved by private transaction. However, where the contract's terms and conditions are so general and unclear, it is difficult for the judge to find a reasonable solution to the problem.

Complicated litigations recently reported by the press are regarded as warnings to the society that result in a social tendency to set up contractual relationships on the basis of well-prepared agreements. Currently, the directing idea that is acknowledged is of having good contracts for seeking profit, and in case of conflict, as a means of defending rights and interests, the contracting party must be active right at the moment of dealings for the formation of the contract. He or she must indeed be knowingly engaged in useful and necessary discussions to clarify his or her own will as well as that of the other party. In other words, to prevent litigation, the contracting party must be ensured that the meeting of wills for the purpose of setting up contractual relations must be concretized in solid terms and conditions described in lucid phrases. For important contracts related to transfer of properties of high value, a legal expert's assistance is necessary, all of which is facilitated, from now on, by a flexible contract regulation set up by Vietnamese contemporary lawmakers.

2.4. Illustration of subjective rights: right to self-protection

Adopting the American experience. To set up the institution of right to self-protection of civil rights, Vietnamese lawmakers have tried to adopt the American experience[6]. In principle, everybody is free to organize his or her life

---

[6] Th. A. Street, *Foundations of Legal Liability – a Presentation of Theory and Development*

within the limit imposed by law. To this effect, the lawmakers recognize that one is entitled to take the necessary measures without resorting to public forces for the protection of one's interests against harmful acts committed by a third party. This rule is formally adopted by the Civil Code of 2015 in Articles 11 and 12. Thus, the land owner is allowed to remove trees or to demolish buildings erected on his or her land without consent. He or she is also allowed to use physical strength to repossess a property belonging to him or her that was stolen by a third party. In contractual relations, the right of self-protection is also recognized as a civil sanction at low cost, easy to implement, and above all very effective. Thus, faced with a non-performing and recalcitrant debtor who does not accept leaving the mortgaged property at the disposal of the mortgagee, the latter can proceed by his own means, without the public forces' assistance, to foreclose on the goods in question with the view of putting them on adjudication in the framework of enforced payment of debt.

However, it cannot be denied that the right of self-protection can lead the holder to an irregular situation in the event of abuse. Therefore, lawmakers should regulate laws in such a way that this right is exercised with prudence and serious reflection.

According to Article 12 of the Vietnamese Civil Code, the self-protection of civil rights must be in reasonable consideration with the nature and extent of the infringement on civil rights and must not be contrary to the fundamental principles of civil law provided for in Article 3 of this Code.

For example, it is quite reasonable to cut off water and electricity supply if the tenant does not pay rent. However, it is absolutely unreasonable to block entry into the house as a self-protection of the lessor's interests against a defaulting tenant, since this is clearly contrary to the constitutionally established principles of guaranteeing the right to housing and freedom of movement.

Moreover, it is noted that the right to self-protection in Vietnamese law is a right of defense. It is only used where there is harm or threat of harm inflicted on

---

of Common Law, Northport, N.Y, Edward Thompson Company, 1906, tr. 280–281.

someone's rights and interests. The concept of harm, for its part, is perceived in the broadest sense. It may simply be passive attitude, such as non fulfillment of an obligation. However, it may also be proactive behavior that adversely affects other's rights and interests, as in case of robbery. Thus, the right of self-protection in Vietnamese law is similar to self-help, which is acknowledged in English law and different from that admitted in American law as the right to use physical force under personal management to protect one's rights and interests without "breach of the peace"[7].

3. Redefinition of Judicial Functions in the Context of a New Concept of Subjective Rights

Prohibition of denial of justice. For a long time under the socialist regime, the judge was allowed to refuse making a decision in case of absence of the necessary rule for settlement of a dispute. The justification of that behavior is as follows: under the centralized social management system, individuals are only entitled to do what they are authorized by statutes. Consequently, all acts done in the absence of legal authorization are considered irregular. There may, of course, be irregularities that cannot be sanctioned due to the lack of relevant regulation. But it is certain that the perpetrators of irregular acts cannot be protected and when they strike at the door of the court to seek legal protection against the violation of the interests involved in the acts in question, the judge may judiciously turn their back.

The integration of the country into the global legal thinking has resulted in the adjustment of the judge's functions. It is ultimately the person to whom one might have recourse in the event of crisis or conflict. Once seized, the judge is

---

[7] For a description of self-help in English law in the matter of protection of property: F.H. Lawson and B Rudden, *The Law of Property*, Oxford University Press, 2002, p. 54 and 55. For an analysis of this institution in US law: R. Mc Robert, *"Defining "Breach of the Peace" in Self-Help Repossessions"*, Washington Law Review, Vol 87:569, 2012, ps. 569 to 594.

required to specify who is right, and, therefore, deserves the protection granted by the public authority subject to sanction. The judge, in the name of justice, has the right, as he or she has an obligation, to pronounce judgment, even in the event of insufficiency or obscurity or even contrariety of the statutory law rules, as specified by the French Civil Code in Article 4.

Currently, the Vietnamese judge must always observe the statutory law in the exercise of his or her functions. However, eventually faced with the difficulty in application of the statutory law, he or she is bound to make a decision on the subsidiary basis of customary law. Where it is impossible to conceive of a solution of any legal issue in the light of statutory law or customary law, it is necessary to resort to equity. Formally prescribed by the lawmakers in the form of a provision inserted in the new Civil Code and the new code of civil procedure, this rule implies the Vietnamese national leaders' firm determination to revamp the legal system and, in particular, the judicial system within the framework of construction of the state, based on rule of law according to the criteria of modernity and global integration.

Chapter 5

THE LAO LEGAL SYSTEM:

Structures, Challenges and Legal Education
toward Strengthening the Rule of Law

Alounna Khamhoung*

(National University of Laos)

Law and legislations of Lao PDR are the outcomes of the development process of Lao's multi-ethnic people over periods of time. After the long-standing aspiration and strong determination of the national community, Laos has finally been launched the state power of people democracy which contributes to the development of the rule of law state of the people, by the people and for the people, following the guidance of Lao People's Revolutionary Party.

This report is the overview of history and evolution of Lao Law from the past until present, aiming to describe briefly the identity of political structure of Lao PDR, also the legal system and challenges, and, summarizing how legal research application promotes the rule of law.

1. Overview of Lao People's Democratic Republic

1.1 Background information

Lao People's Democratic Republic, or Laos, with an area of 236.800 sq. km,

---

* Lecturer, Faculty of Law and Political Science, National University of Laos.

is a landlocked nation in Southeast Asia occupying the northwest portion of the Indochinese peninsula, surrounded by China, Vietnam, Cambodia, Thailand, and Myanmar. Laos is a mountainous country, especially in the north, where peaks rise above 9.000 ft (2.800 m). Dense forests cover the northern and eastern areas. The Mekong River, which forms the boundary with Myanmar and Thailand, flows through the country. The population is 6.9 million with 50 officially recognized ethnic groups[1] and around 90 per cent of the population is Buddhist.

The Lao People's Democratic Republic is a unitary State. Under the Constitution, the country is the state of Lao multi-ethnic people, by the people and for the people. The right of the multi-ethnic people to be master of the country is exercised and guaranteed through the functioning of the political system, with the Lao People's Revolutionary Party as the lead component, as a legacy state that *"The Party leads, Government manages, people owns"*.

The State pursues the policy of promoting unity and equality among all ethnic groups. All ethnic groups have the right to protect, preserve and promote the fine customs and cultures of their own tribes and of the nation. All acts creating division and discrimination among ethnic groups are prohibited. The State implements every measure to gradually develop and upgrade the socio-economic levels of all ethnic groups.[2]

1.2 Lao People's Revolutionary Party

Lao People's Revolutionary Party (LPRP) was established in 1955, following the Communist Party of Vietnam, which was founded in 1930 with the ideology of Marxism-Leninism Communist.

The executive administration is the Politburo, consisting of 11 party members and the Central Committees of LPRP. Both are elected during the Party's

---

[1] In accordance with the 6th ordinary session of the National Assembly's agreement, document number 108/NA dated on 5 December 2018, approved that Brou as an ethnic group, including them in the Mone-Khmer family, which brings the number of ethnic groups in Laos to 50.

[2] Constitution of the Lao People's Democratic Republic (Amended). 2015, Article 8.

Congresses every five years.

Party Congresses are major political events, not only because they choose the LPRP leadership, but also because they determine policy goals and orientations.

1.3 Current political situation

The Lao People's Democratic Republic was proclaimed in 1975. The organs of government are the President, the Prime Minister and the National Assembly. The Government operates under the guidance of the Lao Peoples' Revolutionary Party (LPRP) through five-yearly Party Congresses, the Politburo and the Central Committee. The 10th Party Congress was held in January 2016 and a National Assembly election in April 2016. The National Assembly, the main legislative organ, currently comprises 158 members.[3] The National Assembly elected a new President, H.E. Mr. Bounhang Volachith, and, a new Prime Minister H.E. Mr. Thongloune Sisoulith in April 2016.

1.4 Divisions & Level of Administration

The country consists of 17 provinces and the Capital, Vientiane. The security situation is considered stable.

The administration of Laos is divided into 17 provinces (*Khoueng*) and one prefecture or the Capital city. Each Laotian province is subdivided into districts (*Muang*) and then subdivided into villages (*Baan*). There are 4 levels of administration namely: Central, Provinces/Capital, Districts and Villages.

The government delegates responsibility to the local administration authorities to manage the territory, natural resources and population in order to preserve and develop into a modern, civil and prosperous society.[4]

The personnel of each provincial or city administration comprises:

- The governor or mayor;
- The vice-governor(s) or vice-mayor(s);

---

[3] www.na.gov.la retrieved Nov 20, 2018.
[4] Law on Local Administration. 2003, Article 2.

- The chief and deputy chief of such provincial or city cabinet;
- The director and deputy director of the local divisions; [and]
- Other personnel in such provincial or city administration.[5]

Provincial [administrations] and city administrations have the [following] roles, functions and operational procedures: to manage political, economic, [and] sociocultural affairs and human resources; to protect, preserve and utilize natural resources, the environment and other resources; and to manage national and local defense and security, and foreign affairs as assigned by the government.[6]

1.5 Judiciary system

The legal system is based on traditional customs, French legal norms and procedures, and socialist practice.

The judicial powers of Lao courts are akin to civil law courts, rather than common law courts. Courts have greater leeway in re-hearing evidence on appeal and judges are active in the investigation of the case. In conclusion, Laos is a civil law country and, as such, jurisprudence is not recognized as a source of law and is not part of the legal system. Only the People's Courts are authorized to strictly adjudicate cases in accordance with the laws.

The hierarchy of the Lao PDR court system is: 1) The People's Supreme Court; 2) The appellate courts; 3) The people's provincial and city courts; 4) The people's district and municipal courts; and 5) The military courts.[7]

People's Court

The people's courts make decisions at the following three levels:

(1) At first instance;

(2) On appeal [or at second instance]; and

(3) On cassation.[8]

---

[5] Ibid. Article 8.

[6] Ibid. Article 7.

[7] Law on the People's Court. 2013, Article 15.

[8] A distinction is made between appeals from first instance decisions and appeals from ap-

The people's district and municipal courts each have the jurisdiction to make decisions as the courts of first instance in accordance with the evidence and the laws. The people's provincial and city courts each have the jurisdiction to make the following decisions in accordance with the evidence and the laws:

- Decisions at first instance; and
- Decisions on appeal from decisions at first instance made by the district and municipal courts.

The appellate courts have the jurisdiction to make decisions based on the evidence and the laws.

The People's Supreme Court has the jurisdiction of cassation as provided by the laws.[9]

Military Court

The High Military Court and Regional Military Court adjudicate criminal cases involving offences that pertain to military matters or occur within the compounds of an army base.[10]

2. Constitutional Architecture of the Legal System

2.1 Basic rights in law for Lao citizens

Law is legislation that is developed by the authorized authority, adopted by the National Assembly and promulgated by the President of the Republic [and] that defines principles, regulations and measures governing social relationships in many areas or in a specific area, and is effective nationwide and is long last-

---

peals, which are referred to as "cassation".

[9] Law on the People's Court. 2013, Article 12.

[10] Southeast Asian Legal Research Guide: The Constitution, Legislation and Caselaw (Lao PDR). 2018, The University of Melbourne, https://unimelb.libguides.com/asianlaw retrieved Dec 3, 2018.

ing.[11]

Lao citizens are all equal before the law irrespective of their gender, social status, education, beliefs and ethnic group.[12]

All cases in the people's courts shall be heard in public, except for cases that concern secrets of the State or the society, which shall be heard in proceedings closed to the public.[13]

The accused person in a criminal case and the parties in a civil case have the right of action to litigate their matters personally or to have a lawyer or a legal representative to protect their rights and benefits in proceedings. The procedures [to be observed by] the lawyers and the legal representatives in proceedings are regulated by the criminal and civil procedure laws.[14]

2.2 Law concept of Laos

Buddhism concept

Buddhism is the primary religion of Laos, some consider it as a philosophy because their principles derived from the teaching of Buddha are truly law in the sense that they are recognized as binding in the Buddhist community and not as mere moral precepts.[15]

Marxism concept

The Marxist view of law, is based on the concept of public property, and thus laws are created that promote equal rights. Marxists believe law arises from class conflicts caused by property, and the need for law itself will dissolve once a communist society is established. Furthermore, the working class must rule under the guidance of the Marxist-Leninist political party, giving the party final authority

---

[11] Law on Making Legislation. 2014, Article 17.

[12] Constitution of the Lao People's Democratic Republic (Amended). 2015, Article 35.

[13] Law on the People's Court. 2013, Article 9.

[14] Ibid. Article 10.

[15] Andrew Huxley, "Thai Law: Buddhist Law", Bangkok, 1996, p. 20.

on morality and law.[16]

Hence, law in Lao PDR identifies itself with the real needs and interests of the workers and farmers under the guidance of Lao People's Revolutionary Party.

2.3 Source of Lao law

In historical era (14–19th Century)

Starting from the middle of the 14th Century, during the time of King Fa Ngum the great, our ancestors found the unified Lanexang country "Kingdom of the Million Elephants" (later called Laos) and built it into a prosperous land. Under his suzerainty, it is recognized as a rising of new orders; his sermon mentioned the ethics of governors, punishments against marriage immorality, and also became the person who gave the country its historical borders which are recognized until today. Furthermore, Theravada Buddhism was introduced into Laos during his reign; it means that the Buddhist doctrine influenced the basic code of ethics accepted by lay followers in Lanexang such as the five precepts: killing living creatures, stealing, sexual misbehavior, deceiving and intoxication; Lao people developed mind and character in order to make progress on the path to enlightenment.

According to legal historians, spoken law and humans have evolved together hand in hand. The contents of law comprise of 3 sources or also known as the 3 tier laws: 1) law of the people; 2) law of lawyers; and 3) technical law.

— **Law of the people:** It is the first generation of law, where in this period the law shows itself through a consistency in practice, which results in being well known among and recognized by the people. Gradually the law transformed itself into traditions. On top of this, distinguishing what is right from wrong can be made through a use of common logical reasoning (or a use of common sense); a sermon of the King Fa Ngum was considered as the very first handwritten law of Laos. Therefore, if an infringement of the law occurs the offender(s) is often punished or criticized by people within the group or

---

[16] https://www.allaboutworldview.org/marxist-law.htm retrieved Nov 18, 2018.

village. Moral condemnation = law offence.

Example: Traditionally it is forbidden to have children before marriage in Laos. Especially in the past, Lao people really despised women who had children before marriage and they would be gossiped about, to the point of not being able to integrate back into society.

— **Law of lawyers:** This is the period where artificial juristic reasoning comes into influence. Many legal principles occur from various dispute resolution cases that begin to define penalties. Nevertheless, back in Lanexang Kingdom period, all binding documents were only made by royalists and nobles since most of grassroot people were analphabetic. The process of law making was also based on ethics in Buddhism and was done by a specific committee assigned by the king.

Example: The Law of the Great Throne *Dhāmmāsat Luāng*[17] created during the King Souriyavongsa period divided its contents into 5 sections according to the 5 precepts of Buddhism, which are: 1) Section *Pāṇātipat* on taking life; 2) Section *Adinnādan* on stealing; 3) Section *Kāmesumicchan*[18] on sexual misconduct; 4) Section *Musāvad* on deception/ false speech; and 5) Section *Surāme* of intoxicants as tending to cloud the mind, where in each of these sections there are articles that specify penalties according to the degree of severity.

— **Technical law:** is the third generation of law that does not occur from tradition but a result from developed societies that consist of possibility of having various complex problems or disputes that needed to be solved. For instance, traffic law and family law.

---

[17] The ancient Lao customary law book was adapted from ancient palm leaves manuscripts, mention on social life and customs during the Lanexang period, consist of 431 articles, re-written in modern Lao by Grand-Master Samlit Buasisavat in 1993.

[18] According to the local myth, King Souriyavongsa executed his own son as a crown prince for having seduced one of his concubines.

In contemporary era (20th Century-Present)

A very first constitution, adopted in 1945 then amended in 1947 with 44 articles, was a constitutional monarchy called "Constitution of the Kingdom of Laos" which formed the separation of powers but later abandoned with the monarchy regime. Shortly after independence from the French Colonial, a long civil law finally ended the regime after the Communist Party "Communist Pathet Lao" movement came to power in 1975 and proclaimed the Lao People's Democratic Republic. Since its creation, there have already been three versions of the Constitution namely the 1991 Constitution, 2003 Amended Constitution and the recent version is the Amended Constitution in 2015; consisting of 14 chapters and 119 articles.

The primary source of law is legislation, there are two types: 1) Legislation of general application; and 2) Legislation of specific application.[19]

— **Legislation of general application:** is legislation that governs the state, economy and society without focusing on a particular organization or individual, and is enforceable throughout the country or a certain region/area. Legislation of general application consists of:

(1) The Constitution;
(2) Laws;
(3) Resolutions of the National Assembly;
(4) Resolutions of the Standing Committee of the National Assembly;
(5) Ordinances of the President of the Republic;
(6) Decrees of the Government;
(7) Resolutions of the Government;
(8) Orders and Decisions of the Prime Minister;
(9) Orders, Decisions and Instructions of the Minister and Head of a Government Authority;
(10) Orders, Decisions and Instructions of the Provincial Governors/City Governors;

---

[19] Law on Making Legislation. 2014, Article 3.

(11) Orders, Decisions and Instructions of the District and Municipality Chiefs;

(12) Village Regulations;

International treaties are legislation that shall be implemented in accordance with the provisions of specific legislation.[20]

— **Legislation of specific application:** is legislation that governs administrative activities that focus on a certain organization or individual. Legislation of specific application includes a:

(1) Presidential Decree on the Promulgation of a Law;

(2) Presidential Decree, Decree or Decision on the award or appointment of a certain person for a certain position or specific activity;

(3) Notice.[21]

The development and amendment of legislation shall be implemented according to the following basic principles:

- Consistent with political orientation, the Constitution and laws, and actual economic and social situation;
- Consistent with agreements and treaties to which Lao PDR is a party;
- Under the mandate of the authorized [State] authority issuing legislation;
- Has a development plan and complies with procedures on the making and amendment of legislation;
- Ensures transparency, openness, and cooperation with relevant sectors, broadly expands democracy, and comments are extensively sought;
- The national, scientific and community characteristics [of the legislation] are secured.[22]

2.4 Legislative process

A law is legislation that is developed by the authorized authority, adopted by

---

[20] Ibid. Article 4.
[21] Ibid. Article 5.
[22] Ibid. Article 7.

the National Assembly and promulgated by the President of the Republic [and] that defines principles, regulations and measures governing social relationships in many areas or in a specific area, and is effective nationwide and is long lasting.[23]

Organizations and persons that are eligible to propose drafting a law are:

(1) President of the Republic;

(2) Standing Committee of the National Assembly;

(3) Government;

(4) People's Supreme Court;

(5) People's Supreme Prosecutor;

(6) Lao Front for National Construction and National Mass Organizations[24]

Law making and amending shall be implemented according to the following steps:

- Planning for law making and amendment;
- Drafting a law;
- Reviewing the consistency of a draft law by the Ministry of Justice;
- Reviewing a draft law by the Government;
- Reviewing a draft law and adoption of a law by the National Assembly;
- Promulgation of a law by the President of the Republic.[25]

For the provisions and comments, Domestic and foreign individuals, legal entities and organizations in both the public and private sectors are eligible to provide comments on draft legislation by sending their comments to the authority in charge of making legislation according to the defined time and procedures. The organization in charge of making legislation shall post draft legislation including the constitution, laws and decrees on the website or printing media or other means to ensure that the public can have easy access to them for a period of at least sixty days for comments, except for necessary cases and emergencies

---

[23] Ibid. Article 17.
[24] Ibid. Article 18.
[25] Ibid. Article 19.

as decided by a resolution or other legislation as defined in this law.[26]

3. Legal Policy and Challenges on Legal Development in Laos

3.1 Policy

Laos is one of a handful of Socialist governments and is ruled by a People's Revolutionary Party Government. The policy objectives of the government are focus toward achieving sustainable economic growth and poverty reduction throughout the country.

Lao Government's 8th National Socio-Economic Development Plan (NSEDP) for period 2016–2020 has resulted in a focus on high economic growth that benefits all people and other priorities built upon the achievements made in the implementation of the 7th NSEDP and the shortfalls of the Millennium Development Goal achievements, to realize 4 keys development drivers such as: 1) efficient and effective implementation; 2) strengthen and develop human resources; 3) improve management and governance; and 4) poverty reduction.

The national economy of the Lao PDR relies on a stable multi-sectoral economy which is encouraged [by the government; such economy shall] expand manufacturing capacity, broaden production, businesses and services, transform the natural economy into a trading and manufacturing economy, and modernize; [while] combining with regional and global economies to stabilize and develop the national economy continuously and to improve the material and spiritual living conditions of the multi-ethnic people. All types of enterprises are equal before the laws and operate according to the principle of the market economy, competing and cooperating with each other to expand production and business while regulated by the State in the direction of socialism.[27]

The State manages the economy in accordance with the mechanism of the

---

[26] Ibid. Article 8.
[27] Constitution of the Lao People's Democratic Republic. 2015, Article 13.

market economy to implement the principle of combining centralized management through the consensus of central authorities with the delegation of responsibilities to local authorities in accordance with the laws and regulations.[28]

In order to ensure a comprehensive building and systematic development of the legal system[29], in 2003, the Ministry of Justice, the Supreme People's Court and the Office of the Supreme People's Prosecutor and the Ministry of Public Security, thus, initiated the expedite the development of the Legal Sector Master Plan (LSMP) towards the year 2020. At the same time, the 7th Party Congress (2006) also set the policy: to *"gradually develop Laos as the rule of law state"*. Therefore, the initiated LSMP was adjusted accordingly. The legal sector master plan until the year 2020 was formally adopted by the Government on 11th September 2009 by Decree No. 265/PM. The main spirit of the LSMP is: *"aiming at creation of state of the Lao PDR to become state that secures legal responsibility toward its citizens and ensuring that the citizens fundamentally perform their legal obligations toward the state."*

The LSMP is based upon the four central "pillars" of any legal system: 1) Pillar one is the framework of laws, decrees and regulations; 2) Pillar two consists of the law related institutions that implement that legal framework; 3) Pillar three, the means of educating and training in the use of the system; and 4) Pillar four, the means of assuring that all the laws and regulations are widely disseminated and accessible to both state agencies and citizens.[30]

The State promotes the development of legislation comprehensively in all areas for public administration and social regulations by providing the budget, vehicles and equipment, [and] human resources in the legal field to contribute steadily over time to the development of the Rule of Law State. The State encourages individuals, legal entities and organizations, both public and private,

---

[28] Ibid. Article 18.

[29] Prof. Dr. Chaleun Yiapaoher, "Customary Law and Practice in Lao PDR", 2012, Foreward, Ministry of Justice: UNDP Democratic Governance Thematic Trust Fund.

[30] "The Law making Process in Lao PDR – Baseline Study", 2014, Executive Summary, Ministry of Justice: United Nations Development Programme (UNDP).

to widely and deeply provide comments on draft legislation to ensure that draft legislation has a comprehensive content. The State promotes strict abidance and implementation of existing legislation by all sectors of the society.[31]

3.2 Challenges

Since the national constitution was adopted in Laos in 1991, a number of laws and regulations have been increased but enforcement and citizen awareness remain low because of the lack of a history of rule of law in the country.

Law making process in Laos is based on the demography. As we are aware, Laos is a country of rich diversity and which marked differences between rich and poor; urban and rural; lowland, upland, and highland; and remote or otherwise inaccessible communities. The role of the informal - i.e., customary - justice system is still very strong: reflecting the still limited penetration of the formal system in many areas, as well as the greater familiarity within - and confidence of the majority of people in - traditional structures and practices. Customary law remains an important part of people's lives, particularly with respect to dispute resolution in rural areas, and, therefore, also of the country's justice system. Nevertheless, there remains no official recognition of the customary law system in the national legal framework.[32]

In the meantime, in Article 83 of Making Legislation Law (2014): *"The authority in charge of making legislation print send a copy of the promulgated and enforceable legislation to each sector and organization at the national level, and provincial and capital levels; such [sectors and organizations at the national, provincial and capital levels] shall also send copies within their own sectors from the national to local levels. Legislation issued by the local authority shall be submitted to their higher level for information and storage and shall be sent to organizations within their jurisdiction. The authority in charge of law making*

---

[31] Law on Making Legislation. 2014, Article 6.
[32] "Customary Law and Practice in Lao PDR", 2012, Summary, Ministry of Justice: UNDP Democratic Governance Thematic Trust Fund.

and governmental organization at the national and local levels shall disseminate legislation and educate through different means and methods, including dissemination in ethnic languages, to ensure effective implementation of legislation". In fact, more than 70 per cent of the land in Laos is mountainous, and a third of the villages are not easily reached by road. This makes providing law education a big challenge, multiplied by various local languages and customary practices.

Furthermore, some concerns in the Lao legal sector must be verified:

- Lack of budget and funding: There is support and assistance from friendly countries and the international community to strengthen capacities in educational institutions but it needs more to accomplish the goal toward 2020;
- The daily livelihood of the people is diversified in remote areas, people and ethnic groups have interests in legal information and require active law dissemination throughout country, but people are still poor and have a low level of education and are not fully able to access to legal information;
- The litigation procedure is time consuming;
- The courts' independence cannot be ensured because most of them rely on the financial support from local governments;
- The work on Law dissemination is not able to be immediately evaluated, which affects to the efforts of relevant staff;
- The Law dissemination is the duty of the political system, but many sectors do not properly understand the importance of the activities;
- Lack of law experts/materials: the variety of legal perspectives from graduated employees are limited. When we look at the educational background, foreign languages are the main barriers to study abroad. Most of Lao law practitioners studied in Thailand, Vietnam, Japan, the former Soviet Union, or in the hometown, rarely in Germany, France or the US.[33]

---

[33] Bounkeuth Sangsomsack, "ASEAN Free Area: Opportunity and Challenges of law firms in Lao PDR", lecture on the ASEAN Quiz, held on 3th May 2017 at National University of Laos.

4. Summary on Progress and Challenges in Legal Education towards Strengthening the Rule of Law in Lao PDR

(Adapted from the keynote address on the Legal Research Forum 2018, *"The Relevancy of Research in the Promotion of Rule of Law in Lao PDR"* by Reginald M. Pastrana[34], held on 19th December 2018 at the National University of Laos)

To recall, the Government of Lao PDR places high priority in establishing a rule of law state to support the socio-economic development of the country. To help achieve this objective, the Government officially adopted the Legal Sector Master Plan (LSMP).[35]

Having been adopted and amended constitution and numbers of legislations, the constitutional order in Lao PDR is now institutionalized. The administrative system of the Lao PDR consists of the organs of state powers, namely the National Assembly, the Government, the People's Courts and the People's Prosecutor Offices. There was also established a new Provincial Assemblies tasked to draw policies, oversee the activities in their respective jurisdictions and represent their local constituents on many varied local issues and concerns.

With these developments, and as new laws and administrative decrees are being adopted by the Lao PDR National Assembly, the Government, and the various People's Provincial Assemblies; the need to study, interpret and apply these new laws in the administrative system and to protect and promote the rights of citizens have become essential ingredients to ensure the observance of the rule of law.

---

[34] Chief Technical Advisor, Project LAO/031 - Luxembourg Development Cooperation Agency (LuxDev): Legal Teaching and Training and Promoting of the Rule of Law Concept in Lao PDR.

[35] Prof. Ket Kiettisack, "The Law-making Process in Lao PDR – Baseline Study", 2014, Foreward, Ministry of Justice: United Nations Development Programme (UNDP).

4.1 Legal research in particular

Legal research is the process of identifying and retrieving information necessary to support legal queries. The subject matter of course is law and anything associated with it, like implementing rules and regulations, various decrees, and judicial decisions, among others. Currently, there are universities in Lao PDR that are offering formal law degrees, prominent of which are the Faculty of Law and Political Science (FLP) of the National University of Laos (NUOL) and the Faculty of Law and Administration (FLA) of the Champasak University. In addition, the National Institute of Justice (NIJ), an administrative agency of the Ministry of Justice (MoJ), also offers both formal and non-formal legal education programmes.

The purpose of legal research is to seek legal documents that will aid in finding a solution. One type of legal document which many courts, the Bar and the academe will rely on when solving a problem is categorized as the "primary source." These are generated by, among others, the National Assembly, administrative agencies, and the courts. The ability to conduct legal research is essential for lawyers, judges and the academe. The most basic step in legal research is to identify the law governing the issues in question or the controversies involved. As most researchers know, this is far more difficult than it sounds.

Legal research is indispensable for a systematic investigation of problems of law or any matter connected with that law. Research, therefore, is to be pursued to obtain a better knowledge of that law and to understand, for instance, why it has a sociological or economic impact whether good or bad for the nation, and why legislation may be further needed.

4.2 Research in the academe

Research in the academe, therefore, involves not only the knowledge of the law, but the ability to explain what the law is. It includes knowing the background of the law, the prevailing circumstances when it was proposed, the intention of the National Assembly in passing it and, of course, the rationale of the law. It in this vein that the academicians must nourish their research skills so that they can clarify how the law should be understood by their students. For example, the recent passage by the National Assembly of the Criminal Code may contain vague provisions that must be clarified. Through the skillful research capability of a teacher, he/she can expound what the law is and teach them in its proper appreciation and application.

As the new Criminal Code contains several provisions that may be unfamiliar with the members of the academe, there is thus the need to know the background of the law, the deliberations in the National Assembly and the extraneous circumstance when it was approved. All told, research skills shall take a prominent role in the study of this important piece of legislation so that the legal scholars can interpret properly and accurately.

Legal research, therefore, can teach the correct information gathering, sorting, and critical proper appreciation----basic research skills----necessary for today's legal educators. It can teach life-long skills that will allow students to cope with future legal research environments. Such a process can also provide the skills to understand and to manage the disconnect to how legal reasoning is currently being taught and what students would find when they attempt to apply those reasoning skills to their own legal work.

Thus, academicians play an important role of dissecting needed legislations that will be useful to the policy-formulation process of the country's leaders. The academicians are in the best position to offer unbiased and well-studied legislative policies that can steer the country's economy to achieve the noble aims of the 8th National Socio-Economic Development Plan and the Sustainable Development Goals

4.3 Research in the National Assembly

Legislative research service aims to provide impartial, relevant, timely and authoritative information and analysis to Members of the National Assembly who almost always work under pressure and time constraints. As mentioned, from a situation where they had too little information, the Members now often have too much because of breakthroughs in information and communication technology.

They would find it difficult to distinguish between what is useful and what is not.

This has led to a new stimulus for libraries, research services and archives to help their clients with more advanced analytical services and through new ways of collecting, cataloguing, conserving, retrieving and using information. Research, therefore, becomes an effective way of obtaining unbiased analysis to help improve the quality of policy decisions of the National Assembly.

It is also essential for the National Assembly to have a core team of experts that provides access to analysis and vital information to guide the decision-making process. Thus, the creation of the Institute of Legislative Studies (ILS) is a positive and welcome development for the Lao PDR National Assembly to fill the gaps of information needs vital to its policy-making in forging growth and development for this nation.

4.4 Research for the civil servants, members of the Bar and Bench

The civil servants referred to are government officers and employees working in the MoJ, the OSPP, PSC and other government agencies whose main functions are devolved in the administration of justice and law drafting. There are civil servants in the MoJ who oversee mediation functions, who settle administrative actions, render decisions and resolutions on public petitions relevant to the public petitions law and those who draft proposed laws for consideration by the National Assembly. Government prosecutors refer to those officers and employees in charge of prosecuting criminal offenses. The Peoples' Supreme Court is the court of law which settles actual controversies and renders decisions on criminal matters.

The members of the Bar pertain to the private legal practitioners in Laos. The number of lawyers registered within the Lao Bar Association (LBA) remains extremely low, approximately 150 compared to a population of nearly 6.900.000 inhabitants. This means only one registered lawyer for around 46.000 inhabitants. A further setback, there is few numbers of Lao PDR registered lawyers can never benefit from lifelong learning and specific trainings in research to improve their practice or even enable them to either understand or interpret the law for the benefit of the people.

The Lao Bar Association is a professional organization of lawyers in the Lao PDR established to promote the legal profession, gain solidarity to protect the prestige of lawyers, and guarantee the provision of legal service to the society in a just, broad, and effective manner. The association contributes to the establishment by the State of a rule of law.

These key players in the legal sector need to enhance their legal capability by acquiring skills in legal research and expressing it through in-depth legal writing.

Good legal research of necessity involves more than just what is commonly thought of as research which cites cases and authorities to support a proposition of law. Rather, it entails focus on applying to a case whatever legal precedents or jurisdictions might be relevant. By far the most important part of any research a legal professional does in practice is a detailed examination of the available facts of a case which might be proven if it is thought significant to do so.

This means researching and learning all aspects of what happened in a case. It also involves being able to synthesize the facts and legal precedents which may apply to come up with a coherent and compelling theory of why one side of a case should be favored and the other should not. It means deciding what facts are important and focusing attention on them, and identifying which facts are against you and making them seem less bad and less important.

Therefore, on the part of legal practitioners, lawyers spend a great deal of their time researching by reading and writing, preparing briefs, reports, letters, and they engage in numerous writing projects/assignments. It is important to ensure that the written work produced by a law student or a lawyer is up-to-date and structurally accurate, since the work of the lawyer goes a long way to shaping agreements and policies for public and private sector institutions.

The research materials relevant to lawyers for the execution of their jobs are mostly documents that deal with legal issues, such as legislations, case reports, and legal arguments and agreements. During their legal training, lawyers must learn where and how to find these materials which are known as primary sources. It is after finding and identifying them that the lawyer can develop his/her document based on relevant information collected from the various sources.

4.5 Conclusion

As in the birth of civilization, law continues to be significant now in our modern lives. It provides for and dominates almost all activities of human beings, and has been accepted as the most important instrument of social change. When an individual sells his property or enters into employment or causes injury to someone, fails to pay his dues or obligations, or deals with government on matters affecting his property or personal rights, he comes in contact with law. Either he or his opponent obtains remedy in accordance with existing law and in the absence of such, resorts to the discretion of the courts of law.

The significance of research and the roles it plays to promote the rule of law may be summed up as follows:

- **It will help the government in crafting suitable laws to pursue its economic and social policies.** – The 8th NSEDP needs some enabling legislations in order to level the playing field and meet its important goal of transforming Laos from a least developing country to a developed country through economic growth spurred by "well-researched" laws that favor public and private business, encourage investments, create jobs, initiate infrastructure build-ups, and foster peace and order.
- **It can solve various operational and planning issues and concerns surrounding the environment, business, labor, health, industry and taxation.** – Through effective research, it can draw important solutions to energize business growth, increase availability of jobs and promote an effective tax collection system. Current laws and decrees on investments, labor practices and wage and salary standards, national and foreign corporation requirements for ease of doing business may have to be looked into for some amendments to keep up with the changing times. Research can do this. Present taxation laws may have to be changed also to come up with a more equitable tax code beneficial to the business sector and

the wage earner.

- **It can study and provide solutions to the problems of the People's Court and the various Village Mediation Committees (VMCs).** – It can offer an effective way of managing court cases, record management and promote fairness and justice in disposing court decisions. In the VMCs, it can design an effective technique of settling disputes, including capacity building exercises for the members of the VMCs.

- **It will enable the legal practitioner and civil service officers and personnel to render an in-depth study of the problem at hand, identify the source of the problem, seek the most practical and applicable solution from a menu of options derived from research, and come up with a decision or solution acceptable to the majority of contenders.** – Research can offer evidence-based solutions for tackling legal decisions.

- **It will help the members of the academe to understand the background of the law and interpret what it intends to accomplish and how.** – Research can lead a legal scholar to systematically perform data collection and catalogue practice essential to support an academic legal theory or in interpreting the law through its legislative history---from the time it was introduced in the National Assembly about what it intends to do for beneficiaries, debated upon by Members of the National Assembly, and finally approved by the National Assembly.

- **It can help discover and develop the legal doctrines for publication in textbooks or journal articles which can be accessible to the ordinary people and legal scholars.** – Legal research can help issue-spotting, legal analysis, and the application of law to facts. When taught as a legal skill, legal research reinforces and supports the learning of doctrine and analysis which are essential ingredients in developing and analyzing the law in a given facts and circumstance.

Overall, research permeates every government, legislative and academic activities, not to mention trade and investments practices, labor and health issues, businesses and arts and culture. Adept research skills and techniques should therefore be introduced at the onset of the educational years of the people, particularly for those interested in studying law.

Chapter 6

INTRODUCTION TO THAI LAW:

A Historical Survey

Munin Pongsapan*
(Thammasat University)

1. Introduction

Alan Watson observed:

> For law to be changed there must be a sufficiently strong impulse directed through a Pressure Force operating on a Source of Law. This impulse must overcome the Inertia, the general absence of a sustained interest on the part of society and its ruling élite to struggle for the most "satisfactory" rule.[1]

This statement seems to explain adequately how legal change in Thailand was triggered in the 19th century when commercial and military expansionism forced the Thai government to sign the Bowring Treaty of 1855 with Great Britain. This treaty marked the beginning of Thailand's system of extraterritoriality[2] and became the model for a series of treaties with other Western countries. Con-

---

* Assistant Professor, Faculty of Law, Thammasat University.
[1] Alan Watson, 'Comparative Law and Legal Change' (1978) 37 CLJ 313, 331.
[2] Francis Bowes Sayre, 'The Passing of Extraterritoriality in Siam' (1928) 22 AJIL 70, 70.

sular jurisdiction eventually proved disastrous to the Thai government because it came to be seriously abused by some Western powers. As a result, the Thai king and his government felt a strong impulse to modernize their traditional law to regain full judicial autonomy.[3] The external challenge alone, however, was not sufficient to account for these changes. Contact with Westerners also helped the ruling elite identify the inadequacy and defects of the Thai legal system, which was founded on Indian moral ideologies. External pressure and internal motivation effected a major change in Thai society in general and in modernization of Thai law in particular. Reforms of the legal system began with reorganization and westernization of the judicial system, and later the first law school was established. Codification was the last stage of Thai law's modernization.

This chapter explores establishment of modern Thai law principally through a historical approach. One may easily find information online about different areas of current Thai law, but materials on how it came into existence are rather rare.

2. A Brief History of Thailand

The origin of Thailand, known before 1939 as Siam,[4] is a matter of controversy due to lack of reliable written records. Simon de la Loubère, Louis XIV's extraordinary envoy to Siam in 1687, noted that "Siamese History is Full of Fables."[5] It is commonly believed that ancestors of the modern Siamese were Tai people who began to immigrate south from southern China, beginning in 100 BC. The *Tai* settled in pres-

---

[3] Preedee Kasemsup, 'Reception of Law in Thailand – A Buddhist Society' in Masaji Chiba, *Asian Indigenous Law: In Interaction with Received Law* (KPI 1986) 291; David M Engel, *Code and Custom in a Thai Provincial Court: The Interaction of Formal and Informal Systems of Justice* (UA Press 1978) 1.

[4] In this thesis, 'Siam' and 'Thailand' are used interchangeably. So are 'Siamese' and 'Thai'.

[5] Simon de la Loubère, *The Kingdom of Siam* (OUP 1969) 8.

ent-day Southeast Asia between the 6th and 7th centuries AD.[6] Other ethnic groups were already present, notably the Mon and the Khmer (Angkor).[7] Their settlements, which were in the Chao Phraya River basin[8] and scattered over the region, gradually developed into city-states as primary political units, known in Thai as *mueang*.[9] Notably, the Tai had a distinct language, the foundation of the modern Thai language, which identified them as a separate people.[10] Tai culture, which was intensely connected to religious ideologies, proved the driving force behind Thailand's cultural development over several centuries.[11] Archaeological and historical remains show that Theravada Buddhism was received in Southeast Asia mainly through contacts with Buddhist missionaries from India as early as the beginning of the Buddhist Era,[12] which may be earlier than the reception of Brahmanism (ancient Hinduism).[13] However, the Mon people firmly established a Theravada Buddhist civilization in central Southeast Asia from the 6th to 9th centuries. This Buddhist culture was gradually absorbed into the life of the Tai people who lived on the fringes of the Mon kingdom.[14]

In the early 9th century, the Angkorean kingdom replaced the Mon kingdom to become the single most powerful in central Southeast Asia.[15] Although the Khmer practiced Mahayana Buddhism as early as the 1st century,[16] from the 7th

---

[6] WAR Wood, *A History of Siam: From the Earliest Times to the Year A.D. 1781* (Chalermnit Bookshop 1959) 31–32; HG Quaritch Wales, *Siamese State Ceremonies: Their History and Function* (Quaritch 1931) 13–14; Chris Baker and Pasuk Phongpaichit, *A History of Thailand* (2nd edn, CUP 2009) 3.

[7] David K Wyatt, *Thailand: A Short History* (2nd edn, YUP 2004) 1; Wales, ibid 12; Baker and Phongpaichit, ibid 3.

[8] Wyatt, ibid 2; Baker and Phongpaichit, ibid 4.

[9] Baker and Phongpaichit, ibid. See also Wyatt, ibid 6.

[10] Wyatt, ibid.

[11] ibid 20.

[12] The Buddhist era starts from the death of Gautama Buddha. In Thailand, this is equal to the Christian era plus 543 years.

[13] Wood, *History of Siam* 42–44; Wales, *Siamese State Ceremonies* 12–13.

[14] Wyatt, *Thailand* 19–20.

[15] ibid 21.

[16] Wales, *Siamese State Ceremonies* 19.

century on, Brahmanism became the personal religion of most Khmer kings.[17] Their preferred religion spread over their land, as evidenced by remains of the Angkorean-Brahmanical temples across central and northeastern Thailand and Cambodia, but Theravada Buddhism, well established from the time of the Mon kingdom, largely immunized Tai's culture and religious beliefs against Hinduism.[18] The Brahmanical influence prevailed only in terms of governance and administration; Hindu concepts were borrowed to justify the supremacy of the monarch and the organization of the government.[19] A result of this borrowing was that Brahman priests (*purohit*), who were experts in Hindu law, had an important role to play in the administration of *Tai* states.[20]

From the first half of the 13th century, the Khmer Empire, as well as the Burmese kingdom, suffered a sharp decline, paving the way for some Tai city-states' rapid growth, especially in the Chao Phraya River valley and the upper peninsula, which, mainly by warfare, developed into more powerful political units.[21] These groups of Tai people differed significantly socially and culturally from the northern Tai. They employed Brahmanical beliefs and practices to establish a "relatively more complex, hierarchical social and political organization."[22] Toward the end of the 13th century, these people were, according to Chinese sources, known as Siamese.[23] Sukhothai, one of the early Siamese states, which emerged in the mid-13th century, became the dominant power in the larger part of present-day Thailand for at least half a century. Although it lasted almost 200 years, from the early 14th century, Sukhothai was in decline.[24]

---

[17] Wood, *History of Siam* 46.

[18] Wales, *Siamese State Ceremonies* 19; Wyatt, *Thailand* 24; Baker and Phongpaichit, *History of Thailand* 19.

[19] HG Quaritch Wales, *Ancient Siamese Government and Administration* (Paragon Book 1965) 8.

[20] ibid; Wales, *Siamese State Ceremonies* 19.

[21] Wyatt, *Thailand* 30; Baker and Phongpaichit, *History of Thailand* 7.

[22] Wyatt, ibid 40.

[23] ibid 41.

[24] ibid 41–49.

In about 1351, another Siamese state, the Kingdom of Ayutthaya, was established in the valley of the Chao Phraya River region, south of the Kingdom of Sukhothai.[25] Throughout its 400-year history, Ayutthaya was dominant among Tai states and was one of the most powerful kingdoms in Southeast Asia.[26] By 1550, most of the neighboring states, namely the Malay Kingdom, the Kingdom of Laos, Sukhothai, Chiang Mai, the Khmer Kingdom, and the Shan States fell under the control of Ayutthaya.[27] During the Ayutthaya era, contacts between Siamese and European traders and missionaries were first recorded when Portuguese, Spanish, Dutch, and French were permitted to set up settlements outside city walls. During the reign of Louis XIV, the relationship between France and Siam reached a peak; the two kingdoms exchanged diplomatic missions, and the French won favor with the Siamese king.[28] Some Western visitors to Ayutthaya, particularly during the 16th and 17th centuries, produced written records of their journeys and experiences. These were vital to later Siamese generations in search of their origins. The history of the Kingdom of Ayutthaya is revealed through a number of records of foreigners who visited Ayutthaya beginning in the 17th century,[29] notably Fernão Mendes Pinto (c. 1650s),[30] Jeremias van Vliet

---

[25] Richard D Cushman, *The Royal Chronicles of Ayutthaya: A Synoptic Translation* (Siam Society 2000) 10.

[26] Keith W Taylor, 'The Early Kingdoms' in Nicholas Tarling (ed), *The Cambridge History of Southeast Asia*, vol 1 (CUP 1992) 172; Wyatt, *Thailand* 57.

[27] Virginia Hooker, *A Short History of Malaysia: Linking East and West* (Allen & Unwin 2003) 72.

[28] David Wyatt 'Introduction' in Simon de la Loubère *The Kingdom of Siam* (OUP 1969) v-vi; Dirk van der Cruysse, 'Aspects of Siamese-French Relations during the Seventeenth Century' (1992) 80 JSS 63, 64; Prince Damrong, 'The Introduction of Western Culture in Siam' (1926–1927) 20 JSS 89, 91–92; G Coedès, 'Siamese Documents of the Seventeenth Century' (1921) 14 JSS 7, 7.

[29] Ian Hodges, 'Time in Transition: King Narai and the Luang Prasoet Chronicle of Ayutthaya' (1999) 87 JSS 33.

[30] A Portuguese explorer and writer who travelled to several countries in Asia and wrote an account of his adventures. His memoir, *Pilgrimage* (*Peregrinaçâm* in Portuguese), published in 1614, includes his experience in Siam in the mid-16th century and is one of the earliest

(1633–1642),[31] De la Loubère (1687–1688)[32] and Nicolas Gervaise (1688).[33] These foreign accounts are more reliable than local traditions' highly controversial fables and chronicles.

Although they were Buddhist rulers, kings of Ayutthaya wisely extracted political benefits from Hindu concepts of law and administration to strengthen their power.[34] Following the sack of Angkor Thom, the capital of the Khmer Kingdom, by the Siamese in 1431, Khmer officials and priests were brought to Ayutthaya. These people were instrumental in effecting a change in Siam's social and political systems: the king gained semi-divine status,[35] and the government was centralized. This allowed the ruler to exercise his direct authority over the feudal system previously administered by regional lords.[36] The Hindu-Khmer style of administration remained influential in Siam until the mid-19th century.

---

foreign accounts of Siamese society. See William Wood, 'Fernão Mendez Pinto's Account of Events in Siam' (1926–1927) 20 JSS 25. See also Joaquim de Campos, 'Early Portuguese Accounts of Thailand' (1940) 32 JSS 1.

[31] The director of the Dutch East India Company in Ayutthaya from 1633 to 1642. He wrote three books about 17th-century Siam, namely *Description of the Kingdom of Siam*, *The Short History of the Kingdom of Siam* and *The Historical Account of the War of Succession Following the Death of King Pra Interajatsia, 22nd King of Ayuthian Dynasty*. See Jeremie van Vliet, 'Jeremie van Vliet's Historical Account of Siam' (1938) 30 JSS 95. See also Alfons van der Kraan, 'The Dutch in Siam: Jeremias van Vliet and the 1636 Incident at Ayutthaya' [2000] 2 UNEAC Asia Papers < http://www.une.edu.au/asiacentre/PDF/Kraan_1.pdf> accessed 5 December 2012.

[32] David Wyatt, an eminent expert on Thai history, regards De la Loubère's book, *The Kingdom of Siam*, as the finest work on 17th-century Siam; see Wyatt, 'Introduction' viii. See also Ronald Love, 'Simon de la Loubère: French Views of Siam in the 1680s' (1994) 82 JSS 155; George Sioris, 'Some 16th and 17th Century Interpretations of Japan and Siam Fróis-Álvarez-La Loubère-Gervaise: A Layman's Comparative Reading' (1994) 82 JSS 179, 182–83.

[33] A French missionary who produced a well-known historical account of Siam in 1688 called *The Natural and Political History of the Kingdom of Siam*. See Nicolas Gervaise, *The Natural and Political History of the Kingdom of Siam* (John Villiers tr, White Lotus 1989). See also Sioris, 'Some 16th and 17th Century Interpretations' 183–84.

[34] Baker and Phongpaichit, *History of Thailand* 14.

[35] Gervaise, *Natural and Political History* 125.

[36] Wales, *Ancient Siamese Government* 70.

The city of Ayutthaya was besieged and sacked by the Burmese in 1767, ending the 400-year reign of the great Siamese kingdom. The Kingdom of Thonburi, Ayutthaya's successor, was established on the west bank of the Chao Phraya River. This later merged into Bangkok, but the new kingdom lasted only 15 years. In 1782, the king was executed, and one of his generals succeeded him as the new Siamese king, known as King Rama I. The new monarch built a new capital in the original area of Bangkok, which is on the other bank of the Chao Phraya River and opposite Thonburi, and he established a new dynasty called the House of Chakri. He named his new kingdom "Rattanakosin."[37] Ayutthayan traditions and political systems were considerably maintained in these two successive Siamese kingdoms. The House of Chakri's early kings spent a great deal of time restoring old laws and practices of Ayutthaya.[38] Old social and political traditions were followed and underwent little change until the kingdom's modernization in the mid-19th century.

3. Sources of Thai Law's Pre-codification

The best written evidence for a clear picture of Thai law's pre-codification is *Kojmai Tra Sam Duang* (กฎหมายตราสามดวง) or the Three-Seal Code,[39] the first comprehensive law of Thailand and the compilation of traditional Thai law existing before 1805.[40] This law was in use until Thailand's modern codes were established a hundred years later. Pre-codification Thai law can be divided into

---

[37] Wyatt, *Thailand* 128–29.

[38] ibid 129–30; Wales, *Siamese State Ceremonies* 15.

[39] Andrew Huxley, 'How Buddhist is Theravada Buddhist Law?: A Survey of Legal Literature in Pali-land' (1990) 1 Buddhist Forum 41, 67. See also Andrew Huxley, 'Introduction' in Andrew Huxley (ed), *Thai Law, Buddhist Law: Essays on the Legal History of Thailand, Laos and Burma* (White Orchid 1996) 1, 7.

[40] Sompong Sucharitkul, 'Thai Law and Buddhist Law' (1998) 46 AJCL Supp 69, 75; Viraphol, 'Law in Traditional Siam and China' 1.

written and unwritten law. Traditional Thai law was mainly written law and can relatively easily be documented with written evidence. A study of unwritten law would be a work of anthropology and is not discussed here.

De la Loubère recorded that written law and written records of court proceedings were the normal practice of the Siamese since the time of the Ayutthaya Kingdom.[41] It has generally been accepted that, like several other Southeast Asian states,[42] traditional Thai law was considerably shaped by Indian moral ideologies.[43] There were two main sources of written law.[44] A stone inscription believed to have been erected during the Sukhothai Kingdom (1238–1438) refers to *Thammasat* and *ratchasatra* as the law of the land.[45] The role of *Thammasat* can be compared to that of a modern-day constitution. Its scope transcends the boundary of public law,[46] and it extends even to matters that now fall within the

---

[41] De la Loubère, *Kingdom of Siam* 81, 86.

[42] MB Hooker, *A Concise Legal History of South-East Asia* (Clarendon Press 1978) 17; O'Connor, 'Law as Indigenous Social Theory' 225.

[43] Sawaeng Boonchalermvipas, ประวัติศาสตร์กฎหมายไทย (Thai Legal History) (Winyouchon 2005) 86–87; Viraphol, 'Law in Traditional Siam and China' 93; O'Conner, ibid; T Masao, 'Researches into Indigenous Law of Siam as a Study of Comparative Jurisprudence' (1905) 2 JSS 14, 15; AB Griswold and Prasert na Nagara, 'A Law Promulgated by the King of Ayudhyā in 1397 A.D.: Epigraphic and Historical Studies, No. 4' (1969) 57 JSS 109, 109.

[44] According to Andrew Huxley, a third written source is '*pyatton*', which was found in some parts of Thailand. Huxley describes it as 'a collection of precedents'. *Pyatton* can also mean 'a collection of folk stories describing the exploits of a clever judge'. Andrew Huxley, 'Studying Theravada Legal Literature' (1997) 20 JIABS 63, 72 and 79.

[45] Sukhothai Inscription No 38 cited in R Lingat, ประวัติศาสตร์กฎหมายไทย (Thai Legal History) (Thammasat UP 2010) 48; Boonchalermvipas, ibid 71; Griswold and na Nagara, 'Law Promulgated by the King of Ayudhyā' 110; Huxley, 'Studying Theravada Legal Literature' 69. See the texts of the inscription in Griswold and na Nagara, ibid 120–45. Andrew Huxley argues that this reference does not necessarily mean that *Thammasat* and *ratchasatra* existed during the Sukhothai period and speculates that the words may be borrowed from Burma or Cambodia. See Andrew Huxley, 'Thai, Mon & Burmese Dhammathats - Who Influenced Whom?' in Andrew Huxley (ed), *Thai Law, Buddhist Law: Essays on the Legal History of Thailand, Laos and Burma* (White Orchid 1996) 119.

[46] Lingat, *Thai Legal History* 50; Hooker, *Concise Legal History* 32.

area of private law.[47] *Thammasat* had universally been used by Siamese kings for administration of justice in Siam. It was regarded as the supreme expression of truth and equity, demonstrating how justice should be rightly administered.[48]

Thammasat (*Dhammasattha* in Pali)[49] originated from the Hindu Laws of Manu. Nevertheless, the Siamese did not adopt it directly from the original, but from the Mon Buddhist version (*dhammasattham*) to suit their social and religious conditions.[50] Some original Hindu principles, for example the Manu legend,[51] which helped justify royal power[52] and several provisions concerning debt, property, marriage, and remarriage were adjusted,[53] while some Hindu institutions, especially the caste system, were rejected.[54] Since the spirit of *Thammasat* was grounded in Theravada Buddhism, the Brahmanical concept of the Law of Manu that makes spiritual and secular matters inseparable was also rejected[55] be-

---

[47] Lingat, ibid.

[48] R Lingat, 'Evolution of the Conception of Law in Burma and Siam' (1950) 38 JSS 10, 24–25; Lingat, ibid 56; Viraphol, 'Law in Traditional Siam and China' 100.

[49] 'As the Latin language was to Europe, so Pali was to Buddhist S.E. Asia'. Huxley, 'Introduction' 13.

[50] Prince Dhani, 'The Old Siamese Conception of the Monarchy' (1947) 36 JSS 91, 94; Lingat, 'Evolution' 12; Lingat, *Thai Legal History* 46; Viraphol, ibid 94; MB Hooker, 'The Indian-Derived Law Texts of Southeast Asia' (1978) 37 J Asian Stud 201, 208; O'Connor, 'Law as Indigenous Social Theory' 225; Griswold and Na Nagara, 'Law Promulgated by the King of Ayudhyā' 109. However, through his studies of Burmese literature, Huxley challenged the notion that the Mon were legal pioneers and offered a new explanation that the law of Thai city-states was influenced by the Burmese version of the law of Munu (dhammathat) as early as the late fourteenth century. See Huxley, 'Thai, Mon & Burmese Dhammathats' 81–131.

[51] Manu is, according to the Manusmṛti (Laws of Manu), the progenitor of mankind and the only one who knows 'the effects, the true natue, and the object of [the] universe' and who creates the world. Robert Lingat, *The Classical Law of India* (J Duncan M Derrett tr, UC Press 1973) 78–79.

[52] Lingat, 'Evolution' 17.

[53] Hooker, 'Indian-Derived Law Texts' 205.

[54] O'Connor, 'Law as Indigenous Social Theory' 225.

[55] Lingat, 'Evolution' 16; Viraphol, 'Law in Traditional Siam and China' 94–95. See also Yoshino Ishii, 'The Thai Thammasat' in MB Hooker (ed), Laws of South-East Asia, vol 1 (Butterworth 1986) 195.

cause the "law of a new Manu, greatly different from Brahmanical laws of Manu, by its being merely a civil or lay law," i.e., law, still of a transcending nature, but concerning social organization only'.[56] By virtue of Buddhism, "*Thammasat* describes its ideal of a monarch as a King of Righteousness, elected by the people (the *Mahasammata*)."[57] According to *Thammasat*, an ideal monarch

> abides steadfast in the ten kingly virtues, constantly upholding the five common precepts and on holy days the set of eight precepts, living in kindness and goodwill to all beings. He takes pains to study the Thammasat and to keep the four principles of justice, namely: to assess the right or wrong of all service or disservice rendered to him, to uphold the righteous and truthful, to acquire riches through none but just means and to maintain the prosperity of his state through none but just means.[58]

Ratchasatra or royal ordinances, a supplement to *Thammasat*, put its principles into practice.[59] Kings enjoyed absolute power and could act as they pleased, but their decisions were merely orders that could not contradict *Thammasat* and remained effective as long as the ruler who issued them lived unless they were sanctioned by the new ruler.[60] *Ratchasatra* formed a system of positive law (or "legislation" in Huxley's terms)[61] that was not completely separate from the eternal law of *Thammasat*. In the early period of Siam, its kings collected their predecessors' decisions and ordinances, placing them in books separate from *Thammasat*, in order to make use of them. Such records' value and authority were due

---

[56] Lingat, ibid. See also O'Connor, 'Law as Indigenous Social Theory' 225; Hooker, 'Indian-Derived Law Texts' 205.

[57] Prince Dhani, 'Old Siamese Conception of the Monarchy' 94.

[58] ibid.

[59] Lingat, 'Evolution' 18; Huxley, 'Studying Theravada Legal Literature' 75.

[60] DK Wyatt, *The Politics of Reform in Thailand: Education in the Reign of King Chulalongkorn* (YUP 1969) 8.

[61] Huxley, 'Studying Theravada Legal Literature' 72.

to the king's reputation as a good ruler, for example, a ruler who governed in accordance with the rules of *Thammasat*. Later rulers checked whether old royal decisions and ordinances accorded with *Thammasat*, and if they did, they were then written as sections and placed under the corresponding heading of *Thammasat*. This made them permanent rules, not because they were the king's legislation, but because they reflected eternal law.[62]

In 1767, following the Ayutthaya Kingdom's sack, which mostly destroyed the Siamese legal literature kept in the capital, King Rama I embarked on a project to restore the old law of Ayutthaya. This resulted in compilation of the Three-Seal Code, the integration of *Thammasat* and *ratchasatra* in 1805.[63] The Three-Seal Code was not a mere reproduction of old laws, however.[64] The king corrected old sources by checking whether they accorded with Buddhist morals.[65] The Code covers a wide range of law areas that fall into roughly five categories: public law and administrative law, the administration of courts and procedural law, criminal law and law on delict, private law, and Buddhist law. Until establishment of modern laws and codes in the late 19th century, the Three-Seal Code was the supreme, universal law of the Siamese people.

4. Traditional Thai Private Law

The Three-Seal Code shows that a number of forms of contracts existed historically in Thailand, and they can be compared to modern-day contracts, for

---

[62] Lingat, 'Evolution' 27.

[63] Rama I, กฎหมายตราสามดวง ฉบับราชบัณฑิตยสถาน (The Three-Seal Code: The Royal Institute Edition), vol 1 (Royal Institute 2007) 70–73; Klaus Wenk, *The Restoration of Thailand under Rama I* (UA Press 1978) 35; Direck Jayanama, *The Evolution of Thai Laws* (Royal Thai Embassy 1964) 11.

[64] Ishii, 'Thai Thammasat' 145.

[65] See the Preamble of the Three-Seal Code in Rama I, *Three-Seal Code*, vol 1, 70–71. See also David M Engel, *Law and Kingship in Thailand during the Reign of King Chulalongkorn* (University of Michigan 1975) 4–5; Hooker, 'Indian-Derived Law Texts' 206.

example loan, purchase, hire, bailment, lease, gift and pledge, and guarantee, prior to reception of foreign private law in the 19th century.[66] However, they were not arranged systematically.[67] While loan was contained in a book of the Three-Seal Code titled *Pra Ayakarn Gu Nee* (พระไอยการกู้นี้ or *The Law on Loans*),[68] the other types of contracts were contained in *Pra Ayakarn Bed Set* (พระอายการเบดเสรจ or *The Law on Various Infractions*).[69] Robert Lingat observes that traditional Thai contracts had two important features. First, all types of contracts described in the Three-Seal Code concern transfer of property. Second, a contract was not enforceable until the property was delivered to the other party.[70] The law did not distinguish between contractual, delictual, or criminal liability.[71] The law on purchase, for instance, stipulates that if a purchaser fails to make payment to the vendor pursuant to the property's transfer, he faces both civil and criminal liabilities. The text of the relevant provision states,

> Pursuant to the purchase agreement on which the purchase price has been agreed, the purchaser has received the property but has not paid the vendor for it despite notice given. The vendor shall ask the court to summon him to appear before it. If the vendor's claim is true, the purchaser will be liable for his dishonesty which amounts to twice the price of the property. Half of it will be returned to the vendor for the price of the property. He will also receive half of the remaining sum as compensation while the other half will be

---

[66] See Ishii, 'Thai Thammasat' 188–94.
[67] See Seni Pramoj, 'กฎหมายสมัยอยุธยา (ตอนที่ 2) (Ayuthayan Law (Installment II))' in *Electronic Library of the Thai Court of Justice* 45 < http://elib.coj.go.th/Article/d14_6_5.pdf> accessed 15 April 2013.
[68] Rama I, *Three-Seal Code*, vol 1, 50.
[69] Rama I, *กฎหมายตราสามดวง ฉบับราชบัณฑิตยสถาน* (The Three-Seal Code: The Royal Institute Edition), vol 2 (Royal Institute 2007) 423.
[70] Lingat, *Thai Legal History* 204–05.
[71] ibid 206; Gervaise, *Natural and Political History* 77; Jayanama, *Evolution* 16; Engel, *Law and Kingship* 61–62.

treated as a fine.[72] [Author's translation]

Michael Hooker explains that individual responsibility constituted by a contract was as much a moral, ethical, or religious matter as it was a legal one.[73] In other words, possession of the other party's property caused the possessor a moral obligation to do something in return.[74] In comparing traditional Thai contracts with modern Thai contracts contained in the Civil and Commercial Code of 1925 (Code of 1925), which were products of European legal science, one can claim that Henry Maine's famous generalization that the movement of progressive law and societies is the movement from status to contract[75] appropriately explains development of Thai law and society in the 19th century. In Hooker's terms, pre-codification Thai law was overwhelmingly concerned with "the distribution of obligation between persons of different status," and this "obligation was a function of status and was ascribed on the basis of status rather than on the basis of personal initiative."[76] This is consistent with Huxley's general observation on Theravada legal literature that "no sharp distinction was made between law, morality and good behavior'.[77] The fact that traditional Thai economy was agriculture-based may also explain why traditional Thai private law, especially commercial law, was not as developed as some European private law of the same period. James Low observed in the first half of the 19th century,

> The Siamese are rather an agricultural than a trading people. ... The great body of the people, spread over the country, live chiefly by cultivating the soil; – and the population of their towns, by petty trades and traffick, chiefly

---

[72] Three-Seal Code, s 97 in Rama I, *Three-Seal Code* 446.
[73] Hooker, *Concise Legal History* 10.
[74] Lingat, *Thai Legal History* 287; Ishii, 'Thai Thammasat' 188.
[75] Henry Sumner Maine, *Ancient Law: Its Connection with the Early History of Society and Its Relation to Modern Ideas* (8th edn, J Murray 1880) 170.
[76] Hooker, *Concise Legal History* 10. See also Lingat, *Thai Legal History* 200.
[77] Huxley, 'Studying Theravada Legal Literature' 81.

in agricultural produce. For although Bangkok, the capital, exhibits a busy commercial scene, yet it is to the Chinese that the impulse must be attributed.[78]

In such economic conditions, understandably, traditional Thai private law was concerned more with property transfers and less with commercial activities; it was more interested in protecting farmers' property than facilitating trade. Despite maritime trade significantly generating Ayutthaya's income, especially trade with the Chinese since the 13th century,[79] there was no evidence of law governing commercial activities. Huxley gave two plausible explanations for the absence of written commercial law in traditional Thai society. First, the Siamese political regime in which the monarch had absolute power enabling him to monopolize trade and take whatever he wished encouraged traders to use political rather than legal tools to solve disputes. Second, *Thammasat* may have provided rules governing trade and banking, but "[i]f such rules existed at all, they would be in the oral custom observed between local traders, mixing local rules with borrowings from China, Arabia, and Rome."[80]

5. Administration of Justice before Reform in the 19th Century

According to De la Loubère, the judiciary style and form of pleading in late 17th-century Ayutthaya reflected Siamese society's social and political conditions of Siamese society.[81] The Siamese people were traditionally organized in specific groups for military purposes, and each group had its own chief or master. In cities other than the capital, a complaint had first to go to the plaintiff's master, who simultaneously served as a member of the consultative panel (or assessors) at the

---

[78] Low, 'On the Laws of Muung Thai' 335.
[79] Baker and Phongpaichit, *History of Thailand* 10.
[80] Huxley, 'Introduction' 25.
[81] De la Loubère, *Kingdom of Siam* 85.

court. The complaint was then presented to the city governor, who acted as the sole justice.[82] The governor decided whether the complaint should be admitted. If so, he would assign one of his assessors to direct the trial. When both parties had a common master, the governor often assigned their master to preside at the court.[83] The case was processed, and witnesses were heard in the governor's absence, but before a panel of assessors led by the assignee. At the end of the trial, they gave their opinion, which was written down by a clerk. The judgment, however, was actually made by the governor, who appeared in the court on the last day of the process, after listening to the assessors' opinions and that of another officer who indicated what law was relevant to the fact.[84] As observed by Gervaise in the late 17th century, the governor's decision was usually the same as that of the majority of his assessors.[85] De la Loubère noted that when normal evidence did not suffice, the court resorted to torture, proof by water, proof by fire, and other modes of ordeal, and superstitious proof (with the exception of trials by combat that did not exist in the Siamese system).[86] These extraordinary proofs took place publicly. When the governor decided that the defendant deserved capital punishment, he had to refer the case to the king. Only the monarch had the authority to take a life unless he granted the justice royal permission to issue the death penalty.[87]

In the capital city Ayutthaya, the king acted as governor and supreme judge. Trials often took place in the royal chamber before a prince who represented the king.[88] The prince consulted his assessors before he delivered judgment, in the

---

[82] ibid 82. However, Gervaise's account of the role of the governor as the chief justice implied that there was more than one judge sitting at the court. See Gervaise, *Natural and Political History* 75.

[83] De la Loubère, *Kingdom of Siam* 86.

[84] ibid.

[85] ibid 84.

[86] ibid 86.

[87] ibid 87; Gervaise, *Natural and Political History* 75.

[88] De la Loubère, ibid 88; Gervaise, ibid 77.

same way as a provincial governor.[89] There was no distinction between civil and criminal disputes in the modern sense. A delict case could result in a criminal punishment,[90] likely because even civil cases could undermine public order.[91]

After the fall of Ayutthaya, substantive and procedural laws were put in one place. The 1805 Three-Seal Code dedicated seven books to dealing specifically with legal proceedings and administration of justice. Book Four, *Pra Thammanoon* (พระธำนูน), particularly focused on the court's jurisdiction in the capital. Its provisions show that several courts belonged to different government departments.[92] This was not mentioned by De la Lubère and Gervaise in their memoirs, but Lingat explains that the multi-court system emerged during the late Ayutthaya era, most likely because the royal court, which was the single court in the capital, was unable to cope with the increasing number of disputes.[93] However, trial processes of Ayutthaya and Bangkok did not differ significantly. One of their common features was that various judicial officers were involved in trials, from admission of complaints to formation of judgments. Assessors interrogated parties and witnesses. Judges decided facts and pronounced sentences. Interpreters recommended relevant legal provisions and punishments to judges.[94] As witnessed by John Bowring (1792–1872), then Governor of Hong Kong, who was sent to Bangkok to amend the 1855 treaty with the Siamese government, this complexity of legal proceedings and the separation of judicial duties in a trial continued to exist in accordance with procedural law of the Three-Seal Code until the justice system's 19th-century reform.[95]

---

[89] De la Loubère, ibid.

[90] Lingat, *Thai Legal History* 468; ibid 85.

[91] Lingat, ibid 464.

[92] Rama I, *Three-Seal Code*, vol 1, 75. See also Ishii, 'Thai Thammasat' 166–67.

[93] Lingat, *Thai Legal History* 469; Wales, *Ancient Siamese Government* 180.

[94] Lingat, ibid 470–71; Jayanama, *Evolution* 14–15.

[95] John Bowring, *The Kingdom and People of Siam*, vol 1 (OUP 1969) 170–83. See also Prince Damrong, 'ลักษณะการปกครองประเทศสยามแต่โบราณ (Ancient Siamese Administration)' in Department of Fine Arts (ed), อนุสรณ์ในงานพระราชทานเพลิงศพนายปานจิตต์ เอนกวณิช (In Memory of Mr Panchit Anekvanich) (Department of Fine Arts 1972) 23.

6. Modernization of Thai Law

Modernization of the Thai legal system began with reforms of the administration of justice and legal education. Codification was the last stage of the reform program. Modernization of Thai private law was not an isolated process, but part of a series of reforms of substantive law. To have a full picture of the reform of Thai private law, a brief overview of reforms of administration of justice and legal education is needed.

6.1 Administration of justice in Thailand

The greatest reform of the judicial system during Chulalongkorn's reign took place in 1892 when the Ministry of Justice was established as part of the modernization of the Siamese government.[96] Walter Graham, who lived in Siam during the period of the reform, observed that the "introduction of reforms met with many grave initial difficulties and it was not until the end of 1894 that a new scheme of judicial administration had been drawn up and sanctioned and new courts constituted in accordance therewith, had been established even in Bangkok town."[97] The Ministry of Justice played the central role in judicial administration; it consolidated judicial power formerly vested in various courts and government departments and centralized judicial activities.[98] The entire judicial system was reorganized and systematized. The number of courts was reduced from 16 to seven, all under control of the Ministry of Justice, which took charge of all matters from appointment of judges to administrative work of court officials. In terms of hierarchy, there were two appeal courts and five courts of first instance, but in terms of disputes' nature, the courts of first instance consisted of one criminal court, two civil courts, one revenue court, and one International

---

[96] Government Gazette (10 April 1892) Book 9, 9–11; Engel, *Law and Kingship* 66–67; Hooker, 'Europeanization' 552.

[97] Graham, *Siam* 281–82.

[98] PW Thornely, *The History of a Transition* (Siam Observer 1923) 161; Engel, *Law and Kingship* 60, 67.

Court.⁹⁹ For this reason, a department was established within the Ministry of Justice to admit and classify complaints.¹⁰⁰ This modernization of judicial administration occurred mainly in the capital, while reforms of provincial courts did not begin until 1896.¹⁰¹

Following the Ministry of Justice's establishment, in 1894, Chulalongkorn adopted his foreign General Adviser Gustave Rolin-Jacquemyns's recommendation to establish a government body to take care of legislative work.¹⁰² Under the Legislative Council Act of 1894, a council was appointed and empowered to debate and agree on bills within the scope of its capacity as determined by the monarch who alone had absolute legislative power to pass any law.¹⁰³ The Legislative Council consisted of all ministers and other members, including some foreign advisors, appointed by the king. The Council formed a committee, which usually had at least one foreign member, to draft laws on an ad hoc basis.¹⁰⁴ Many important statutes, mainly procedural law, were drafted by this legislative body prior to codification, for example, the 1895 Law of Evidence, the 1895 Law on the Organization of the Provincial Courts, the 1896 Transitory Civil Procedure Law, and the 1896 Transitory Criminal Procedure Law. The three procedural laws, including the Law of Evidence, were modeled on English law.¹⁰⁵ Enactment of the Transitory Civil Procedure Law of 1896 marked the start of a distinction between civil and criminal cases since the law defined civil cases as

---

⁹⁹ Ministry of Justice, *100 ปี กระทรวงยุติธรรม* (100 Years of the Ministry of Justice) (Ministry of Justice 1992) 26–27.

¹⁰⁰ Ministry of Justice, *100 Years* 27.

¹⁰¹ Engel, *Law and Kingship* 69; Graham, *Siam* 282; Hooker, 'Europeanization' 553.

¹⁰² Salao Rekaruji and Udom Pramuanwittaya, *30 เจ้าพระยา* (30 Chao Phrayas) (Krungton 1961) 595–96.

¹⁰³ King Chulalongkorn, 'Royal Decree on the Establishment of the Legislative Council' in Satien Vichailuck (ed), *ประชุมกฎหมายประจำศก* (Yearly Collection of Laws), vol 14 (Neetivej 1935) 213. See also Engel, *Law and Kingship* 43–48.

¹⁰⁴ Chanhom, 'Codification in Thailand' 116.

¹⁰⁵ Sansern Kraichitti, 'The Legal System in Thailand' (1967) 7 Wahburn LJ 239, 241.

those with no request for criminal punishment.[106] Because its members were senior government officials who were already busy with their day-to-day work, the Council often faced problems of quorum, and its legislative work was transferred to the cabinet in 1900, before being discontinued.[107]

Worth noting is that, because of lack of manpower, Chulalongkorn relied heavily on foreign experts to push Thailand's early legal reforms through.[108] Rolin-Jacquemyns,[109] the king's first foreign General Adviser from 1892 to 1901, was instrumental in making modern Thai law.[110] Westerners also worked in various positions, ranging from judges in courts, advisers in government departments responsible for administration of justice, to law professors. The Ministry of Justice hired 43 foreign advisors between the 1900s and the 1930s: 23 Britons and 19 Frenchmen.[111] The predominance of the British and French reflects the Siamese government's diplomatic policy of balancing these two main powers and the effects of French and British treaties and agreements, which required the Siamese government to appoint French and British nationals as judges in courts and legal advisers. Modernization of Thai law was in fact linked to the ultimate aim of the Siamese government—to preserve the country's independence.

---

[106] King Chulalongkorn, 'Royal Decree on the Transitory Civil Procedure Law' in Satien Vichailuck (ed), ประชุมกฎหมายประจำศก (Yearly Collection of Laws), vol 15 (Neetivej 1935) 157. See also Engel, *Law and Kingship* 79.

[107] Chanhom, 'Codification in Thailand' 118.

[108] Hooker, 'Europeanization' 552, 564; Baker and Phongpaichit, *History of Thailand* 68–69.

[109] Rolin-Jaequemyns (1835–1902) was a Belgian lawyer, diplomat and Minister of Interior Affairs and a founder of *Institut de Droit International* before he came to Siam. His contribution to the modernisation of Siam and the preservation of Siamese independence was greater than that of any other foreigner and was recognised by Chulongkorn, who bestowed a highest non-royal rank of Siamese hierarchy upon him, the *Chao Phya Abhai Raja*. He was the first and only foreigner to receive such highest honour since the seventeenth century. See Walter EJ Tips, *Gustave Rolin-Jaequemyns and the Making of Modern Siam: The Diaries and Letters of King Chulalongkorn's General Advisor* (White Lotus 1996).

[110] Engel, *Law and Kingship* 59.

[111] Ministry of Justice, *100 Years of the Ministry of Justice* 89–91.

6.2 Legal education

Since Rolin-Jacquemyns saw manpower as a crucial factor for successfully modernizing Siam, he proposed Western education programs for Chulalongkorn's sons,[112] including Rabi, who spent 2 years studying Latin, English, and French in Edinburgh from 1886 to 1888[113] and went back to Great Britain a second time to study law at Oxford from 1891 to 1894.[114] In 1897, the Belgian General Advisor recommended that the king establish a law school to produce professional judges and lawyers.[115] Chulalongkorn accepted this recommendation, and that year Rabi, then Minster of Justice, established the first law school in Siam. The law school was not a government body,[116] but rather the prince's private school; he took care of both its administration and curriculum himself and allowed it to run in the Ministry of Justice's premises.[117] Since the school was associated with the Minister and Ministry of Justice, it was known as the Law School of the Ministry of Justice. The school mainly taught English law and some traditional Thai law, especially of the Three-Seal Code.[118] Rabi gave lectures on various subjects and authored several books on principles of English law used at the school.[119] Visiting European legal advisors of the Siamese government sometimes gave civil law lectures.[120] Those who passed the law school's final examinations were recognized as

---

[112] ibid 88.

[113] National Archive of Thailand, Department of Royal Private Secretary, Special Book No 17, 'หนังสือจากกรมหลวงเทวะวงศ์วโรปการ ถึงพระยาไชยสุรินทรและหมอกาแวน (Letter from Prince Devavonse to Phraya Chaisurindhorn and Dr Peter Gawan' (29 June 1885) 99–100.

[114] Nikorn Tatsaro, พระเจ้าบรมวงศ์เธอ พระองค์เจ้ารพีพัฒนศักดิ์ กรมหลวงราชบุรีดิเรกฤทธิ์ (Prince Rabi) (Nanmee Books 2006) 83.

[115] Laor Kriruk, เรื่องของเจ้าพระยามหิธร (Chao Praya Mahidhorn's Stories) (Trironnasarn 1956) 51.

[116] Luang Saranaiprasas, พัฒนาการการศึกษากฎหมายในประเทศไทย (The Development of Legal Education in Thailand) (Thammasat University 1956) 3.

[117] Leelamien, 'Legal Education in Thailand' 79.

[118] Thanin Kraivixien, การปฏิรูประบบกฎหมายและการศาลในรัชสมัยพระบาทสมเด็จฯ พระจุลจอมเกล้าเจ้าอยู่หัว พระปิยะมหาราช (The Reforms of Law and Judicial Administration during the Reign of King Chulalongkorn) (Ministry of Justice 1968) 28.

[119] Leelamien, 'Legal Education in Thailand' 82.

[120] National Archive of Thailand, 'Georges Padoux's Memorandum on the Question on Legal

Siamese barristers,[121] and almost all served as judges in different courts.[122] Given the prince's academic background, his profound influence at the Ministry of Justice and Law School, and the general trend of sending Thai students to study law in England, English law's predominance in Thai legal education before codification is not surprising. Also not unexpected is that lawyers and judges produced by the first Thai law school were learned men of English law.

English law's dominance in early Siamese legal education apparently contrasted with the government's policy of adopting European codes as models for Thai codes. This displeased French diplomats and advisors, as illustrated by the proposal for Siamese legal education reform by Georges Padoux, a French legislative adviser to the Thai government and the head of the draftsmen of the Thai Penal Code of 1908 and the later drafted civil and commercial code. Four years after the first code, the Penal Code of 1908, modeled mainly on European codes, came into force, Padoux submitted a memorandum on the Question of Legal Education in Siam to the Minister of Justice. He described the legal education system in Siam, saying:[123]

> The largest number have been educated in Bangkok or have taken their degrees in the Bangkok law school [the Law School of the Ministry of Justice]. They have learned the Siamese Family, Inheritance and Land law from Siamese professors. As to the general theories of law, lectures have been delivered in the Bangkok law school by Siamese lawyers educated in England or sometimes by European Advisers. Those who know the English Language have completed their training by reading English Law books. The best men have been sent to England where they have spent several years studying English law finally being admitted as Barrister-at-law. In one way or the other

---

Education in Siam' (20 Dec 1913) Kor Tor 35.10/10, 142.

[121] Leelamien, 'Legal Education in Thailand' 87.

[122] ibid 95–97.

[123] It is worth noting that by 1913, when Padoux submitted his memorandum, Prince Rabi no longer held any position at the Ministry of Justice and the Law School.

the technical training of the Siamese Judges is almost exclusively based on English methods and English Law.[124]

Padoux saw Japanese legal education as a good example of a legal education system consistent with the style of codes modeled mainly on European codes and balancing three major systems—German, French and English law—each of which had a native professor at the Japanese law school.[125] He found the contemporary law program at the Siamese law school inadequate and therefore proposed reform of legal education modeled on a European program.[126]

Now, it is a very important point for the Siamese government that the new legal system to be derived from the Codes be properly applied. The enactment of a large and comprehensive body of Civil, Commercial and Criminal Law would have but an unsatisfactory effect if the Judges entrusted with the decision of the cases were not familiar with the spirit and characteristics of the Code system.[127]

Chulalongkorn's successor King Vajiravudh (Rama VI) readily approved the proposal.[128] Two changes were introduced.[129] First, the government began to send Thai students to study in other Western countries, for instance, France and the United States, and, second, it attempted to reform the curriculum. However, these changes did not produce any dramatic effect, as demonstrated by the number of Thai students sent to study law abroad from 1913 to 1925. Of 16 students,

---

[124] 'Georges Padoux's Memorandum on the Question on Legal Education' 142.

[125] ibid 149.

[126] ibid.

[127] ibid 145.

[128] National Archive of Thailand, Ministry of Justice Doc No Yor 1/1, 'พระราชหัตถเลขา พระบาทสมเด็จพระมงกุฎเกล้าเจ้าอยู่หัว พระราชทานกรมหลวงสวัสดิ์วัตนวิศิษฎ์ (Letter from King Vajiravudh to Prince Svastiwatvisit)' (18 March 1913).

[129] Leelamien, 'Legal Education in Thailand' 111.

12 went to England, but only four studied in France and the United States,[130] including Pridi Banomyong ("Pridi"),[131] who was sent to France in 1920 and later became instrumental in French jurisprudence's rise in the Thai legal system.[132] The curriculum, especially in relation to private law, did not undergo a significant change since Thailand did not have a civil and commercial code until 1923. We also need to consider that by the time changes were introduced, almost all Thai judges were already familiar with English law.

A major reform of Thai legal education happened after promulgation of the Civil and Commercial Code of 1923 (the controversial code by French draftsmen), which was repealed 2 years later. In 1924, the king appointed a council of jurists named "สภานิติศึกษา" (the Council of Legal Studies) to administer the Law School of the Ministry of Justice and its programs of study according to the civil law system.[133] The Council introduced French law courses as alternatives to English law courses. English law was no longer the predominant foreign law taught at the Law School, but the new legal education policy did not significantly reduce English law's influence. The Law School, in fact, maintained balance between these two legal systems since in the first three terms, law students had to study certain foreign law courses in both English and French versions.[134] The reason for maintaining English law and introducing only French as an alternative foreign law was political. The British agreement of 1925 required that the Siamese government hire English law professors to teach at the Law School, and in the

---

[130] National Archive of Thailand, Ministry of Justice Doc No Yor 2 10/3, 'จำนวนนักเรียนไทยไปศึกษากฎหมายในต่างประเทศระหว่าง 22 มีนาคม 2455 และ 22 พฤษภาคม 2468) (The Number of Thai Students Sent to Study Law Abroad between 22 March 1913 and 22 May 1925)'.

[131] Pridi Banomyong (1900–83), a doctor of law from Paris, was a leader of the revolution of 1932, which changed the system of government from an absolute monarchy to a constitutional monarchy. He was Prime Minister briefly in 1946. He established Thammasat University to promote free higher education and democracy in 1934.

[132] Chanchai Sawaengsak, อิทธิพลของฝรั่งเศสในการปฏิรูปกฎหมายไทย (French Influence on the Reforms of Thai Law) (Nititham 1996) 117.

[133] Government Gazette (10 August 1924) Book 41, 53–55.

[134] Luang Saranaiprasas, *Development of Legal Education* 43–46.

absence of Thai civil and commercial law, Siamese courts had to apply English law,[135] while France asked the Siamese government to establish a Department of Legislative Redaction, reform the curriculum, and hire Frenchmen to be the managing director, law professors of the Law School, and the legislative adviser to the Ministry of Justice.[136]

In 1933, King Prachadhipok (Rama VII), Vajiravudh's successor, transferred the Law School of the Ministry of Justice to a newly established faculty at Chulalongkorn University titled "คณะนิติศาสตร์และรัฐศาสตร์" (Faculty of Law and Political Science).[137] Nevertheless, in 1934, on Pridi's initiative, Thammasat University[138] was established, and it took over Chulalongkorn University's Faculty of Law and Political Science,[139] making Thammasat University the only Thai university offering a bachelor's degree in law until 1971.[140] Pridi became the first President of Thammasat University and profoundly influenced university management and administration of education.[141] Thammasat University's curriculum of legal studies was considerably remodeled according to the civil law system, especially

---

[135] Ministry of Foreign Affairs, Letter from Prince Tridos to Chao Phraya Mahidorn (2 July 1925) cited in Foran, 'Amendment of Extraterritoriality Clauses' 181.

[136] Ministry of Foreign Affairs, Letter from Prince Tridos to Chao Phraya Mahidorn (10 September 1923) cited in Foran, ibid 158–59.

[137] Prasit Kowilaikul, 'การศึกษากฎหมายในคณะนิติศาสตร์ จุฬาลงกรณ์มหาวิทยาลัย (Legal Education in Chulalongkorn University Faculty of Law)' in *100 ปี โรงเรียนกฎหมาย* (A Hundred Years of the Thai Law School) (Institute of Legal Education of The Thai Bar 1999) 130.

[138] The original name of Thammasat University (มหาวิทยาลัยธรรมศาสตร์) is the University of Moral and Political Science (มหาวิทยาลัยวิชาธรรมศาสตร์และการเมือง). The name was changed by the military government after a *coup d'état* in 1947.

[139] Thammasat University Act of 1934, art 5.

[140] Ramkhamhaeng University was established in 1971 with a law degree offered, and in 1972 Chulalongkorn University successfully established a law faculty.

[141] Sawaengsak, *French Influence* 136. See also Charnvit Kasetsiri, 'ปรีดี พนมยงค์กับมหาวิทยาลัยธรรมศาสตร์และการเมือง (Pridi Banomyong and the University of Moral and Political Sciences)' in Thamrongsak Petchlertanan (ed) *ปรีดี ป๋วย กับธรรมศาสตร์และการเมือง* (Pridi and Puey and the University of Moral and Political Sciences) (Thammasat University Archive 2006) 10–30.

French law.[142] As a result, English common law's influence in Thailand declined despite many Thammasat law professors being judges educated in England or students of English law. French law replaced English law as the predominant foreign jurisprudence in Thailand. By 1987, France was the most popular destination for higher legal education among Thammasat law scholars.

6.3 Codification of civil and commercial law in Thailand

Chulalongkorn realized that the judicial system's reorganization was not sufficient to "equip Siam for its Future in the late nineteenth century."[143] Hence, following judicial reforms of administration and establishment of the Law School, the king executed the next modernization phase of Thai law—reform of substantive law. The project began with codification of criminal law in 1898 in the hope that criminal law, by comparison easier to make and understand, would help the Siamese, who had no prior knowledge of the code system, to adapt to the new environment.[144] Nevertheless, before codification began, a question had to be answered: would Siam adopt a common law or a civil law system? There was fierce debate over this question. Rabi, then Minister of Justice and the administrator of the Law School of the Ministry of Justice, was the most influential figure in Thailand's legal community. The English-law-educated prince preferred the English system, while the king's French and Belgian advisers promoted the French system.[145] Rabi wrote to his father urging him to adopt the common law system:

> In my opinion, despite my appreciation of the code system, as everyone may know, codification is an unachievable task. One reason is that making a code is even more difficult than making a railway from Bangkok to Phetchaburi

---

[142] Thammasat University, แนวทางการศึกษาชั้นปริญญาตรี โท และเอก ของ มหาวิทยาลัยวิชาธรรมศาสตร์และการเมือง (Bachelor Master and Doctoral Programmes of Thammasat University) (Sri Krung 1934) 1–69.

[143] Hooker, 'Europeanization' 551.

[144] René Guyon, *The Work of Codification in Siam* (Imprimerie Nationale 1919) 27.

[145] Wyatt, *Thailand* 195.

[a province around 123 km from Bangkok] or making a pond in Bangkok. It took the Germans 20 years to make the BGB and the Japanese 15 years to make a civil code, while the code of India has yet to be finished. Another reason is that codification is costly, and it is almost certain that the finance department won't be happy with this. ... Although we can successfully make a code, government officials won't be satisfied with it; the code may be useful to the people, but it is too rigid for the officials who will be required to work along the same lines. I suspect that our government system is not ready for it.[146] [Author's translation]

Despite this plea, the king found traditional Thai law, particularly the Three-Seal Code, similar to European codes and decided to adopt the code system as the model for modern Thai codes. This decision dismayed Rabi, who later withdrew from drafting the Penal Code.[147] His withdrawal allowed French domination in the work over the next 20 years.

Drafting of the Penal Code, which began in 1898, went relatively smoothly and was completed in 1908. The first drafting committee chaired by Rabi had no French nationals, and although it completed a draft of the Penal Code, this draft was never implemented due to some disruptions, for example, the quorum problem of the Legislative Council and negotiation between the Siamese and French governments to revise the extraterritorial clause.[148] Following the French agreement signed in 1904, the Siamese government accepted the French proposal to appoint Padoux as a legislative adviser in exchange for an amendment of

---

[146] National Archive of Thailand, Ministry of Justice Doc No Yor 23/3, 'พระราชหัตถเลขากรมหมื่นราชบุรีดิเรกฤทธิ์ ถวายพระบาทสมเด็จพระจุลจอมเกล้าเจ้าอยู่หัว (Letter from Prince Rabi to King Chulalongkorn)' (2 December 1904).

[147] National Archive of Thailand, Ministry of Justice Doc No Yor 12 1/1, 'พระราชหัตถเลขากรมพระสวัสดิ์วัฒนวิศิษฎ์ ถวายพระบาทสมเด็จพระมงกุฎเกล้าเจ้าอยู่หัว เรื่องข้อเสนอปาดูซ์เกี่ยวกับการจัดระบบการศึกษากฎหมาย (Letter from Prince Svastiwatvisit to King Vajiravudh on Georges Padoux's Memorandum on the Question on Legal Education in Siam)' (15 March 1914).

[148] Chanhom, 'Codification in Thailand' 167–79.

the Franco-Siamese Treaty,[149] and it set up a new drafting committee led by the Frenchman.[150] Despite Padoux's predominance in the committee, the Code was drafted in English, the common language between Thai and foreign officials, before being translated into Thai.[151] Codification of criminal law was completed in 1907, and the Penal Code came into force in 1908. The 1908 Penal Code did not focus on any particular legal system, but its previous draft and a variety of foreign criminal laws were considered, with dominance by Belgian, Indian, Italian, French, Dutch, Egyptian, and Japanese Penal Codes.[152]

Following promulgation of the 1908 Penal Code, Padoux was tasked with drafting a civil and commercial code. He was assisted by four other Frenchmen, including René Guyon (1876–1963), who was active in all subsequent drafting committees of the civil and commercial code.[153] Realizing that the Thai government was struggling to end extraterritoriality and urgently needed contract law to deal with commercial activities, Padoux proposed that his drafting committee should rush to finish codification within 4 years (in early 1913) and start by drafting the law of obligations, which may be promulgated earlier than other parts.[154] In 1910, government bodies responsible for codification were reorganized. The government established the codification commission with six divisions, but drafting responsibility remained with the French draftsmen led by

---

[149] National Archive of Thailand, Miscellaneous Doc No Bor 9/115, 'หนังสือจากกรมหลวงเทวะวงศ์วโรปการ ถึงพระเจ้าน้องยาเธอกรมขุนสมมตอมรพันธ์ (Letter from Prince Devavonse to Prince Sammuta Amornbhan)' (9 December 1904).

[150] J Stewart Black, *Report for the Year 125 (1906–07)* (Ministry of Justice 1907) 9–10.

[151] Black, ibid 10; G Padoux, *Report on the Proposed Penal Code for the Kingdom of Siam Submitted to His Royal Highness Prince Rajburi Direckrit, Minister of Justice* (Ministry of Justice 1906) 7.

[152] Padoux, ibid 8.

[153] National Archive of Thailand, Miscellaneous Doc No Bor 9/89, 'หนังสือจากพระยาจักรปาณีศรีศีลวิสุทธิ์ กราบบังคมทูลพระบาทสมเด็จพระจุลจอมเกล้าเจ้าอยู่หัว (Letter from Phraya Chakkapani to King Chulalongkorn)' (16 April 1907).

[154] National Archive of Thailand, Ministry of Justice Doc No Yor 12 1/8, 'บันทึกนายยอร์ช ปาดูซ์ เรื่องข้อเสนอในการจัดทำประมวลกฎหมายแพ่งและพาณิชย์ (Georges Padoux's Proposal on the Drafting of the Civil and Commercial Code)' (20 July 1909) 2–3.

Padoux.[155] In 1913, codification was disrupted by Padoux's resignation and return to France, and the First World War made it difficult for the Thai government to find a replacement for him. By the time he left the country, Padoux managed to draft 1335 articles that provided the basis for subsequent drafts of the Civil and Commercial Code of 1923.[156] Even though another French lawyer was appointed the new chief draftsman a year later, from the contemporary Minister of Justice's viewpoint, his ability was by no means comparable to Padoux's. From 1914 to 1916, the drafting of the civil and commercial code went nowhere.[157]

In 1916, a major change was made to the drafting committee. The French chief draftsman was dismissed and replaced by Prince Svastiwatvisit, then President of the Supreme Court; three eminent Thai jurists—Phraya Jindabhirom Rajasabhabordi (Chitr),[158] then Chief Justice of the Central Civil Court; Phraya Noranaeti Banjakit (Lad), then judge of the Supreme Court; and Phraya Dhebvitoon Pahoolsarutabordi (Boonchoi), then Attorney General—were added to the drafting committee of three French draftsmen.[159] Chitr, Lad, and Boonchoi had all received their legal education at the Law School of the Ministry of Justice and

---

[155] National Archive of Thailand, Ministry of Justice Doc No Yor 12 1/2, 'หนังสือจากพระองค์เจ้าจรูญศักดิ์ กฤดากร กราบบังคมทูลพระบาทสมเด็จพระจุลจอมเกล้าเจ้าอยู่หัว (Letter from Prince Charoonsak to King Chulalongkorn)' (8 August 1910).

[156] See National Archive of Thailand, Office of the Council of State Doc No 9, 'การร่างและพิมพ์ประมวลกฎหมายแพ่งและพาณิชย์') (The Drafting and Publishing of the Civil and Commercial Code)' (around January 1925). This document is apparently a Thai translation of an English memorandum mostly likely written by Guyon because it accompanies the Thai translation of an English letter from Guyon to Francis Sayre, then Foreign Affairs Advisor to the Thai Government. Unfortunately, the English copy was missing. See National Archive of Thailand, Office of the Council of State Doc No 9, 'Letter from René Guyon to Francis Sayre' (10 January 1925)

[157] National Archive of Thailand, Ministry of Justice Doc No Yor 12 1/2, 'บันทึกของพระองค์เจ้าจรูญศักดิ์ กฤดากร กราบบังคมทูลพระบาทสมเด็จพระมงกุฎเกล้าเจ้าอยู่หัว (Letter from Prince Charoonsak to King Vajiravudh)' (5 May 1916).

[158] *Phraya* was a Siamese noble rank for commoners, second only to the rank of *Chao Phraya*. The system of noble ranks was abolished in 1942. 'Jindabhirom Rajasabhabordi' was, for example, an official name given by the monarch.

[159] Government Gazette (7 May 1916) Book 33, 40.

INTRODUCTION TO THAI LAW

then in England and were all English barristers. The drafting committee chairman gave Guyon the important role of chief advisor, which was effectively chief draftsman.[160] The drafting committee revised and translated the Padoux draft of the law of obligations and the law of contract.[161] Codification would have made progress if chairmanship of the drafting committee had remained unchanged, but Prince Svastiwatvisit's resignation in 1918 caused disruption. Vajiravudh decided to introduce another major reform to the codification commission. The king thought that a commoner, rather than a royal who was usually occupied with day-to-day work, should direct codification and, in 1919, asked Chao Phraya Abhai Raja, then Minister of Justice, to be president of the codification commission as well. Chao Phraya Abhai Raja reorganized the commission by reducing its divisions from six to three: drafting (the drafting committee), the translation, and the Thai revisions.[162] The members of the Drafting committee members remained unchanged, except that Guyon was appointed chief draftsman.[163] The codification commission's president also appointed Phraya Manavarajasevi (Plod), Chitr's younger brother, secretary of the commission, a position previously held by a French draftsman. Plod, a Thai and an English barrister, became instrumental in the Siamese government's policy switch from French-oriented to German-oriented codification and played a leading role in successfully drafting the Code of 1925. Plod's role in creation of the Code is the focus of this thesis and receives careful scrutiny in the next chapter.

Under Guyon's direction, in 1923, the committee completed the draft of the first two books of the Civil and Commercial Code, which contained 387 provisions. The English draft was then translated to Thai by the translation committee

---

[160] Guyon, *Work of Codification* 10.

[161] Pakdi Phagagrong, 'การจัดร่างประมวลกฎหมายแพ่งและพาณิชย์: พ.ศ. 2451–2478 (The Drafting of Siamese Civil and Commercial Code: 1908–1935 AD)' (MA Thesis, Silpakorn University 1994) 53.

[162] National Archive of Thailand, Ministry of Justice Doc No Yor 12 1/2, 'พระราชหัตถเลขาพระบาทสมเด็จพระมงกุฎเกล้าเจ้าอยู่หัว ถึงกรมหลวงเทวะวงศ์วโรปการ (Letter from King Vajiravudh to Prince Devavongse)' (21 April 1919).

[163] Guyon, *Work of Codification* 10.

(known as the High Revising Committee) comprised of a number of royals who were also head of ministries and department.[164] The draft of a civil and commercial code, which was prepared by the draftsmen led by a Frenchman and with the French majority, was principally based on the French Civil Code. Plod found the French draft unsystematic and incomprehensible and convinced the king and his ministers to redraft a new civil and commercial code modeled on German and Japanese law.[165] An agreement between French and Thai governments, signed in September 1923, requiring the latter to establish a department specifically responsible for legislative redaction,[166] gave the Thai government an opportunity to change the drafting committee's French-dominated composition. In October 1923, the codification commission became the Department of Legislative Redaction, run by a committee of, mostly, previous draftsmen. However, Guyon was no longer chief draftsman and had only a role as chief advisor. Abhai Raja, then Minister of Justice, headed the committee himself.[167]

In November 1923, for political and technical reasons, the Thai government decided to put the French draft into effect. The government could not simply announce that French draftsmen's work was imperfect; widespread criticism from the Thai legal profession, especially judges, was needed to justify setting it aside. While waiting for this feedback, the government put the French draft into effect to show the French government goodwill. Then, strong criticism of the Civil and Commercial Code gave the king an excuse to postpone its effective date.[168] The new drafting committee, dominated by Thai jurists, then proceeded to draft a new civil and commercial code. They spent about 7 months redrafting

---

[164] National Archive of Thailand, Ministry of Justice Doc No Yor 12 1/2, 'หนังสือเจ้าพระยาอภัยราชาฯ กราบบังคมทูลพระบาทสมเด็จพระมงกุฎเกล้าเจ้าอยู่หัว (Letter from Chao Phraya Abhai Raja to King Vajiravudh)' (28 August 1919).

[165] Phraya Manavarajasevi, บันทึกคำสัมภาษณ์พระยามานวราชเสวี (Transcript of the Interviews with Phraya Manavarajasevi) (Thammasat University 1982) 3–4, 28–30.

[166] Foran, 'Amendment of Extraterritoriality Clauses' 159.

[167] Government Gazette (28 October 1923) Book 40, 128–30.

[168] This will be discussed in greater detail in the next chapter.

two books, and the new draft, mainly founded on German jurisprudence, came into effect in 1925. It is still in use today. The drafting of the Code of 1925 is the main focus of this thesis since it shows how modern private law in Thailand developed, and the thesis considers whether Watson's theory of legal transplants adequately explains legal change in Thailand. These issues are therefore thoroughly discussed in subsequent chapters.

Worth noting is that due to lack of publications of legal texts and statutes in Thailand, Thai law was almost unknown to the public and even Thai lawyers. In 1909, Padoux observed,

> Every foreigner who has to deal with Siamese legal questions knows that it is extremely difficult to get reliable information about the existing Siamese statute law...Very few Siamese lawyers have a full knowledge of Siamese law...From my personal practice as a Judge in the Bangkok Appeal Court I knew that even in matters governed by rather modern texts, I mean laws enacted during the last 15 years, it is most common to the ordinary Judge to give judgment without quoting the law or even making any allusion to its existence.[169]

Before promulgation of the Code of 1925, it was common for Thai courts to adopt English law and the principle of judicial precedent to decide civil and commercial disputes, which had foreigners involved on a case-by-case basis.[170] When Thai courts applied English law, they simply stated, without any acknowledgment of the law's source, "according to the law," rather than "according to English law."[171] The agreement between the British and Siamese governments required Siamese courts to apply English private law only where there was no

---

[169] 'Georges Padoux's Proposal on the Drafting of the Civil and Commercial Code' 15–16.

[170] ibid 16; Kasemsup, 'Reception of Law in Thailand' 292.

[171] Preedee Kasemsup, นิติปรัชญา *(Philosophy of Law)* (Thammasat University Faculty of Law 2000) 49. See also Kittisak Prokati, การปฏิรูประบบกฎหมายไทยภายใต้อิทธิพลยุโรป (The Modernisation of Thai Law under the European Influence) (2nd edn, Winyouchon 2006) 112.

applicable Thai law, but they usually resorted to English law despite the availability of Thai law.[172] The predominance of English law at Siamese courts was not surprising given that Siamese judges and lawyers' legal education prior to promulgation of the Code of 1925 was overwhelmingly influenced by English jurisprudence.

7. Conclusion

Reforms of law in Thailand from the late 19th century to the early 20th century were directed by ruling and professional elites who felt impelled to modernize the country to regain full judicial autonomy. Most steps taken by Thai governments to reform the traditional Thai legal system were influenced by external pressure, for example, extraterritoriality and agreements with foreign governments that usually required involvement of their own people in the modernization process. This condition had implications for reception of foreign private law in Thailand and development of Thai private law. However, to understand fully why Watson is correct, one needs to consider social and political conditions of traditional Thai society—a paternal society ruled by an absolute monarch. Legislation had long been kept from ordinary Thai people and was only allowed to be published and circulated a few decades before modernization of Thai law began.

---

[172] 'Padoux's Proposal on the Drafting of the Civil and Commercial Code' 16.

Chapter 7

MYANMAR'S CURRENT LEGAL SYSTEM AND INHERITANCE UNDER THE MYANMAR CUSTOMARY LAW

Khin Phone Myint Kyu[*]

(University of Yangon)

Introduction

Myanmar, officially known as the Republic of the Union of Myanmar, is a sovereign state and parliamentary republic and the second largest state in Southeast Asia. It shares borders with Bangladesh, India, China, Laos, and Thailand. The country is delineated and constituted with seven regions, seven states, and union territories. The Seven states include Kachin State, Shan State, Kayah State, Kayin State, Mon State, Chin State, and Rakhine State. The Seven regions are Sagaing Region, Mandalay Region, Magway Region, Bago Region, Yangon Region, Ayeyawady Region, and Taninthayi Region. Nay Pyi Taw is the only union territory and is recognized as the capital city of Myanmar under sections 49 and 50 of the 2008 Constitution of the Republic of the Union of Myanmar. Yangon is the former capital city and remains the commercial capital city.

The total Area of Myanmar is 676,590 km², with a total population of 55,252,033 (over 55 million) people. Myanmar is a country where multinational races collectively reside. Primarily, there are eight major ethnic groups: Kachin,

---

[*] Professor, Department of Law, University of Yangon, Myanmar.

Kayah, Kayin, Chin, Mon, Bamar, Rakhine, and Shan. Under section 34 of the 2008 Constitution, the citizens are allowed to freely profess a number of different religions[1]. The official language is Myanmar (Burmese).

The politics practiced in Myanmar is "a multi-party democratic system," which means that its legislative, executive, and judicial powers are separated for the purpose of reciprocal control, checking, and balanceing among themselves. These three branches of sovereign power are shared among the union, regions, states, and self-administered areas.[2]

1. History of Myanmar's Legal System

The legal system of Myanmar has its roots in the common law family. However, it is not an identical common law family. Hence, it can be said that Myanmar's legal system is a unique combination of the common and civil law systems. It uses the principles of common law and implants them into the codified laws or statute laws, which are promulgated by the legislature.

Myanmar's legal system included different origins in different periods of the country's history. Based on studies, the history of Myanmar's legal system can be divided into three parts, namely; the reign of the monarchy, the British colonial period, and after independence.

1.1 Under the Reign of the Monarchy

Myanmar was a monarchy until the British annexed the entire country in 1885. Myanmar's kings, who ruled the country for over a thousand years until the late 19th century, governed their people as absolute monarchs, and this system in the Myanmar (Burmese) language is called the *thet-oo-san-paine* system.

Myanmar had its own legal system under the reign of the kings.The supreme

---

[1] Section 34, the Constitution of the Republic of the Union of Myanmar.
[2] Ibid, Section 11.

powers of the legislative, executive, and judiciary branches of government were vested in the hands of the King.

1.1.1 Executive

The highest authority was vested in the king and he was assisted by ministers (*Wonmin*), mayors (*Myosar*), town-chiefs (*Thanbyin*), village-headmen (*Kalan* or *Ywarsar*), and government servants (*Luhlin Kyaw*).

1.1.2 Legislature

The legislative power was vested to the king and he was assisted by the "Hluttaw" (i.e., the Parliament).

It can be said that the laws of Myanmar were composed of three great elements: *Yazathat*, *Dammathat*, and *Phyathton*. The most important kind of legislation was the *Yazathat* or order of the king. *Dammathats* were somewhat similar to the customary laws of the land. Traditional and customary rules of personal and family character were codified in *Dammathat*, which was written by famous monks and scholars. Those may be rightly called collections and records of social customs. *Phyathtons* were the records of judicial decisions rendered by various monarchs and judges.

1.1.3 Judiciary

The highest authority in the judiciary was held by the king, followed by the supreme queen, crown prince, princes, and then the ministers in the Parliament. Judges appointed by the king, mayors, town-chiefs, and village-headmen assisted the king.

In ancient times, trial by ordeal was practiced in both criminal and civil proceedings and most criminal punishments were fines. Only four types of crimes were punishable by death, that is, murder, rebellion, insurgency, and rape. Since this period, the criminal and civil jurisdictions have been considered separate. Prevention of threat to the peace and public security were considered a part of administrative functions of governments. Hence, administrative officials of the state dispensed criminal justice. On the other hand, civil justice was administered by judges appointed by or under the king and by arbitrators chosen by parties. Naturally, appeals lay as a last resort to the king or the queen, but from the decision of an arbitrator, there was no appeal. Naturally, appeals lay as a last resort to the king or the queen, but from the decision of an arbitrator, there was no appeal. Neither was there an appeal when the trial was by ordeal.

1.2 During the British Colonial

In the 19th century, Myanmar fought three wars against British colonialists; the first war was fought in 1826, the second in 1852, and the last in 1885. It was finally annexed to the British Empire on the January 1, 1886, as a province of British India. After annexation, the monarchy system was abolished in Myanmar, and the last king, King Thibaw, was exiled.

1.2.1 Executive

The British controlled their new province through direct rule, making many changes to the previous governmental structure. The Constitution accorded to Myanmar in 1923 was referred to as a dyarchical constitution under which certain subjects, known as **reserved subjects**, were administered by two executive members, who were officials appointed by the governor. On the other hand, two ministers, who were elected members of the Legislative Council, administered certain other subjects, known as **transferred subjects**.

In 1937, Myanmar separated from India and became a separate, self-governing colony. The Government of Burma Act of 1935 accorded a new constitution to Myanmar. Under this Constitution, the chief executive was the governor who represented the Majesty. There was a council of ministers, not exceeding 10 in number, to aid and advise the governor in the exercise of his functions. Those ministers were chosen by the governor and held office during his term.

1.2.2 Legislature

Steps were initiated for the establishment of a uniform system of laws throughout the country to affect a greater unity in the judicial administration in British India. In 1834, a law commission was appointed to codify the law applicable to British India. The British introduced several laws that were used in British India, that is, criminal and civil laws including the Indian Penal Code (1860), the Criminal Procedure Code (1862), the Indian Evidence Act (1872) and the Civil Procedure Code (1859). Thus, gradually, the statutory laws, which were designed based on the British Common Law models for use in India, were extended to Myanmar as well.

However, the impact of English law has not affected appreciably by ancient Hindu, Mohammedan, and the Myanmar Customary Laws, which form the rule of decision in any question to be decided by the court regarding succession, inheritance, marriage, or any religious usage or institution.

After passing the Government of Burma Act, 1935, the legislature comprised His Majesty, represented by the governor and two chambers—the Senate and the House of Representatives.

Hence, before Myanmar gained complete independence, acts were passed by the British Parliament and British Governor. Although Myanmar broke away from the British Empire, the Indo–British Legal System, which had its roots in the British conception of justice, equity, and good conscience, continue as a basis for our legal system. However, some obsolete and inconsistent laws, in terms of social, cultural, and economic objectives, have been amended and repealed as and when necessary.

1.2.3 Judiciary

The British established the Court of the Judicial Commissioner for Upper Myanmar in Mandalay. The Court of Lower Myanmar was established in 1900 as the highest appeals court. In 1922, the High Court of Judicature at Yangon was established after the abolishment of the aforementioned two judicial organs. Sub-divisional courts, district civil and session courts, and township courts were also established with specific jurisdiction. Although the 1935 Government of Burma Act was enacted, the High Court of Judicature at Rangoon (Yangon) continued as the highest court in the territories of Burma.

1.3 After Independence

Myanmar gained complete independence on January 4, 1948. For the purpose of studying the legal system after independence, this section will be divided into four periods, according to the practice of political and legal system, as follows:

(1) The Parliamentary Democracy Period (1948–1962, under the Constitution of the Union of Burma);

(2) The Socialist Period (1962–1974, under the Revolutionary Council);

(3) The Socialist Period (1974–1988, under the Constitution of the Socialist Republic of the Union of Myanmar); and

(4) The Democracy Period (1988–2011, under the Military Government).

1.3.1 The Parliamentary Democracy Period (1948–1962, under the Constitution of the Union of Burma)

On January 4, 1948, when Myanmar gained independence and became a sovereign independent state, the Constitution of the Union of Burma was adopted. However, it continues the concept of the Indo–British legal system as a basis of the legal system.

1.3.1.1 Executive

Myanmar was included in the category of parliamentary executive of the union government under the 1947 Constitution of the Union of Burma. The president was elected by both chambers of Parliament in joint session by secret ballot. The term of his office was five years and no more than two terms in all. The president had the authority to:

(1) appoint a Prime Minister, on the nomination of the Chamber of Deputies; the prime minister was the head of the union government;

(2) appoint other members of the union government, on the nomination of the prime minister; and

(3) accept the registration or terminate the appointment of any member of the

union government, on the advice of the prime minister.

1.3.1.2 Legislature

According to the 1947 constitution of the Union of Burma, the legislative power of the Union was vested in the Union Parliament, which comprised the president and two chambers—the Chamber of Deputies and Chamber of Nationalities. These two chambers enjoyed equal legislative powers except for in relation to two matters. First, the budget, which, after much debate, was adopted in the Chamber of Deputies. Second, the responsibility of the government lay with the Chamber of Deputies. Thus, it can be said that, during this period (i.e., 1948–1962), Myanmar's legislature was practiced through a bicameral system. Though the legislative power was vested in the Parliament, the president had the power to promulgate ordinances when both chambers of Parliament were not in session, and when he was satisfied that circumstances existed that rendered it necessary for him to take immediate action. This ordinance had the same effect as an Act of Parliament assented to by the president. However, the president had to present that ordinance to both chambers of parliament within 45 days from the date of promulgation thereof. That ordinance would cease to operate at the expiration of 15 days from the reassembly of the Chamber of Deputies or the Chamber of Nationalities.

1.3.1.3 Judiciary

The Supreme Court, High Court, and courts at different levels were established in this period, wherein judicial independence was highly remarkable. The Constitution of the Union of Burma provided that "all judges shall be independent in the exercise of their judicial functions and subject only to the constitution and the laws." The Supreme Court was the final appellate court and had jurisdiction throughout the entire Union. Its decisions were bound by all courts. Under the Constitution, the High court had exclusively original jurisdiction in all matters arising under any treaty made by the Union in all disputes between the union and a unit or between one unit and another, and in other such matters, if any, as may be defined by law.

In 1948, the Union Judiciary Act was enacted and the courts were established according to its provisions. The Supreme Court was the court of final appeal from all courts within the Union, but leave to appeal had to first be obtained from the High Court. The Supreme Court had supervision over all courts in the Union. Moreover, occasionally, the Supreme Court had the power to promulgate rules consistent with the Constitution and the Union Judiciary Act for enabling it more effectively to exercise the jurisdiction and the power of supervision conferred upon it by or under the Constitution or any other law for the time being in force. In addition, the Supreme Court had the power to review the bill or any specified provision thereof that was presented to the president by the State Council.

The High Court had ordinary original civil jurisdiction within such local limits, as may be declared by the president, and until such local limits of the ordinary original civil jurisdiction of the High Court of Judicature at Rangoon, immediately before the commencement of the Constitution. Moreover, it had ordinary original criminal jurisdiction within the local limits of ordinary original civil jurisdiction, and in the exercise of such jurisdiction, it had the power to try all persons brought before it in due course. It was also a court of appeals from all Courts of the Union other than the Supreme Court. It was a court of reference and revision from the criminal court. Hence, it was the principal court of appeals in both criminal and civil cases. Occasionally, it also had the power to make rules consistent with the Constitution and any other law, for the time being, in force applicable to the High Court for enabling it more effectively to exercise the jurisdiction conferred upon it by or under the Constitution and the Union Judiciary Act.

At different levels of courts, there were four classes of criminal courts and four classes of civil courts. Besides these courts, there were the City Civil Court at Rangoon, the Small Causes Courts, other Special Civil Courts, Juvenile Courts, Special Crime Courts, and Special Crime Appellate Courts.

1.3.2 The Socialist Period (1962–1974, Under the Revolutionary Council)

On March 2, 1962, the Revolutionary Council took over the State power and legislative, executive, and judicial powers were vested in the hands of the Chairman of the Revolutionary Council. The Revolutionary Council declared Socialism to be the aim of the state. This was presented as the Burmese way to Socialism, which desired to alter Burma into a democratic socialist state.

1.3.2.1 Executive

On March 3, 1962, the Revolutionary Council dissolved the Chambers of Deputies and Chamber of Nationalities, along with the State Council of various federal states. On May 9, 1962, the old system of administration was replaced by new machinery. The Security and Administrative Committees of various levels were established. The local Committees were as follows:
- The Central Security and Administrative Committee;
- The State/Division Security and Administrative Committee;
- The Township Security and Administrative Committee and
- The Ward/Village Tract Security and Administrative Committee.

These Committees were responsible for security, administrative, economic, and social matters of various localities.

1.3.2.2 Legislature

On March 7, 1962, the Revolutionary Council issued Declaration No. 14 to the effect that existing laws shall, with effect on March 2, 1962, continue to be in force until they are repealed. The government neither repealed nor suspended the Constitution. On June 28, 1971, the Council adopted the drafting of the new Constitution based on the principles of socialism. The Revolutionary Council enacted the necessary law relating to the holding of the national referendum for confirmation of the new Constitution. In addition, the Council published the draft so that the people could study before participating in the referendum. On January 3, 1974, the Constitution came into force by the overwhelming majority of the people. From 1962 to 1974, it was promulgated by the legislature not in the form of "Act", but in the form of "Law".

1.3.2.3 The Judiciary

On April 1, 1962, the Revolutionary Council abolished the former High Court and the Supreme Court. To be in line with socialism, their powers and functions were amalgamated into a newly established court known as the Chief Court. The Chief Court continues to function as the highest court of appeals in matters both civil and criminal and deals with suits in Rangoon (Yangon) city, in exercise of its original jurisdiction, subordinate courts were unchanged until 1972. The People's Judiciary System was introduced. Courts were composed of representatives of the Worker's and Peasant's Council. Various judicial committees were established as follows-

– The Central Judicial Committee;
– The State/ Division Judicial Committee;
– The Ward/Village Tract Judicial Committee.

These committees had jurisdiction on criminal matters, and from June 1973, they had jurisdiction on civil matters.

1.3.3 The Socialist Period (1974–1988, under the Constitution of the Socialist Republic of the Union of Myanmar)

After the promulgation of the 1974 Constitution of the Socialist Republic of the Union of Myanmar, the State adopted a single-party system. The Myanmar Socialist Programme Party, which was the sole political party, led the State. Under the Constitution, the sovereign power resided with the people. In accordance with the Constitution, the *Pyithu Hluttaw* (People's Assembly) exercised the sovereign power invested in it by the people and delegated to the organs of State Power. The Council of State was formed for directing, supervising, and coordinating the works of the central and local organs of State Power and of bodies of public services.

The central organs of State Power were the Council of Ministers, the Council of People's Justices, Council of People's Attorneys, and the Council of People's

Inspectors. In each state, division, ward, and village tract, there was a People's Council.

1.3.3.1 Executive

The *Pyithu Hluttaw* delegated the executive power of the state to central and local organs of State Power. The Council of Ministers was the highest executive organ of the State and was responsible to the *Pyithu Hluttaw* when the *Pyithu Hluttaw* was in session and to the Council of State when the *Pyithu Hluttaw* was not in session.

1.3.3.2 Legislature

Supreme power was vested in the *Pyithu Hluttaw*, which exercised the sovereign powers of the State on behalf of the people. The regular term was four years from the date of the first session. The legislative power of the State was vested in the *Pyithu Hluttaw*. It delegated the executive and the judicial powers of the state to central and local organs of State Powers. The *Pyithu Hluttaw* had the authority to decide on whether to declare war or make peace only by a 75% majority vote. Moreover, it had the power to decide to hold a referendum where necessary.

The Council of State was responsible to the *Pyithu Hluttaw*. The head or chairman of the Council of State was the President of the State. Laws enacted by the *Phithu Hluttaw* were signed and promulgated by the president. Laws operated during the period 1974–1988 were according to the 1974 Constitution. Under the Constitution, only the *Pyithu Hluttaw* could approve enacted laws and rules. During the *Pyithu Hluttaw* (1974–1988), 128 laws were enacted and published yearly. The Council of State had powers to interpret laws other than this Constitution for uniformity; to make decisions concerning the establishment of diplomatic relations with foreign countries, severance of such relations, and the appointment and recall of diplomatic representatives; to make decisions concerning the entering into, ratification or annulment of international treaties, or the withdrawal from such treaties with the approval of the *Pyithu Hluttaw*; and to make decisions concerning international agreements—abrogate the decision and orders of the central and local organs of State Power if they were not consistent with the law:

1.3.3.3 Judiciary

In this era, judicial organs were constituted as the Council of People's Justices, and the members were nominated and appointed by the *Pyithu Hluttaw*. The Central Court was the final appeals court of the country, under which there were state/division people's courts, township people's courts, and ward/village tract people's courts. People's courts comprised members of the people's councils of various levels, respectively.

The Council of People's Justices supervised all judicial organs and courts within the State, and formed the necessary judicial courts only with its members and administered justice. Therefore, the Council of People's Justice was the highest judicial organ of the State.

People's attorneys were responsible for assisting the people's courts and protecting the legal interests of the people.

Hence, the 1974 Constitution defined Myanmar as a socialist democracy. It also provided for a unicameral legislature and the state adopted a single-party system. Consequently, the Myanmar Socialist Programme Party became the only legally recognized political party dominating all the three separate branches of government.

1.3.4 The Democracy Period (1988–2011, under the Military Government).

In 1988, the general discontent among the people had risen due to economic declination, leading to a countrywide civil disturbance. Administrative machinery broke down and on September 18, 1988, the State Law and Order Restoration Council (SLORC) took over the power of the State. It suspended the 1974 Constitution and abolished the *Pyithu Hluttaw* and various responsible councils, along with the Council of People's Justice and the Central Court. Legislative, executive, and judicial powers had been vested in the SLORC and it administered martial law. The SLORC abolished the single-party system and socialist economic system, paving the way for a multi-party democratic State based on political democracy and a market-oriented economic system.

The SLORC enacted the Judiciary Law in 1988 to transform the aforementioned socialist judicial system. Under this law, the Supreme Court was established and it became the highest judicial organ, under which there were state or divisional courts and township courts.

The SLORC called a National Convention in 1993, but it was suspended in 1996 when the National League for Democracy boycotted it. The National Convention was again called in 2004. Myanmar remained a sovereign state without a constitution until 2008.

On November 15, 1997, the State Peace and Development Council (SPDC) was instituted. In 2000, the Judiciary Law was enacted by the SPDC to transform the formation of courts. According to its provisions, the Supreme Court was still the highest judicial organ of the Union of Myanmar, with state or division courts, district courts, and township courts.

After the promulgation of the 2008 Constitution of the Republic of the Union of Myanmar. in accordance with section 443 of the Constitution of the Republic of the Union of Myanmar, the SPDC enacted the Judiciary Law of 2010 to implement the judicial works smoothly in accordance with the Constitution of the Republic of the Union of Myanmar. This law became enforced commencing from the day on which the Constitution came into force.

2. The Current Legal System (2011–Present)

2.1 Constitution of the Republic of the Union of Myanmar

The Referendum for approval of the draft Constitution of the Republic of the Union of Myanmar was held in 2008. After successfully holding the referendum, the Constitution of the Republic of the Union of Myanmar was ratified and promulgated on May 29, 2008. The Constitution comprises 15 chapters, including a Preamble; in total, there are 457 sections, with five schedules.

The Constitution is based on the principle of separation of powers and does not accept the doctrine of unified power. The three branches of sovereign power are separated and exert reciprocal control, checking, and balancing among themselves. These powers are shared among the union, regions, states, and self-administered areas.

2.2 Executive

The Government of Myanmar is basically formed with the president, vice-presidents, ministers of the union, and the attorney general of the union.[3] The executive power of the **Union** is distributed among the union, regions, states, and self-administered areas as prescribed by the Constitution. The head of the executive is the president who takes precedence over all other persons throughout the Union.[4] The president may appoint as well as dismiss the ministries of the union government and designate the number of Union Ministers as necessary with the approval of the *Pyidaungsu Hluttaw*.[5] Furthermore, he may appoint the attorney general of the Union to seek legal advice and assign duties on legal matters, with the approval of the *Pyidaungsu Hluttaw*, and the deputy attorney general to assist the attorney general.[6]

The **Region and State Government** is formed respectively with the chief minister, the ministers, and the advocate general of the region or state.[7] Generally, these region or state governments have the responsibility to assist the union government in preserving the stability, peace, tranquility, and prevalence of law and order of the Union.[8]

The administrative body of a **Self-Administered Division or Self-Administered Zone** is called the leading body[9], which is comprised of at least 10

---

[3] Section 20, the 2008 Constitution.
[4] Section 58, Ibid.
[5] Sections 202, 232, 233, 234, 235, Ibid.
[6] Sections 237, 239, Ibid.
[7] Section 248 (a) and (b), Ibid.
[8] Section 250, Ibid.
[9] Section 275, Ibid.

members. The president has to appoint the chairperson of the Self-Administered Division or the Self-Administered Zone concerned.

As for the administration of Nay Pyi Taw, the Union Territory, the president has to form a Nay Pyi Taw Council and appoint a chairperson and the members of the Nay Pyi Taw Council.

2.3 The Legislature

The legislative authority is vested in the *Pyidaungsu Hluttaw* (The National Parliament), which comprises two Hluttaws, namely, the *Pyithu Hluttaw* (The People's Assembly) and the *Amyotha Hluttaw* (The National Assembly).[10] The *Pyithu Hluttaw* is formed with a maximum of 440 seats; it comprises not more than 330 elected representatives and not more than 110 representatives who are the Defence Services personnel nominated by the Commander-in-Chief of the Defence Services. The *Amyotha Hluttaw* is formed with a maximum of 224 seats and comprises 168 elected representatives and 56 representatives who are the Defence Services personnel nominated by the Commander-in-Chief of the Defence Services.

The Region or State Hluttaw shall have the right to enact laws related to matters prescribed in Schedule two of the Region or State Hluttaw's legislative list.

The legislative power relating to the matters listed in Schedule three for the respective Self-Administered Division or Self-Administered Zones are allotted to the respective division or zone Leading Bodies.

2.4 Judiciary

The Courts of the Union are established under the 2008 Constitution and these include the Supreme Court of the Union, high courts of the region, high courts of the state, courts of the self-administered division, courts of the self-administered zone, district courts, township courts, and other courts constituted by law; courts-martial; and the Constitutional Tribunal of the Union.[11] On October

---

[10] Section 74, Ibid.
[11] Section 293, Ibid.

28, 2010, the Union Judiciary Law was enacted to implement judicial works of the aforementioned courts in the present judicial system.

2.4.1 The Supreme Court of the Union

The Supreme Court of the Union, which is the highest court, is situated in Nay Pyi Taw and headed by the chief justice of the Union. A minimum of seven and a maximum of 11 judges of the Supreme Court including the chief justice can be appointed. The president can appoint the chief justice and judges of the Supreme Court of the Union after seeking approval from the *Pyidaungsu Hluttaw*, which has no right to refuse the person nominated by the president for the appointment unless it can clearly be proved that the persons do not meet the qualifications for the post.

The Supreme Court has original jurisdiction in matters arising out of bilateral treaties concluded by the Union; in disputes, except the Constitutional problems, between the union government and the region or state governments, or among the regions, among the states, between the region and the state, and between the union territory and the region or the state. It has the appellate jurisdiction to decide judgments passed by the High Courts of the regions or the states and judgments passed by the other courts in accordance with the law. In addition, it has the revisionary power over any judgment or order passed by any subordinate court and the jurisdiction on confirming the death sentence as well as appealing against the death sentence. Furthermore, it has the jurisdiction to transfer a case from a court to itself or to any other court. It possesses the power to issue Writ of Habeas Corpus, Writ of Mandamus, Writ of Prohibition, Writ of Quo Warranto, and Writ of Certiorari. However, this power to issue writs is suspended in areas where a state of emergency is declared. The decisions of the Supreme Court are final as well as conclusive, and thus it is the final court of appeal in the Union.

2.4.2 High Courts of the Region and High Courts of the State

A high court is established for every region and the state of the Union. Each high court is headed by the chief justice of the high court of the region or the chief justice of the high court of the state. A minimum of three and a maximum of seven judges including the chief justice of the high court can be appointed. The president can appoint the chief justice and the judges of the high court, in coordination with the chief justice of the Union and the chief minister of the respective region or state, after seeking approval from the respective Region or State Hluttaws, which has no right to refuse the person nominated by the president for the appointment unless it can clearly prove that the individuals do not meet the qualifications for the post.

Every high court of the region or state has jurisdictions to adjudicate on an original case, appeal case, revision case, and other matters prescribed by any law. It has the appellate jurisdiction on the judgments, decrees, and orders passed by all other subordinate courts. In addition, it has the power to supervise district courts and township courts in the region or the state and court of the self-administered division, as well as court of the self-administered zone, if there are self-administered areas in the region or state. Moreover, it has the jurisdiction to transfer a case from a court to itself or to any other court within the respective region or state. It has unlimited jurisdiction to hear and decide both criminal and civil suits.

2.4.3 District Courts, Courts of the Self-Administered Division, and Courts of the Self-Administered Zone

District courts, courts of the self-administered division, and courts of the self-administered zone have the jurisdiction to hear criminal, civil, appeal, and revision cases, as well as other matters prescribed by any law. The respective high court of the region or state supervises the appointment of judges at this level of courts. Judges at this level are granted the right to try serious criminal cases and civil suits not exceeding 500 million kyats (over 300 thousand US dollars) as original jurisdiction.

2.4.4 Township Courts

Township Courts have the jurisdiction to try both criminal and civil cases as well as other matters prescribed by any law. The respective high court of the region or state supervises the appointment of judges at this level of courts. These levels of courts are mainly courts of original jurisdiction. Judges at this level can pass a sentence up to seven years of imprisonment. They can try civil suits wherein the amount in dispute or value of the subject matters does not exceed 10 million kyats (approximately 6000 US dollars). They also exercise jurisdiction over juvenile cases.

2.4.5 Courts-Martial

The Courts-Martial were established under the 2008 Constitution of the Republic of the Union of Myanmar to adjudicate defense services personnel. The establishment and composition of different levels of Courts-Martial are provided in the Defence Services Act of 1959.

2.4.6 The Constitutional Tribunal of the Union

The Constitutional Tribunal of the Union has nine members. Its essential functions are to interpret the provisions under the Constitution, decide constitutional disputes in the union, and review whether the laws promulgated are in conformity with the Constitution. The president can appoint the chairperson and its members after seeking approval from *Pyidaungsu Hluttaw*, which has no right to refuse the persons nominated by the president for the appointment unless it can be clearly proved that they are disqualified for the post.

The president, speaker of the *Pyidaungsu Hluttaw*, speaker of the *Pyithu Hluttaw*, speaker of the *Amyotha Hluttaw*, chief justice of the Supreme Court of the Union, and chairperson of the Union Election Commission have the right to submit any constitutional matter to the Constitutional Tribunal and seek an interpretation, resolution, and/or opinion.

Moreover, the chief minister of the region or state, the speaker of the Region or State Hluttaw, the chairperson of the self-administered division leading body or the self-administered zone leading body, and representatives numbering at least 10% of all the representatives of the *Pyithu Hluttaw* or *Amyotha Hluttaw* may also have the right to submit constitutional matters to the Constitutional Tribunal in accordance with the prescribed procedures and obtain an interpretation, resolution, and/or opinion. A court, which submits any case involving constitutional issue to the Constitutional Tribunal in accordance with the prescribed procedures for its opinion, has to stay the trial until it receives such a resolution. In addition, its resolution is final and conclusive.

2.4.7 Other Courts

There are also other courts with specific jurisdiction, namely, juvenile courts to try offenses committed by minors, municipal courts to try municipal offenses, and motor vehicle courts to try road traffic offenses.

In terms of hierarchy, township courts and other courts are courts of first instance; district courts, courts of the self-administered division, and courts of the self-administered zone are courts of first appeal; the high courts of the regions and the high courts of the states are courts of second appeal; and the Supreme Court is the court of final appeal.

3. Inheritance under the Myanmar Customary Law

3.1 Myanmar Customary Law

The Myanmar Customary Law applies to all Buddhists in Myanmar as the personal law that is mainly concerned with family matters, such as marriage, divorce, inheritance, and matrimonial rights. The Myanmar Customary Law is the social and secular law based upon the customs and usages that are historically accepted by ancient Myanmar. Therefore, it is the law based on long established customs practiced throughout the history of the people of Myanmar and is the body of customs practiced by Myanmar Buddhists.

The sources of the Myanmar Customary Law are the *Dhammathats*, judicial precedents, customs, and enacted laws.

The *Dhammathats* are "treatise of rules which are in accordance with the custom and usage and referred to in the settlement of disputes relating to person and property." They are a principal source of the Myanmar Customary Law.

Judicial precedents are the decisions of the highest court that are the landmarks in the development of the Customary Law.

The prevailing customs of Myanmar is one of the sources of the Myanmar Customary Law. Custom is the rule.

Some of the Myanmar Customary Laws, as set forth in the *Dhammathats* and precedents, do not coincide with the prevailing situations. Thus, the legislative body has to enact the laws relating to social matters.

There are three enacted laws relating to social matters:
1. The Registration of Kittima Adoption Act, 1939;
2. The Myanmar Buddhist Women's Special Marriage Law; and
3. The Monogamy Law.

3.2 Succession and Inheritance

There is a slight difference between succession and inheritance. Succession is the power or right of coming to the inheritance of ancestors and liabilities of a deceased person to his or her heirs. On the other hand, inheritance is a perpetual or continuing right to an estate invested in a person and his heirs. Hence, succession is not only succession of the deceased person's estate but also the taking the place of the deceased by his or her heirs and inheritance is only the succession of the deceased person's estate.

3.3 The Basic Principle of Succession

If a Myanmar Buddhist dies, the estate left behind is to be distributed among the successors of the deceased in accordance with the Myanmar Customary Law. Therefore, it is important to know the legal successors.

According to the Myanmar Customary Law, there is a definite provision of who may be the heir according to the order of succession and what portion of the estate may be inherited when one person dies. Subsequently, one may get this right as soon as the death of a deceased ancestor occurs, which vests in him separately and individually. This right of legatee is called a vested right.

Hence, the Myanmar Customary Law of inheritance is complete and systematic. As the essence of the Myanmar Customary Law, there are six basic principles as follows:

1. Intestate succession;
2. On the death of a husband or wife, without children, the surviving spouse succeeds to the whole of the deceased's estate;
3. Inheritance shall not ascend when it can descend;
4. The nearer shall exclude the more remote;
5. In a competition between equidistant, the full blood excludes the half-blood; and
6. Conduct can indeed operate as disqualification, but it is in no sense a necessary qualification to obtain the right of inheritance.

3.3.1 Intestate Succession

A Myanmar Buddhist does not have the right to dispose his property by means of a will (*thedansa* in Burmese). Inheritance, therefore, is by intestate succession only.

Here "will" refers to the legal declaration of the intention of a testator with respect to his property, which he desires to be carried into effect after his death. A will is the legally enforceable declaration of a persons' intention of what he desires to be done after his death—which declaration is revocable during his lifetime, which is operative for no purpose until death, and which is applicable to the situation that exists at the will-maker's death.

The principle that a man may select the person on whom his property is to be devolved after his demise is not available in the *Dhammathats*. In fact, the word *thedansa* does not appear in the *Dhammathats*.

When conscious of their approaching death, parents call their heirs together and make a formal division, orally or in writing, of their properties among the heirs, exhorting them to accept the allocation without dispute. This is the idea conveyed by the word *thedansa*. Therefore, the idea conveyed by *thedansa* is not the same as that conveyed by the English word "will." Therefore, it has been a settled law that Myanmar Buddhist inheritance is by intestate succession only.

Although a Myanmar Buddhist cannot dispose of their estate by making a will, there have been some attempts to circumvent the rule against testamentary disposition.

In Ma Thin Myaing v. Maung Gyi[12], "where a mother made a gift of land by a deed of sale to three out of her five children, subject to a condition that the gift was to take effect on her death, the parties being Buddhist. In this case, the Yangon High Court had held that a Myanmar Buddhist cannot dispose of his or her property after his or her death by Will, and no Myanmar Buddhist can under the guise of making a gift be allowed in effect to make a Will. He or she cannot set at naught the provisions of his personal law as to inheritance of his property after his death."

However, a Myanmar Buddhist can make a gift during his or her lifetime according to section 122 of the Transfer of Property Act. Hence, for a gift to be valid there must be delivery of possession during the lifetime of the donor. Therefore, we may firmly say that a Myanmar Buddhist cannot dispose of their property by writing a will, which cannot be evaded by an attempted transfer *inter vivos* to take effect upon the death of the donor.

However, they can dispose their property by an arrangement of special contract (i.e., family arrangement) before their death among those heirs, whereby they bind themselves to accept a certain method of partition. Nevertheless, such an arrangement will not usually give them a right to recover the property from their parents during their lifetime and such arrangements are not binding until the parents die and the heirs act upon it and are thereby stopped from challenging its validity. The parties to a family arrangement must be persons who have a right to the property regarding which arrangement is made, and there must be mutuality among them in the arrangement to make the arrangement binding on all of them. The main objective of the family arrangement is to prevent the emergence of multiple suits concerning inheritance and to evade the quarrel on

---

[12] Ma Thin Myaing v. Maung Gyi, 1 Ran., P. 351.

that matter. Thus, the making of a family arrangement is the appropriate idea for a Myanmar Buddhist. Though a Myanmar Buddhist can make a family arrangement, the family arrangement cannot be seen in other family laws (i.e., Mahhomedan, Christian, and Hindu).

3.3.2 On the death of a husband or wife, without children, the surviving spouse succeeds to the whole of the deceased's estate

The second general principle of the Myanmar Customary Law of inheritance is that "on the death of a husband or wife, the survivor, in the absence of children, succeeds to the whole of the deceased's estate." This principle will be explained in detail later.

3.3.3 Inheritance shall not ascend when it can descend.

One person has two lines of succession: First, the descendant line, for example, children and their descendants and second, the ascendant line, for example, parents and their representatives.

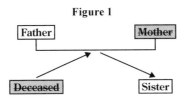

Figure 1

If the father and sister of the deceased contested to inherit the estate of the deceased, the right of the father of the deceased cannot be maintained against the right of the sister, because the sister is in the descending line and the father is in the ascending line. (**Figure 1**)

For instance, half-brothers or half-sisters and maternal grandmother of the deceased contested to inherit the estate of the deceased. In such a case, the right of the maternal grandmother of the deceased cannot be maintained against the right of half-brothers or half-sisters of the deceased because half-brothers or half-sisters are in the descending line and the maternal grandmother is in the as-

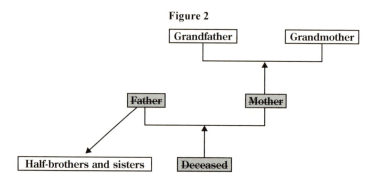

Figure 2

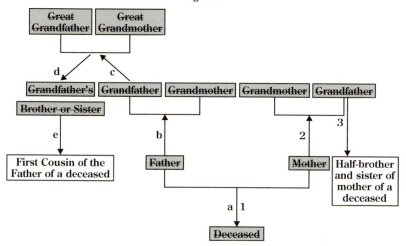

Figure 3

cending line. (**Figure 2**)

However, where the deceased person dies leaving no descendants the inheritance may ascend, but it shall not ascend more than is necessary. A descendant, however remote, will exclude an ascendant, however near.

In a claim between a half-brother and sister of a mother of the deceased and full cousin of the father of the deceased, the first group excludes the latter group. This is because to reach the half-brother and sister, the line of inheritance ascends twice and descends once, while to reach the full cousin, it has to ascend three times and descend twice. (**Figure 3**)

3.3.4 The nearer shall exclude the more remote

Subject to the previous principle, the estate of a deceased man or woman will devolve upon the person who is most closely related to the deceased. According to this principle, the nearest relation of the deceased can succeed the legacy. To know the nearness and remoteness of relations, one can measure by placing the deceased in the center.

An aunt on the father's side and cousins of the deceased on both the father's and mother's side competitively claim the deceased's estate. (**Figure 4**)

Figure 4

Lineal steps from the deceased to his aunt

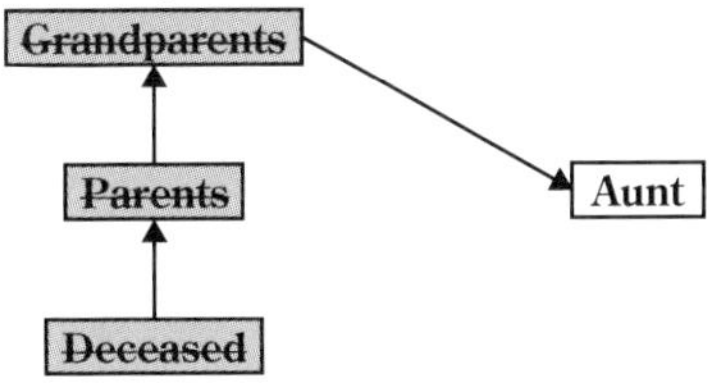

```
Grandparents ─────┐
     ▲            ▼
  Parents        Aunt
     ▲
  Deceased
```

(1) From the deceased to his parents   -1 step (ascending)
(2) From parents to grandparents   -1 step (ascending)
(3) From grandparents to aunt   -1 step (descending)
                                Total   3 steps

Lineal steps from the deceased to his first cousin

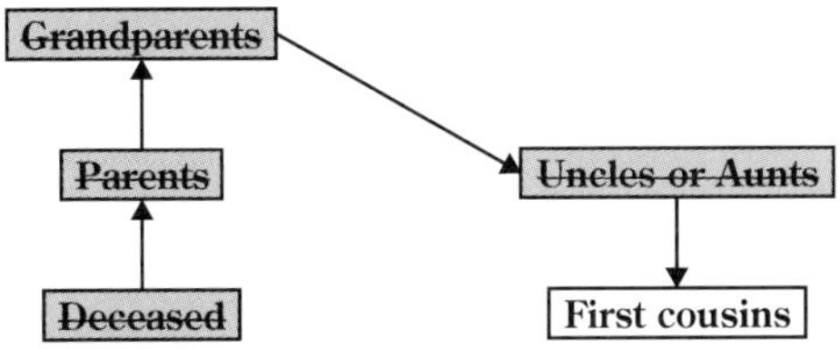

```
Grandparents ─────┐
     ▲            ▼
  Parents      Uncles or Aunts
     ▲            ▼
  Deceased     First cousins
```

(1) From the deceased to his parents   -1 step (ascending)
(2) From parents to grandparents   -1 step (ascending)
(3) From grandparents to uncles or aunts   -1 step (descending)
(4) From uncles or aunts to first cousins   -1 step (descending)
                                   Total   4 steps

There are only three lineal steps from the deceased to his aunt (or uncle), but there are four lineal steps from the deceased to his first cousin. Therefore, according to the principle of "the nearer excludes the more remote," the aunt (or uncle) excludes first cousins of the deceased.

A nephew of the deceased and an uncle of the deceased competitively claim the deceased's estate. (**Figure 5**)

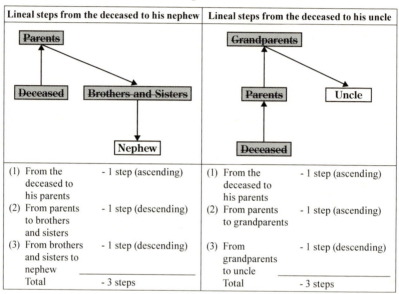

Figure 5

Lineal steps from the deceased to his nephew		Lineal steps from the deceased to his uncle	
(1) From the deceased to his parents	- 1 step (ascending)	(1) From the deceased to his parents	- 1 step (ascending)
(2) From parents to brothers and sisters	- 1 step (descending)	(2) From parents to grandparents	- 1 step (ascending)
(3) From brothers and sisters to nephew	- 1 step (descending)	(3) From grandparents to uncle	- 1 step (descending)
Total	- 3 steps	Total	- 3 steps

To the nephew, there is one ascending line and two descending lines. Then to the uncle, there are two ascending lines one descending line. So, both are in equal lineal steps from the deceased. Hence, the matter cannot be decided according to the principle of the "nearer excludes the more remote." Therefore, it is to be decided by citing the previous principle. Therefore, relatively, the nephew may be said to be in the descending line and excludes the uncle who can be said to be in the ascending line. In other words, if both the classes are in the degree of proximity in the propositus, it is to be decided by referring the principle of "inheritance shall not ascend when it can descend." Moreover, if both are in equidistant collaterals of the same level, they share equally.

There are some exceptions to this principle.

According to the Myanmar Customary Law, in the case of the death of a son or daughter, unmarried and without children, his or her property devolves upon his or her brothers and sisters in preference to his or her parents, whether the deceased was at the time of his or her death living with the parents or separately. (**Figure 6**)

Figure 6

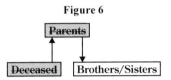

This matter does not abolish the principle of the "nearer excludes the more remote." In such a case, to brothers and sisters, there is one ascending line and one descending line. To the parents, there is one ascending line. Hence, parents are closer lineal steps than brothers and sisters. However, brothers and sisters are more closely related than parents.

Representation is not a principle of the Myanmar Customary Law. The basic rule is that the nearer heir excludes the more remote, and that the partial representation allowed to grandchildren in competition with children is merely an exception to that general rule, and is the only exception to it. (**Figure 7**)

Figure 7

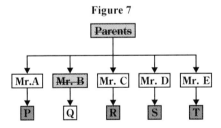

In the above example, Mr. B passed away before his parents. After the death of both parents, the estate of the parents is claimed by Mr. A, Mr. C, Mr. D, Mr. E, and grandchild Q. To Mr. A, Mr. C, Mr. D, and Mr. E, there is one descending line. While to grandchild Q, there are two descending lines. Thus, Mr. A, Mr. C, Mr. D, and Mr. E are a closer lineal step than grandchild Q. Although grandchild Q is more remote than the others, he can inherit the grandparent's estate as a representative of Mr. B. (**Figure 8**)

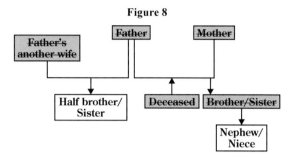

Figure 8

Another exception is that "A brother or sister of half-blood stands in the same degree of relationship for the purposes of succession as a nephew or niece of full blood." In this situation, to the nephew, there is one ascending line and two descending lines. To the brother or sister of half-blood, there is one ascending line and one descending line. Hence, a half-blood relation is a closer lineal step than nephew or niece. However, they would share equally.

3.3.5 In a competition between equidistant, the full blood excludes the half-blood.

Persons who are born from the same father and mother are called full blood relations. Persons born from the same father but different mother or the same mother but different father are called half-blood relations.

When both are in the same degree of propinquity, full blood relations shall exclude the half-blood relations. (**Figure 9**)

To the full blood nephew or niece, there are two ascending lines and three descending lines. Then to the half-blood nephew or niece, there is one ascending line and two descending lines. Hence, the half-blood nephew or niece is nearer in degree than the half-blood nephew or niece. However, they inherit the estate together. This was decided in Maung Htun Htun Aung v. Daw Pyone Yi[13]. This decision is contrary to the Myanmar Customary Law's principle of the "nearer excludes the more remote."

---

[13] 1976 B.L.R., P. 38.

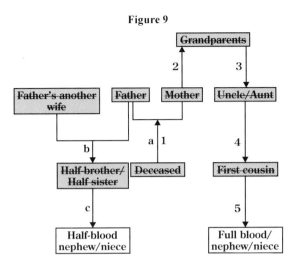

Figure 9

However, a full blood relation will not exclude a half-blood relation, when the latter is nearer in degree than the former. (**Figure 10**)

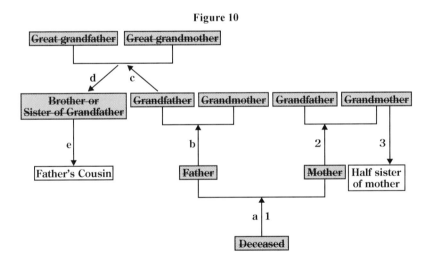

Figure 10

In the event of half-brothers and half-sisters of the mother of the deceased and the father's full cousin, the first half-blood related person excludes the latter. This is because to the mother's half-brothers and half-sisters, there are two ascending lines and one descending line. However, to the full blood cousin of the father, there are three ascending lines and two descending lines. Therefore, half-blood relations of the mother are closer lineal steps than full blood relations of the father. This is the exception to this principle.

3.3.6 Conduct can indeed operate as disqualification but it is in no sense a necessary qualification to obtain the right of inheritance

The general principle is that "conduct can indeed operate as disqualification but it is in no sense a necessary qualification to obtain the right of inheritance." Hence, conduct can operate as a disqualification for a person to obtain the right to inheritance.

3.4 General order of Succession

When a Myanmar Buddhist dies, succession must be in accordance with the above principles.

Hence, it is necessary to know the order of succession in the inheritance of property. By summing up the above general principles of inheritance, the surviving spouse, subject to the right of an *Orasa*, is the original and the first in priority, who is entitled to the deceased's estate.

"Orasa" is a word derived from the Sanskrit word "aurasa," which literally means "child born of the body," which in other words means "child born out of the bosom" or "a child that comes from the breast," in Myanmar, "*Yin Hnit Phyit Taw Thar*" The *Orasa*, therefore, is a legitimate child of a union contracted with parental sanction on both sides, who will be entitled to inherit not only the estates of his or her parents but also of the grandparents.

When a Myanmar Buddhist dies, leaving no surviving spouse, the general order of succession, is in the order as numerically indicated below. (**Figure 11**)

3.5 Inheritance of Surviving Spouse

The widow did not lose her vested interest in the joint estate of the marriage in favor of her mother-in-law. The rule will also hold for the widower; thus, in spite of the fact that the couple lived with the parent, who held possession of

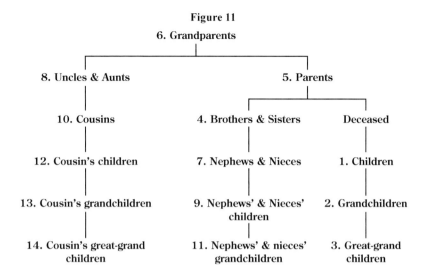

the joint property of the couple, the survivor will be entitled to his or her vested interest in the joint property of the couple, as against his or her parent-in-law in possession.

The Myanmar Customary Law of inheritance states, "on the death of the husband or the wife, without *Orasa* child, the survivor succeeds to the whole of the deceased's estate." Therefore, it is obvious that the right of inheritance of a surviving spouse depends on whether they have *Orasa* child or not.

The estate of the husband or wife goes upon the death of one to the other by succession and not by survivorship.

The ordinary rule of the Myanmar Customary Law is that the surviving spouse succeeds to the deceased's estate to the exclusion of all the children (except the *Orasa*, if there be any), and that so long as he or she remains unmarried, no child (except the *Orasa*) can claim any share of the property left by the deceased.

When a husband or wife dies and they have children, it is necessary to see whether there is a child who can claim the status of *Orasa*, because an *Orasa* is a privileged child who can claim one-fourth of the deceased's estate, once a parent of the same sex dies. Therefore, an *Orasa* can claim the parental estate from the surviving opposite sex parent when the same sex parent dies.

If there is an *Orasa* child at the time of death of the husband or the wife, the widow or widower has no right to claim as the sole successor of the deceased, because the *Orasa* son or daughter has the right of inheritance at that time. In that instance, the *Orasa* child can claim a quarter share of the parental estate from the surviving parent of the opposite sex. Hence, the widow or widower can inherit three-fourths of their joint estate.

When one a spouse dies, leaving behind Kanittha children but no *Orasa*, the surviving spouse inherits the entire joint estate if he or she does not remarry.

Myanmar Buddhist marriage is said to be polygamous (polygyny), which meant that a man could take more than one wife at the same time. All wives can get equal status, whether or not they live with the husband, and inherit his estate on an equal footing. However, in 2015, the *Pyidaungsu Hluttaw* enacted the **Monogamy Law**. According to **Section 16** of this law, if a husband who is married according to any law or a religion or a custom, enters into another marriage with another woman while the original union is still legally recognized, such marriage is not legal, and thus the second wife shall not be entitled to inherit when that husband dies. Moreover, the husband who marries and lives together with another spouse shall not be entitled to inherit from the first and the second wives. After promulgating that law, the Myanmar Customary Law of marriage was changed from polygamy to monogamy and the legally married first wife can inherit from her husband as mentioned hereinbefore.

After the death of one parent, if the surviving parent remarries, the *Orasa* can claim a quarter share of the parental estate from the surviving parent if the *Orasa* did not claim his quarter share on the death of the same sex parent. In addition, the *Kanitthas* (younger children) can also claim quarter shares from the surviving parent on the remarriage of the surviving parent. Thus, the surviving spouse can get half of the deceased's estate.

When on the death of one parent the *Orasa* has already taken his or her quarter share from the surviving parent, he or she cannot claim a fresh share on the remarriage of the surviving parent.

The real reasons for allowing partition on remarriage lies in the apprehension that the stepparent may not have due regard for the stepchildren's interests and may deal with the property to the other's detriment. Even without committing actual waste, the stepparent may gradually convert the properties as their own properties, and thus injure the stepchildren's interest.

The trend is that on the death of one parent if the survivor remarries, not only the *Orasa* but also the *Kanitthas* may claim a share of the parental estate from the surviving parent. If there is no *Orasa* and only *Kanitthas*, in such a case, half of the parental estate shall go to the surviving parent, one-fourth to the eldest child, and the remaining one-fourth to the other children collectively.

On the death of the husband or wife, even the *Orasa* child is an only child; the widow or widower can inherit three-fourths of the estate. However, on the death of one parent having no children except an *Orasa* child, if the surviving parent remarries, the survivor is entitled to claim half of the estate.

Hence, Myanmar Buddhist husbands and wives are equal before the law and are entitled to inherit without any discrimination based on sex. Hence, according to the Myanmar Customary Law of inheritance, equality of sexes has been an age-old concept of the society in Myanmar. In addition, it has become a distinct characteristic of the Myanmar Customary Law.

3.6 Inheritance of Children

Children who are entitled to inherit are:
- *Orasa* child;
- Eldest child;
- *Kanittha* children;
- *Kittima* children;
- *Apatittha* children;
- *Pubbaka* children (Stepchildren).

In the Myanmar Customary Law of inheritance, non-discrimination of sex is accepted. In other words, the son and daughter have equal rights to inherit the parental estate.

3.6.1 *Orasa* child

The word "Orasa" includes not only the sons but also the daughters, who enjoy this vested right.

(1) The essential conditions for the existence of the status of Orasa are:

(2) The child must be the first-born;

(3) The child must be legitimate;

(4) The child must be natural born;

(5) The child must attain majority prior to the date of the death of the same sex parent; The child, if a son, must help in the acquisition of the family property and the discharge of the father's responsibilities; if a daughter, must help the mother in the care of the property and the control and management of the household, which lie particularly within the mother's duties.

There cannot be two *Orasas* in the same family; that is to say, there cannot be an *Orasa* son and an *Orasa* daughter or two *Orasa* sons or two *Orasa* daughters at the same time in the same family.

If there is an *Orasa* child at the time of death of the husband or the wife, the widow or the widower has no right to claim to be the sole successor of the deceased because the *Orasa* son or the *Orasa* daughter has the right of inheritance at that time.

The *Orasa's* estate comes into existence as soon as the parent dies. In other words, the *Orasa's* share vests at the moment of the parent's death.

The claimant for *Orasa*-ship may be either a son or a daughter who is not a minor. However, a *Kittima* child cannot claim to be an *Orasa*.

The *Orasa* is entitled to: -

(a) claim a quarter share of the parental estate on the death of one parent, from the surviving parent of the opposite sex.;

(b) claim a quarter share of the parental estate on the remarriage of the surviving parent after the death of the parent; and

(c) transmit, by dying before his or her parents, to his or her children a right superior to that of an ordinary grandchild by a predeceased child.

An *Orasa* son cannot claim a quarter share of the parental estate on the death of his mother from the surviving father. In addition, an *Orasa* daughter cannot claim a quarter share of the parental estate on the death of her father from her surviving mother.

3.6.2 Inheritance of the Eldest Child

Inheritance under the Myanmar Customary Law of the eldest-born child occupies an extraordinary favored position as compared with the younger children.

In Maung Po Kin and one v. Maung Tun Yin and two[14], it was held that "The eldest child, on the remarriage of the surviving parent, becomes entitled to a quarter shares in the joint estate of the parents, if he or she has not already taken a share as *Orasa*."

Hence, the eldest child cannot claim a quarter of the shares like an *Orasa* at the time of one parent's death. He or she can only claim his quarter share on the remarriage of the surviving parent.

3.6.3 *Kanittha* Children

The Sanskrit word "Kanistha" has been distorted into the Pali word "Kanittha," which means younger. Hence, all the children of a married couple, except the *Orasa*, are called *Kanittha*, which now means younger children.

The rights of *Kanittha* are inferior to those of *Orasa*. When one spouse dies, leaving behind *Kanittha* children but no *Orasa*, the surviving spouse inherits the whole of the joint estate if he or she does not remarry. It can be considered a rule of the Myanmar Customary Law that not only the eldest child but also an *Orasa*, if an *Orasa* has not already taken his share on death of the same sex parent, are entitled to a quarter share on the remarriage of the surviving parent. In addition, the *Kanittha* of the surviving parent.

Only in the case of remarriage can the children of the first marriage rightfully claim a partition of property arises. They collectively acquire a vested interest

---

[14] Maung Po Kin and one v. Maung Tun Yin and two, 4 Ran., P. 207

in the joint property of the marriage to the extent of the deceased parent's share which is half.

3.6.4 *Kittima* Children

In the Myanmar Customary Law and the society, in general, adoption plays an important role. According to the Myanmar Customary Law, there is no law prohibiting a Myanmar Buddhist from adopting children and as many as the individual sees it fit.

According to the *Dhammathats*, there were four kinds of adoption. They were:

(i) the *Kittima*, the child adopted publicly;

(ii) the *Apatittha*, the casually adopted children;

(iii) the *Sahoddha*, the child purchased and brought up in the family; and

(iv) the *Chatta-bhatta*, the destitute child taken out of pity into the adoptive parent's family.

Though the *Dhammathats* mention four classes, there are only two kinds of adoption that have practical importance today, that is, the *Kittima* and *Apatittha*.

The word "*Kittima*" comes from the Sanskrit word "*Kritrima*" or the Pali word "*Kitima*," which means fictitious. The *Kittima* is the full adoption of a son or daughter with the intention that the child shall inherit. Hence, it can be noted that, in the case of a *Kittima* adoption, the intention to give the right of inheritance is the paramount.

A *Kittima* adopted child can inherit like a natural son or daughter from the adoptive parents. Similarly, he or she can also inherit from the relatives of the adoptive parents. They can claim a quarter share from the surviving parent on the remarriage of the adoptive surviving parent after the death of the other. They can claim a share in the estate of the parent of their adoptive parent when the adoptive parent, having acquired the status of *Orasa*, had predeceased his or her own parent. For the purpose of partition among brothers and sisters or between uncles and nephews, a *Kittima* child is treated exactly like a natural child. In the absence of any heir, such as a son, grandson, great-grandson, or great-great-grandson, the *Kittima* son becomes the sole heir.

The *Kittima* child's position is inferior to that of the natural children. If there is any property to which the parents were entitled by inheritance, but which had not yet come into their possession, the *Kittima* son cannot obtain the whole of such property. He shall get only half and shall relinquish the other half to the parent's co-heirs. However, if the surviving child is a natural- born child, he or she can inherit the whole estate at this situation.

A *Kittima* child cannot claim to be *Orasa* and sue for a quarter share of the adoptive parent's estate on the death of one adoptive parent from the surviving adoptive parent because the *Kittima* child is not by any means regarded as being on equal footing with one's own child.

There is another instance of the *Kittima* son's or daughter's inferiority to the natural-born children. When Myanmar Buddhist married couples embrace Christianity, their Myanmar Buddhist natural-born children are still their heirs if they die intestate. However, after the adoption of a child, if the Myanmar Buddhist adoptive parents become Christians and die as intestate Christians, their adopted Myanmar Buddhist child cannot claim to inherit their estate as their adopted child because when a person changes his or her religion and embraces Christianity, his or her personal law changes and the Succession Act governs the right of succession to his or her estate. Even though Myanmar Buddhist parents change their faith to Christian, their natural-born children cannot lose their vested rights of inheritance. Hence, an adopted child is inferior to the natural one.

Another position of inferiority is that the *Kittima* adopted child of a Myanmar national couple, who is a foreigner, cannot automatically become a citizen of Myanmar.

3.6.5 *Apatittha* Children

The word "*Apatittha*" comes from the Sanskrit word "*Apabiddha*" or the Pali word "*Apabidda,*" which means rejected. An *Apatittha* child is one who has been adopted casually and without any intention expressed on the part of the adoptive parents that the child shall inherit. So, an intention, either expressed or implied, on the part of the adoptive parents that the adopted child shall or shall not inherit forms the dividing line between a *Kittima* child and an *Apatittha* child. *Apatittha* adoption is a compassionate one. The position of the *Apatittha* child is quite different from and inferior to that of the *Kittima* child. An *Apatittha* child does not get any right to inherit from the adoptive parents because the person who adopts him has no intention to give him any such right.

Although an *Apatittha* child is not entitled to share in the estate of the adoptive parents when there are natural or *Kittima* children, in the absence of the natural or *Kittima* children, the *Apatittha* child is entitled to inherit the estate of his adoptive parents when both of them are dead. However, he or she has no right to share in the adoptive parents' estate when one parent is dead and the other is surviving.

3.6.6 *Pubbaka* (Stepchildren)

Pubbaka or stepchildren are the children of another husband or wife by a former marriage or marriages. In case a man has more than one wife at the same time and the wives reside in separate houses, the children of one wife are not entitled to a share in the estate of the other wife or wives at her or their death. However, if the children do not claim their share on the remarriage of the surviving parent, the children of a former marriage will claim their share as stepchildren or *Pubbaka*.

In the Myanmar Customary Law, stepchildren are entitled to inherit. On the death of their surviving parent, stepchildren are entitled to claim a partition with their stepparent if they did not claim on the remarriage of the surviving parent. When on the remarriage of the surviving parent if the children claimed the estate from their surviving parent, they retain no further claim either in the share taken by the surviving parent to the new family or in the jointly acquired property of the surviving parent and the stepparent. On a partition on the death of a father, the division between the children of the first marriage and their stepmother is always *per stirpes*.

3.6.7 Inheritance of Grandchildren

According to the Myanmar Customary Law, there are two kinds of grandchildren, namely in-time grandchildren and out-of-time grandchildren. In the case of in-time grandchildren, their parents died after the death of their grandparents, that is, grandchildren by a post-deceased child. On the other hand, out-of-time grandchildren are those whose parents died before either both or one of the grandparents, that is, grandchildren by a predeceased child.

According to the basic principle of the Myanmar Customary Law of succession, the heirs succeed the deceased's estate in their own rights and not by representation. The fundamental rule is that "the nearer shall exclude the more remote." Nevertheless, providing grandchildren the right to inherit at all in competition with their parent's brothers and sisters is right of representation to some extent, which is the exception in the Myanmar Customary Law of succession.

The rights of out-of-time grandchildren are different. In the case of the death of a Myanmar Buddhist couple leaving grandchildren born of different children, who predeceased the couple, the grandchildren inherit and succeed in their own-right, and divide the grandparent's estate equally *per capita* among themselves. Similarly, among grandchildren of the same parents, the eldest is not entitled to a larger share than the others. They share equally.

The inheritance rights of out-of-time grandchildren and in-time grandchildren also differ. In-time grandchildren are not entitled to inherit the grandparents' estate as grandchildren.

In the case of partition between out-of-time grandchildren and their uncles and aunts, if the out-of-time grandchildren's parent is an *Orasa*, they will get more rights than the grandchildren born of the other sons and daughters. The out-of-time grandchildren of an *Orasa* son in collection get one share, which is equivalent to that of each of their uncles or aunts.

When either parent of the out-of-time grandchildren is not an *Orasa*, then such out-of-time grandchildren take between them only a quarter of what their parent would have taken had he or she survived. The remaining three-quarters revert to the estate. These three-quarters shall be divided between the uncles and aunts.

3.6.8 Inheritance of Great-grandchildren

Great-grandchildren, when in competition with children or grandchildren, are not entitled to any share in the great-grandparents' estate. They can inherit only in the absence of children and grandchildren.

3.6.9 Inheritance of Collaterals

According to the Myanmar Customary Law of inheritance, if there are no descendant lines, such as the surviving spouse, children, grandchildren, great-grandchildren, adopted children, and stepchildren, the collaterals will inherit their estate.

Collateral consanguinity is that which subsists between two persons who are descended from the same ancestor, but neither of whom is descended in a direct line from the other.

The general rule of Myanmar Customary Law of inheritance is that the husband succeeds to the wife's property and vice versa. Out of the husband and wife, the collaterals of one person who died first have no right of inheritance. The collaterals of one person who died last have a right to inherit the estate of the couple.

According to the law of inheritance, where the deceased has no direct descendants, the order of succession to the estate of the deceased is as follows:

(1) brothers and sisters;

(2) parents;

(3) grandparents;

(4) nephews and nieces;

(5) uncles and aunts;

(6) nephews' and nieces' children;

(7) first cousins;

(8) nephews' and nieces' grandchildren;

(9) first cousins' children;

(10) first cousins' grandchildren;

(11) second cousins; and

(12) first cousins' great-grandchildren.

3.6.10 Stranger

"Stranger," especially in this context, refers to

(1) a stranger in blood;

(2) a relative who is not in the ordinary line of succession; or

(3) one who, though a natural heir, has lost, for some reason or other, the ordinary right of inheritance.

A stranger is sometimes allowed to inherit a deceased person's property wholly or in part, exclusively or as sharers with ordinary heirs, in return for care and support during illness and performance of burial rites.

To get the rights of inheritance by strangers, the following conditions must be satisfied, namely:

(1) that the heirs desert and intentionally and deliberately neglect the ordinary duties of affection and kindred;

(2) that the heirs fail to pay attention to the deceased person during his last illness; and

(3) that the stranger gives support and gives assistance in sickness and performs the funeral ceremonies upon death.

Moreover, it is accepted that the stranger may inherit at least in preference to the Government to whom the estate escheats in the total absence of heirs.

Conclusion

The Myanmar legal system is complex and based on a combination of statutes and regulations with their origins in different periods of Myanmar's history and includes colonial period laws (pre 1948), parliamentary laws, Revolutionary Council laws, *Pyithu Hluttaw* (People's Assembly) laws, SLORC, and SPDC laws.

In Myanmar, there are three constitutions. The three sovereign powers such as executive, legislative, and judiciary are practiced separately by three organs, i.e., the executive, the legislative, and the judicial. Moreover, check and balance principle was used in 1947 constitution and 2008 constitution but not in 1974 constitution.

In the executive branch, the president is the highest of the executive organ in both the 1947 and 2008 Constitutions. In the 1974 Constitution, the president and the prime minister were the highest in the executive organ.

By studying these constitutions, it was established that Myanmar's Parliament was a bicameral system in the 1947 and 2008 constitutions. Both these Constitutions were designed to apply the parliamentary democracy. The 2008 Constitution allocates the legislative power to the regions, states, and self-administered areas or zones. This is different from the 1947 Constitution. The 1974 Constitution was the pathway to establish the Socialist Republic of the Union of Burma. It practiced the one-party system. At that time, the unicameral system was used and there was no separation of powers.

In the judiciary branch, the Supreme Court was the highest court in the union according to the 1947 Constitution. The Supreme Court and the high court are constituted under the 1947 Constitution. Other subordinate courts are organized under the Judiciary Act of 1948. The Central Court was the highest court of the Union in line with the 1974 Constitution. In addition, there were various levels of subordinate courts at that time. The current 2008 Constitution constitutes the Supreme Court of the Union, high courts of the region, high courts of the state, courts of the self-administered division, courts of the self-administered zone, district courts, township courts, and other Courts constituted by law (such as Juvenile Courts, Municipal court, and so on); Courts-Martial and the Constitutional Tribunal of the Union, which was not constituted before the 2008 Constitution.

Inheritance under the Myanmar Customary Law is complete and systematic. There are definite provisions about who may be the heir according to the order of succession and what portion of the estate may be inherited. Inheritance under the Myanmar Customary Law is pure intestate succession. Thus, they can dispose their property by making a family arrangement. A Myanmar Buddhist married couple is considered equal before the law and are entitled to inherit without discrimination of sex. With the exception of an *Orasa,* the children cannot inherit in the case of the death of one parent; however, they can inherit when the surviving spouse decides to remarry. In the absence of descendant lines, the collaterals will inherit. In case of no legal heir, the Government takes the estate of the deceased person. However, the Myanmar Customary Law is ever-changing with the developing circumstances of the society.

PART III
USE OF COMMON TOPICS TO IMPROVE COMPARATIVE LAW AND LEGAL EDUCATION

Chapter 1

USE OF COMMON TOPICS TO IMPROVE COMPARATIVE LAW AND LEGAL EDUCATION IN ASIA

Hiroshi Matsuo*

(Keio University)

1. Introduction

The improvement of legal education has attracted the attention of governments throughout Asian countries as an indispensable process to vitalize the rule of law for their sustainable economic, political, and social development.[1] Following extended legislation since the 1990s enacting changes to civil, commercial, and criminal codes and codes of civil and criminal procedure, applying them to cases has become crucial for achieving the rule of law in business and civic life. To improve the application of law to cases, the comparative study by using common topics seems effective. "Common Topics" shall refer to common legal questions based on cases.[2] It is a comparative analysis of how laws are applied to

---

* Professor, Keio University Law School; Director, Keio Institute for Global Law and Development (KEIGLAD).
[1] On the relation between promoting the rule of law and legal education, see Hiroshi Matsuo, "Why and How Should Comparative Legal Education Be Promoted in an Asian Context?", in: KEIGLAD (ed.), *Comparative Legal Education from Asian Perspective* (Program for Asian Global Legal Professions [PAGLEP] Series I), Keio University Press, 2017, pp. 3–5.
[2] See Sections 2.2 to 2.6 below.

common questions assumed to arise in each country.

The comparison of relevant legal provisions should also include comparative legal interpretation of those provisions for the solutions of examined cases. Common topics is a new method of comparing legal system of different countries to improve understanding of comparative law. It will be useful for legal education in each country and a new referent of comparative legal education among universities, notably those involved in Programs for Asian Global Legal Professions (PAGLEP).[3]

The method of teaching and learning comparative law is worth improving. Comparison of legal provisions and their functions is indispensable knowledge for law students. The comparative case analysis of the common topics deepens understanding of similarities and differences in the application of law. It is a method of understanding comparative law through micro analysis of processes of applying legal rules to particular cases and thus the working legal system of each country.

Comparative legal education using the common topics would promote pedagogy and legal education materials in Asian universities, where international student and teacher exchanges are commonplace.

The common topics will be presented to students as a part of legal education in universities in each country or in a class of students from different countries. They can present solutions of each question in the common topics by applying the laws of their respective countries and discuss solutions from comparative viewpoints. It would be productive to compare characteristics of legal provisions and precedents in each country and to identify its singularities of legal thinking, legal interpretations, and solution to cases. It would further develop the legal system of each country.

---

[3] For theoretical and practical perspectives on comparative legal education to improve pedagogical methods, see Hiroshi Matsuo, "Why Is It Worth Challenging for Studying Law Abroad in the Asian Region?", in: KEIGLAD (ed.), *Challenges for Studying Law Abroad in the Asian Region* (Program for Asian Global Legal Professions [PAGLEP] Series II), Keio University Press, 2018, pp. 3–22.

2. Creating Common Topics

2.1 Perspectives

Creating the common topics used for comparative case analysis is important. First, the content of topics should be arranged for easy and appropriate use in classrooms of different countries. Second, they should reflect major fields of law. In the field of civil law, for instance, topics may be chosen from property, contract, tort, family relations, and succession law. Third, topics should cover major content such as (drawing from civil law) who can be subjects of rights, what can be objects of rights, and how the transformation of rights shall be defined and given effect among parties and against a third party. Forth, they should correspond to the principles overarching each field of law.

Followings are samples of common topics used in joint seminars of law students in the Mekong region and Japan as part of PAGLEP arranged by Keio Institute for Global Law and Development.[4]

2.2 A Group of Persons as a Subject of Rights

[Case 1] Legal Personality of the Group MT

Ms. A, a foreign designer, planned to open a boutique of silk products. Mr. B and Ms. C, domestic entrepreneurs, agreed with A to establish a group named "Monsoon Textiles" (MT) and to invest US$20,000 in MT. The original asset (paid-in capital) of MT was US$60,000.

On behalf of MT, B rented a house from Mr. D for the MT's office and shop at US$1,000 per monthly. B borrowed US$20,000 from Bank E for operating funds. These contracts were concluded by B as a representative of MT.

C bought silk fabric from Company F for US$5,000. C ordered Ms. G to produce 30 pieces of carpet using the fabric for the price of US$200 per piece. These contracts were concluded by C as an agent of MT. G delivered 30

---

[4] For the activities of PAGLEP, including joint seminars undertaken by Keio Institute for Global Law and Development (KEIGLAD) see [http://keiglad.keio.ac.jp/en/paglep/].

pieces of silk carpet to MT, which sold 20 pieces to customers for US$1,000 per piece.

When MT entered default, its remaining assets were 10 pieces of silk carpet and a claim of US$2,000 against Company H from the sale of silk carpets. Creditors of MT were D (unpaid rent of US$1,000), E (unpaid loan of US$2,000), F (US$6,000 for silk fabric), and G (unpaid production contract of US$3,000).

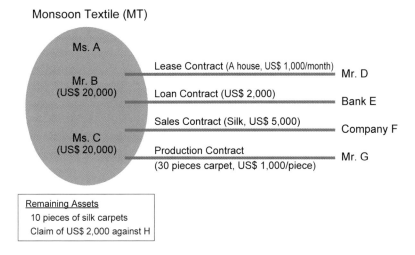

[Question 1]

What is the nature of group MT—partnership, association, or other possibility?

What are the requirements for MT to become a legal person?

What are differences distinguish partnerships and associations? What criteria distinguish them if MT has not acquired a legal personality?

[Purpose of Question 1]

This question seeks to clarify the source of legal personality of juristic persons. Is it a matter of registration or of the organization being substantially independent from its members? What are the requirements for obtaining legal personality? If MT has not completed the requisite procedure, what can MT: a partnership or an association?

[Question 2]

What claims can D, E, F, and G make against MT? What rights do they have regarding MT's remaining assets (10 pieces of carpet and a claim of US$2,000 against H)?

[Purpose of Question 2]

D, E, F, and G are creditors against MT, and their claims are pecuniary. In this case, the purchase price of the remaining assets (10 pieces of carpet) at public auction may be distributed among them in proportion to the amount of each claim: 1,000/12,000 for D, 2,000/12,000 for E, 6,000/12,000 for F, and 3,000/12,000 for G. May some creditors have priority before the law? Can the claim for US$2,000 against H be divided and distributed among D, E, F, and G in proportion to the amount of each claim? Are there differences between the carpet kept in the building leased by D and MT's monetary claim against H?

[Question 3]

Should A, B, and C be individually responsible for MT's debt?

[Purpose of Question 3]

This question tries to clarify the ultimate source of limited or unlimited liability of members of a group of persons if the group cannot repay its debt. Are there differences between members of a partnership and members of an association even though both have no legal personality?

2.3 Transformation of Property Rights: Acquisition of Property

[Case 2] Double Transactions of Immovable Property

Mr. A, a landlord, negotiated with Company B to sell a piece of land that A owned and concluded a sales contract at the price of US$200,000. B paid US$20,000 as part of the purchase money to A and took possession of the land. However, the transfer of ownership was not registered because the contract specified that registration was to be made in exchange for the remaining purchase money. Thereafter Company C asked A to sell the same land for US$220,000. A decided to transfer ownership of the land to

C and registered the change of title from A to C in exchange for receiving US$220,000 from C.

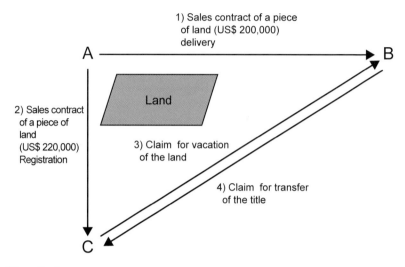

[Question]

C claimed against B for vacating the piece of land on the basis of ownership acquired from A, which was registered. What defense can B make against A by proving what facts?

[Purpose of the Question]

This question compares requirements for transfer of ownership of immovable property and treatment of parallel transactions. Treatment of third party C, who knew of the preceding transaction between A and B, would be most important and interesting from the viewpoint of comparative law.

2.4 Contractual Liabilities

[Case 3] Debtor's Liability for Non-Performance of Contract

On October 10, 2018, Company A, a dealer of fresh fruits, concluded a contract with Company B, a manufacturer of canned fruits, to sell 500 boxes of oranges at US$50 per box. A promised B to deliver them by October 30, 2018, to B's warehouse. B promised to pay the purchase money in exchange for delivery. On October 15, 2018, B concluded a contract with C to sell 1,000 cans of oranges to be made from those oranges at the price of US$5 per can.

[Question 1], [Question 2], and [Question 3] are different questions.

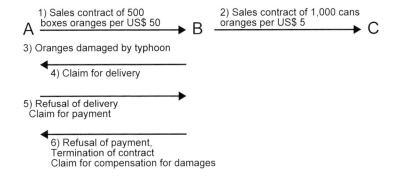

[Question 1]

On October 20, 2018, a typhoon hit the orange field from which A was to buy oranges to sell to B. All the oranges fell or were damaged beyond use as canned oranges. As a result, A could not deliver the oranges to B as A had promised.

In this case, what claim can B make against A? What defense can A make against B's claim?

[Purpose of Question1]

Question 1 concerns the impossibility of performance of the contract that occurs after its conclusion. In this case the contract was valid when concluded between A and B. The point of the question is to determine how and to what extent B can claim compensation for damages against A caused by non-performance of the contract, and whether A can make a defense for the reason that non-performance was caused by a natural disaster not attributable to A.

[Question 2]

On October 8, 2018, a typhoon hit the orange field from which A was to buy oranges to sell to B in accordance with the contract that was concluded afterward. All the oranges had fallen or been damaged beyond use as canned oranges. Without knowledge of this damage, A concluded the sale of 500 boxes of oranges with B on October 10, 2018, as in [Case 3]. B was unaware of the damage from the typhoon at the conclusion of the contract.

What claim can B make against A? What defense can A make against B's claim?

[Purpose of Question2]

Question 2 is concerned with a case involving initial impossibility. That is, performance of contractual obligation had been impossible at its conclusion. Treatment of initial impossibility may differ between civil law countries and common law countries.

[Question 3]

On October 20, 2018, a typhoon hit the area near the orange field from which A was to buy oranges to sell to B. It caused a flood that halted traffic, delaying collection and transportation of the oranges 15 days. B could not manufacture the orange cans by the date promised to C, which caused damages of US$1,000 on the part of B. B claimed against A for compensation for damages of US$1,000 caused by the delayed delivery.

What defense can A make against B's claim? What re-defense can B make against A's defense?

[Purpose of Question3]

Question 3 asks whether the responsibility of a debtor (obligor) should be the same in a case of impossibility of performance and of delay of performance. Treatment of this case is concerned with the principle of risk allocation.

2.5 Non-contractual Liabilities, Succession, and Status of Fetus

[Case 4] Claim for Compensation for Damages Caused by the Traffic Accident

A, a 40-year-old man, drove his wife B, a 35-year-old woman, in his car to the hospital. Another car driven by C crossed the center line and collided with A's car. The accident was due to C's inattentive driving. A suffered a broken leg and was hospitalized one month and had to go to hospital from home for three months even after the hospitalization. B was pregnant and scheduled to give birth, so she had to have a medical check at the hospital. B died the next day because of this accident.

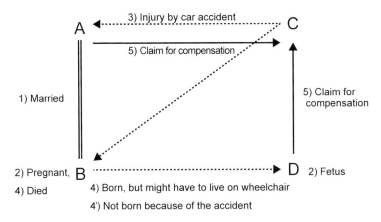

[Question 1]

D, a fetus at the time of this accident, was delivered by emergency operation. What can A and D claim against C? Answer under the premise that A's and B's annual incomes were US$60,000 respectively, and A and B had no children other than D.

[Purpose of Question1]

Question 1 tries to confirm the legal status and treatment of a fetus in each legal system. It asks about requirements for supporting claims for compensation for damages caused by a tortious act of another person, the content and coverage of a claim for compensation for damages (mental damages and economic loss), and how to calculate the amount of compensation.

In addition, Question 1 asks whether B's heirs can pursue a claim for compensation for damages (including pecuniary damages and mental damages) because he died due to the accident.

[Question 2]

What can D claim against C if D was injured by this accident caused by C and suffered a broken leg such that D might have to live in a wheelchair?

[Purpose of Question 2]

Question 2 asks about the content of a claim for compensation for damages of after-effects (sequelae) of the accident by using the example of reduced working ability.

[Question 3]

If the fetus could not be born because of the accident caused by C, what claim can A make against C?

[Purpose of Question 3]

Question 3 asks about legal treatment of a fetus that could not be born alive because of the accident. Is it recognized as a subject of rights? If so, the same rules governing B's claim in Question 1 may be applied. If not, another possibility of claim for the loss of the fetus may be sought.

3. Use of Common Topics and Its Outcomes

3.1 Implementation of Common Topics

These samples of common topics have been used in joint PAGLEP seminars[5] at the National University of Economics and Law in Ho Chi Minh City in Vietnam (UEL)[6], Pannasastra University in Cambodia (PUC)[7], Keio University Law School in Japan (KLS)[8], Thammasat University in Thailand (TU)[9], and Hanoi Law University in Vietnam (HLU)[10] from March 2017 to August 2018.

During the joint seminars students from different countries presented solu-

---

[5] As for the PAGLEP, see 2.1 and Footnote 3 above.

[6] On 8 March 2017 for [Case 5], and on 15 March 2018 for [Case 1].

[7] On 13 March 2017 for [Case 5], and on 9 March 2018 for [Case 1].

[8] On 29 August 2017 for [Case 3].

[9] On 14 September 2017 for [Case 3].

[10] On 24 August 2018 for [Case 4].

tions to the common topics by applying laws of their countries. Presentations were followed by discussion among all participants and by comments from teachers.

3.2 Findings

First, we have found that a variety of legal provisions regulate cases provided by the Common Topics. Legal rules governing the same questions are not always identical and depend on conditions of each country, shown in the following chapters.[11] In addition, relationships between substantive and procedural law and distinctions between civil (private) and criminal law differ. In some jurisdictions compensation for damages caused by tortious action, for instance, can be claimed under procedures attached to the criminal proceeding because it often is hard for victims of the tort to collect necessary evidence for trial. Evidence collected by public prosecutors may be available to the victim to claim compensation.

Second, we have confirmed there are differences in value judgments about who should win a case and how conflict should be solved under conditions of different societies.

Third, we have found there are different approaches to solutions of cases when explicit provisions of law are lacking and interpretation of the relevant provisions or general principles are required. Even when explicit provisions exist, the strictness or the flexibility of their interpretation seem to differ.[12]

3.3 Further Development of Case-based Comparative Law

Common topics in this chapter are trial samples for case-based comparative analysis of the application of laws in each country. Common topics must be revised, extended, and coordinated to elicit characteristic features of legal systems in each jurisdiction. They should include, for example, treatment of intangible

---

[11] See sample answers to each common topic from Chapters 2 through 7.
[12] See On-site Reports in this Volume (pp. 313–329) and Volume I (pp. 157–174) and in Volume II (pp. 161–189).

things (e.g., a photo or a picture of a property and of a person), the good faith (bona fide) of a possessor as a requirement for prescription, etc.

After we analyze similarities and differences in legal rules, thought, and interpretation among jurisdictions, we may be able to confirm whether there are truly *common principles of law in the dynamic process of legal development* even in a variety of patterns of application of laws to concrete cases by considering differences in social conditions.

Chapter 2

USE OF COMMON TOPICS TO IMPROVE COMPARATIVE LAW AND LEGAL EDUCATION:

Application of Japanese Law

Hiroshi Matsuo*
(Keio University)

1. A Group of Persons as a Subject of Right

[Case 1] Legal Personality of the Group MT (Chapter 1, 2.2 above)
[Question 1] The nature of MT; requirements for becoming a legal person; differences and distinguishing criteria between partnerships and associations

Under Japanese law, MT may be a partnership [*kumiai*] or an association without legal personality [*kenrinouryoku-no-nai-shadan*], unless MT has completed the necessary procedure to acquire legal personality.

To acquire legal personality, MT must follow the procedure provided by law. MT may become a company (profit-seeking legal person) such as a general partnership company, limited partnership company, limited liability company (these three types of company are called "Membership Company") or a stock company in accord with the provisions of Company Law (Law No. 86, 2005) (CA).[1] MT

---

* Professor, Keio University Law School; Director, Keio Institute for Global Law and Development (KEIGLAD).

may become a general legal person of association (a non-profit legal person) in accord with the Law on the General Legal Person of Association and the General Legal Person of Foundation (Law No. 46, 2006: LGLP). These laws stipulate registration is necessary to acquire legal personality (Art. 49 CA for a Stock Company, Art. 579 CA for a Membership Company, and Art. 22 LGLP for a General Legal Person).

If MT does not have legal personality, as is given in [Case 1], and if MT is recognized as an association without legal personality, its creditors shall claim against MT for performing its obligation. Creditors cannot claim for performing MT's obligation against each member of MT individually because MT, as an association, is an independent body distinguished from its individual members.[2]

To be recognized as an association, MT must have (a) a regular collective meeting for its own decision-making as an independent body, (b) a representative, and (c) a set of rules to manage its own property so that the organization can continue to exist when its members change.[3]

If not recognized as an association, MT is regarded a partnership. In this case, its creditors may claim for performing its obligation against MT and against each member of MT individually in the same proportion unless creditors do not know the portion of responsibility of each member if any (Art. 675 Japanese Civil Code (JCC hereafter).

[Question 2] Claims of creditors D, E, F, and G against MT and for its remaining assets

D, E, F and G are creditors against MT, and their claims are pecuniary claims, although amounts of each claim differ. In principle, when D, E, F and G claim payment from MT by attaching its remaining assets, the 10 pieces of carpet

---

[1] A company shall be a legal person (Art. 3 CA).
[2] Supreme Court Decision, 1973, October 9, Minshu 27–9–1129.
[3] Supreme Court Decision, 1964, October 15, Minshu 18–8–1671.

shall be sold at public auction and the purchase price distributed among the creditors who applied for it in proportion to the amount of each claim: 1,000/12,000 for D, 2,000/12,000 for E, 6,000/12,000 for F, and 3,000/12,000 for G. The claim for US$2,000 against H is divisible among creditors who applied for it in proportion to the amount of each claim as above.

If the 10 pieces of carpet are sold at US$1,000 per piece and the claim for US$2,000 is collected from H, total assets of US$12,000 shall be distributed as follows: US$1,000 for D, US$2,000 for E, US$6,000 for F and US$3,000 for G.

However, if the carpet was sold at US$400 per piece (US$4,000 in total), and the remaining assets totaled US$6,000 (US$4,000 from the carpet and US$2,000 from the claim against H), total distribution from the remaining assets shall be: US$500 for D, US$1,000 for E, US$3,000 for F, and US$1,500 for G respectively. They have to try to claim additional payment from A, B, and C individually.

Priority for the 10 pieces of carpet located in the building leased from D and produced by G may be given to D and G through the provisions of law (Art. 312 JCC and Art. 324 JCC). Priority between D and G shall be given to D by the provision of law (Art. 330 (1) JCC). If these provisions are applied to this case, D can be prioritized first to collect the claim of US$1,000 from the purchase money of 10 pieces of carpet, and G can be prioritized second to collect the claim of US$3,000 from the remaining purchase money of the carpet. If any purchase money remains from auctioning the carpet, it shall be distributed among E and F in proportion to the amount of their claims.

[Question 3] Individual responsibility of members of MT for its debt

If D, E, F and G cannot collect their claims from the remaining assets of MT and MT is recognized as a partnership, A, B, and C are responsible for the unpaid claims held by D, E, F, and G in equal proportion among A, B, and C (Art. 675 (2) JCC). For example, were F paid only US$3,000 from MT's remaining assets and F still has the claim of US$3,000, then F can ask A, B, and C for US$1,000 each. The same principle shall be applied to other creditors who have unpaid claims.

2. Transformation of Property Rights: Acquisition of Immovable Property

[Case2] Double Transactions of Immovable Property (Chapter 1, 2.3 above)
[Question] Claim of first purchaser B against second purchaser C and vice versa

The basis of C's claim is ownership of the land acquired from A via the contract between A and C. However, B will make the defense that B had already acquired ownership of that land from A via contract between A and B before C concluded the contract with A. According to Art. 176 JCC, ownership may be transferred from the transferor to the transferee only by expressing the will to transfer it.

C will assert that even had B acquired ownership from A before C contracted with A, B's acquisition of ownership shall not be opposable against C as a third party unless B's acquisition of ownership is entered in the registration book (Art. 177 JCC). The registration procedure is provided by the Law on the Registration of Immovable Property (Law No. 123, 2004: LRIP hereafter).

However, if B can prove successfully that C concluded the contract with A knowing B had already acquired ownership of the land from A (in bad faith) and it can be regarded as against the principle of good faith (Art. 1 (2) JCC), B's acquisition of ownership is opposable against C without the registration. B can refuse to vacate and claim to transfer the title of owner against C.[4] For instance, in such cases as C was an agent or broker for B, or C intended damage to B, or C conspired with A to gain unreasonable profit from B fraudulently, C can be

---

[4] Supreme Court Decision, 1968, August 2, Minshu 22–8–1571; Supreme Court Decision, 1969, January 16, Minshu 23–1–18.

regarded as acting in bad faith and against the principle of good faith as provided by Art. 1 (2) JCC.

If B cannot prove C acted in bad faith and against the principle of good faith (Art. 1 (2) JCC), B will claim compensation against A for breach of contract by proving the amount of damage B suffered through non-performance of the contract (Art. 415 JCC). It is under discussion whether B may be able to claim the amount of purchase money that A acquired from C as a surrogate for the piece of the land (Art. 422–2 JCC).

* Additional information about patterns of transfer of ownership under Japanese law

(1) If A made a fictitious manifestation of intent to transfer ownership of A's piece of land to B in collusion with B and B contracted with C to transfer its ownership and C was unaware of the fictitious transaction between A and B (in good faith), C can acquire ownership of the land *by force of law* (Art. 94 (2) JCC).

This provision of Art. 94, Paragraph (2) has been *analogically applied* to cases where A did not fictitiously transact in collusion with B, but A could be regarded as responsible for the incorrect outlook of the transaction with B (for example, by leaving the incorrect registration of the change of title of the land from A to B with prior knowledge).[5]

(2) If A concluded a contract with B to transfer ownership of A's land to B *by mistake*, and B contracted with C to transfer ownership and C did not know of A's mistake in the transaction between A and B (in good faith) without negligence, C can acquire ownership of the land even though A avoided the contract with B by reason of *mistake* (Art. 95 (4) JCC).

The same protection of a third party is provided in such case as A concluded a contract with B to transfer ownership of A's land to B *by fraud* of B and B contracted with C to transfer ownership and C did not know of B's fraud in the

---

[5] Supreme Court Decision, 1970, September 22, Minshu 24–10–1424.

transaction between A and B (in good faith) without negligence, C can acquire ownership of the land even though A avoided the contract with B for reason of *fraud* (Art. 96 (3) JCC).

The central point in the additional explanations in (1) and (2) above is how to coordinate the interest of A, the true owner or who will recover ownership, and the interest of C, a third party to the transaction between A and B. Also in [Case 2], the central point is how to coordinate the interest of B, the first acquirer, and C, the second.

3. Contractual Liabilities

[Case 3] Debtor's Liability for Non-Performance of Contract (Chapter 1, 2.4 above)

[Question 1] Debtor's liability for the impossibility occurring after the conclusion of contract (impossibility after contract) due to natural disaster

If B claims for delivery of 500 boxes of oranges, A can refuse to deliver them on the basis of impossibility to perform in accord with the contract and common sense in the transaction (Art. 412–2 (1) JCC).

If A claims payment of purchase money against A, B may refuse to pay by asserting A did not provide promised delivery of the oranges and the impossibility of delivery cannot be attributed to B (Art. 536 (1) and 567 (1) JCC).

In addition, B can terminate the contract for reason of impossibility (Art. 542 (1) [1] JCC) and claim compensation by proving B suffered from non-performance of the contract (Art. 545 (4) and 415 (1) JCC).

A can defend against B's claim for compensation by proving that non-performance of delivery cannot be attributable to A in accord with the contract and common sense in the transaction (Art. 415 (1) proviso JCC).

[Question 2] Debtor's liability for the impossibility occurring before the conclusion of contract (initial impossibility) due to natural disaster

The difference between [Question 1] and [Question 2] is the timing of the typhoon that struck the oranges field and made A's performance of obligation impossible. In [Question 1] the impossibility occurred after conclusion of contract. In [Question 2] it had occurred before conclusion of the contract.

After the Amendment to the Civil Code (Law No. 44, 2017), the same rule is applied to the case in [Question 1] (initial impossibility of performance) with that applied to case in [Question 2].

Before the Amendment, according to majority opinion the contract shall be void in the case of initial impossibility so that obligations generated by the contract shall be invalid. As a result, B cannot claim for the performance of delivery, nor can A claim payment of purchase money. B can claim only compensation for damages due to the reliance on a valid contract (e.g., expenses for contractual document, transportation for the negotiation of contract) on the basis of *culpa in contrahendo*, which is recognized by Japanese law on the basis of the principle of good faith (Art. 1 (2) JCC).

[Question 3] Debtor's liability for delayed performance of contractual obligation due to natural disaster

B can claim compensation for damages of US$1,000 that may have been caused by the loss of profit to be acquired from the transaction with C (Art. 415 (1) JCC).

A will make a defense by proving the delay was attributable to the typhoon, which was not attributable to A, in accord with the contract and common sense in the transaction (Art. 415 (1) proviso).

However, B may mount a re-defense that typhoons have frequently and repeatedly caused similar damages in the past and A could foresee the possibility of delay or non-performance of its obligation. Therefore the delay can be regarded as attributable to A even though it was due to the natural disaster unless an exemption clause had been included in the contract.

4. Non-contractual Liabilities, Succession, Status of the Fetus

[Case 4] Claim for Compensation for Damages Caused by the Traffic Accident (Chapter 1, 2.5 above)
[Question 1] Claim for compensation by the victim A (who was wounded by the accident), B (A's wife who died due to the accident), and D (a fetus who was delivered after the accident)

A and D can claim (1) compensation for damages caused to A and D and (2) compensation for damages caused to B, which A and D inherited equally (Art. 900 [1] and [4] JCC).

B's claim for compensation consists of loss of income to be earned during her life, which shall be calculated on the basis of her annual income of US$60,000 and the average of workable years (Art. 709 JCC)[6] and mental suffering due to the injury caused by C (Art. 710 JCC). B's compensation for economic and mental loss can be succeeded by A and D.[7]

A's compensation for damages will include expenses for treatment and hospitalization for one month and for treatment and travel to the hospital for three months, the loss of income during hospitalization, visits to hospital if any (Art. 709 JCC), and mental loss (Art. 710).

Although D's injury was caused by C before birth, it can be compensated under the provision of law that a fetus shall be deemed to have been born with respect to the claim for compensation for damages (Art. 721 JCC). D's claim

---

[6] However, living expenses and interim interest shall be deducted from total lifetime income earned by B.
[7] Supreme Court Decision (Grand Bench), 1967, November 1, Minshu 21–9–2249.

for compensation shall be exercised by A as a parent authorized to manage the child's property by law (Art. 824 JCC). D's loss will include the economic loss estimated to have been earned had D not been injured (Art. 709 JCC) and mental loss (Art. 710 JCC).

[Question 2] Claim for compensation by victim D, who suffers aftereffects of the accident

D can claim compensation for expenses necessary to live in a wheelchair and the income to be earned had D not broken a leg calculated by reduction of working ability and average life expectancy (Art. 709 JCC) and for mental loss (Art. 710 JCC).

[Question 3] Claim for compensation by A against C when the fetus could not be born due to the accident

The fetus cannot acquire rights if it was not born, because it could not acquire legal personality. However, A can claim mental suffering for the unborn child caused by C's tortious action (Art. 710 JCC). This claim may be based on the analogical application of Art. 711 JCC (which provides "a person who has taken the life of another person must compensate for damages to the father, mother, spouse and children of the victim, even in cases where the property rights of them have not been infringed") to A who may be equated to "father" of "another person" and the fetus may be equated to "another person" whose life was taken. Although the fetus is not yet "another person" and A is not yet "father" of the victim, loss of the chance to have a child shall be equated to the loss of a child.

Chapter 3

USE OF COMMON TOPICS TO IMPROVE COMPARATIVE LAW AND LEGAL EDUCATION:

Application of Vietnamese Law

Doan Thi Phuong Diep[*]

(University of Economics and Law Vietnam National University in Ho Chi Minh City)

1. General Introduction to Civil Law in the Bachelor's Degree Program at University of Economics and Law (UEL), National University-Ho Chi Minh City, Vietnam

Civil law is a principal subject for all law students. The bachelor's degree program at UEL is designed for four academic years in compliance with the Higher Education Law (2012). In this four-year program, instruction in civil law include numerous subjects:

- General regulations in civil law,
- Property law,
- Family law,
- Contract law,
- Law on property in family (including succession law),
- Liabilities law.

There are four law majors in UEL: Civil law, international commercial law,

---

[*] Lecturer and Head of Office of Inspection and Legal Affairs, University of Economics and Law Vietnam National University in Ho Chi Minh City.

business law, and finance & banking law. Family and property law are electives. Civil law courses devote an average of 40 hours to each subject.

2. Sample of Common Topics

2.1. A Group of Persons as Subjects of Rights

[Case 1] Legal Personality of MT Group (Chapter 1, 2.2 above)

[Question 1] The nature of MT; requirements for legal personhood; differences and distinguishing criteria between partnerships and associations

According to Vietnamese law, MT is a partnership. "A partnership means an enterprise of which: At least 02 partners are co-owner of the company who run business together in a common name (hereinafter referred to as general partner). Apart from general partners, the company may have contributing partners" (article 172 Law on Enterprises 2014). Because only with a partnership, the partners can conclude the contract as an agent or representative of the partnership.

A partnership attains legal status from the issuance date of the Certificate of Business Registration.

Among many differences, partnerships have a legal personality and associations do not. Rights and obligations of members also differ. Members of an association have only the right to sign contracts on behalf of the association when authorized by all other members (via an authorization contract). Without it, members take sole responsibility for the contract signed. Members of a partnership can sign contracts for it without authorization.

Partnerships have general partners and contributing partners. General partners take joint responsibility for paying debts of the company if its assets are insufficient to cover them. Contributing partners are liable for the company's debts only up to the amount of capital they contributed to the company.

[Question 2] Claims of creditors D, E, F, and G against MT for its remaining assets

Debt claim

Under Vietnamese law all four parties have rights to "redistribution of assets." When MT defaulted, its remaining assets—10 pieces of silk carpet and a claim of US$2,000 against Company H—were less than its obligations. D, E, F, G will receive distributions in proportion to the debt (Article 54 Bankruptcy Law 2014).

[Question 3] Individual responsibility of members of MT for its debt

If A, B, and C are general partners, they have joint responsibility for MT's indebtedness if assets are insufficient to discharge them. Article 172-1b of the Law on Enterprise 2014 declares "Unlimited liability partners must be individuals who shall be liable for the obligations of the company to the extent of all of their assets"

2.2. Transformation of Property Right: Acquisition of Immovable Property

[Case 2] Double Transactions of Immovable Property (Chapter 1, 2.3 above)
[Question] Claim of first purchaser B against second purchaser C and vice versa

The contract between A and B is sale contract rather than a deposit contract under Vietnamese law. In this case, B has the right to cancel the contract given inability to perform and to claim damages (Article 425 of Civil Code). "Where the obligor cannot perform part or all of its obligations to make the purpose of the obligee may not be reached, the obligee party can cancel the contract and claim damages") and claim for the the fines against the violation (if anticipated in the contract)" (Article 418 of Civil Code 2015).

[Case 3] Debtor's Liability for Non Performance of Contract (Chapter 1, 2.4 above)

[Question 1] Debtor's liability for the impossibility which occurred after the conclusion of contract (impossibility after contract) due to the natural disaster

Because A has violated delivery obligations, B has the right to claim the responsibility for continuing performing obligations and compensation for damage caused by break of contract (Article 351-1 of Civil Code 2015).

A can use Article 351-2 to refuse to execution delivery and provide compensation due *to force majeure* (Article 351). Civil liability arising from breach of civil obligations 1. An obligor which fails to perform or performs incorrectly an obligation has civil liability to the obligee. Breach of obligations means that the obligor fails to perform the obligations on time, perform the obligations incompletely or incorrectly. 2. Where an obligor is not able to perform a civil obligation due to an event of force majeure, it shall not have civil liability, unless otherwise agreed or otherwise provided by law.

[Question 2] Debtor's liability for the impossibility that occurred before conclusion of the contract (initial impossibility) due to natural disaster

B has the right to claim the responsibility for continuing performing obligations and compensation for damage caused by break of contract (Article 351-1 of Civil Code 2015).

According to Article 294 of Commercial Law 2005, " Cases of exemption from liability for breaching acts

1. A party that breaches a contract shall be exempted from liability in the following cases:

a/ A case of liability exemption agreed upon by the parties occurs;

b/ A *force majeure* event occurs;

c/ A breach by one party is entirely attributable to the other party's fault;

d/ A breach is committed by one party as a result of the execution of a decision of a competent state management agency which the party cannot know."

Whereas Article 156-1 of Civil Code 2015 provides "An event of force majeure is an event which occurs in an objective manner which is not able to be foreseen and which is not able to be remedied by all possible necessary and admissible measures being taken." The Article indicates that an event is considered *force majeure* when it occurs after conclusion of the contract. In this case, A can only refer to any liability exemption the contracting parties might have agreed to.

[Question 3] Debtor's liability for delayed performance of contractual obligation due to natural disaster

In this case A can invoke *force majeure* for exemption from liability (Article 294 of Commercial Law 2005).

Given the typhoon struck near the grove from which A was to buy oranges, B might defend against A's claim by showing the *force majeure* event did not directly affect performance of the contract because oranges can have been transported by other routes for timely delivery.

2.3. Non-contractual Liabilities, Succession, Status of Fetus.

[Case 4] Claim for Compensation for Damages Caused by Traffic Accident (Chapter 1, 2.5 above)

[Question 1] Claim for compensation by victim A (injured by the accident), B (A's wife who died due to the accident), and D (a fetus who was delivered after the accident)

This is a case of liability for compensation for non-contractual damages. The liability for compensation in Vietnamese law is not based on the financial capacity of the obligor but on the basis of actual damages incurred. So A and D can claim liability for the damage caused by harm to life. Including:

a) Reasonable costs for treating, nursing and rehabilitating health, and functional losses and impairment of the aggrieved person;

b) Loss of or reduction in actual income of the aggrieved. If his or her income is irregular and unable to be determined, the average income for the type of work performed by the aggrieved shall be applied;

c) Reasonable funeral costs;

d) Support for the dependants of the aggrieved person;

e) Other damage as prescribed by law.

f) Reasonable costs and actual income losses of caregivers of the aggrieved during the period of treatment. If the aggrieved person loses ability to work and requires a permanent caregiver, damages shall include those reasonable costs (Article 591 of Vietnamese Civil Code 2015).

[Question 2] Claim for compensation by victim D who suffers aftereffects of the accident

Article 590 gives D the right to claim compensation for damages caused by harm to health (A and B will represent D to exercise this right):

1. Damage caused by harm to health shall comprise:

    a) Reasonable costs for treating, nursing, and rehabilitating health, and functional losses and impairment of the aggrieved person;

    b) Loss of or reduction in actual income of the aggrieved. If actual income is irregular and unable to be determined, the average income for the type of work performed by the aggrieved shall be applied;

    c) Reasonable costs and actual income losses of the caregivers of the aggrieved during the period of treatment. If the aggrieved loses ability to work and requires a permanent caregiver, damages shall include reasonable costs.

    d) Other damage as prescribed by law.

2. A person causing harm to the health of another must pay items provided in Clause 1 of this Article alongside compensation for mental suffering.

Compensation for mental suffering shall be as agreed by the parties; if they cannot agree, the maximum shall not exceed 50 months of base salary prescribed by the state.

[Question 3] Claim for compensation by A against C when the fetus could not be born due to the accident

No Vietnamese regulation recognizes a fetus as a human being. In this case, Article 16-3 supports a just claim for damages caused by harm to health (Article 590 of the Civil Code 2015). "The legal personality of a natural person commences at birth and terminates at death."

Chapter 4

USE OF COMMON TOPICS TO IMPROVE COMPARATIVE LAW AND LEGAL EDUCATION:

Application of Cambodian Law

Kong Phallack*
Mao Kimpav**

(Paññāsāstra University)

About the application of the Cambodian Law to the Common Topics, see Part I, Chapter 4, 2.2.

---

* Dean and a professor of law at the Faculty of Law and Public Affairs, Paññāsāstra University in Cambodia.
** Manager of Law Programs, Faculty of Law and Public Affairs, Paññāsāstra University in Cambodia.

Chapter 5

USE OF COMMON TOPICS TO IMPROVE COMPARATIVE LAW AND LEGAL EDUCATION:

Application of the Lao Law

Alounna Khamhoung*

(National University of Laos)

1. A Group of Persons as a Subject of Right

[Case 1] Legal Personality of the Group MT (Chapter 1, 2.2 above)
[Question 1] The nature of MT; the requirements for becoming a legal person; and the differences and the distinguishing criteria between partnership and association

Article 80 of Contract and Tort Law (2008) stated that: "Any individual who willfully exercises his rights in excess of a reasonable limit shall be liable to compensate for damage arising from such exercises of rights beyond a reasonable limit." Based on the case, Ms. A, Mr. B, and Ms. C have signed a contract that established MT Company; therefore, MT Company is a partnership company.

The requirement for MT Company to become a legal entity is that it needs an approval from an authorized organization. Based on the Right to establish an enterprise, in Article 14 of Enterprise Law (2014): "Enterprise registration is the approval of legitimate establishment of an enterprise. Conducting business shall

---

* Lecturer, Faculty of Law and Political Science, National University of Laos.

be registered as an enterprise unless otherwise provided. Enterprise registration is done once for the whole business duration of an enterprise."

Differences between partnership and association:

-Based on Article 3.4 of Enterprise Law (2014): "Partnership is a form of enterprise created on the basis of a contract of at least two or more investors for mobilization of capital, with a view to jointly conducting business and sharing the profits"

-Based on Article 2 of the Decree of The Government on Association (2017), "An Association that is established and working under this decree is a social organization that was established with voluntariness, and is active, non-profit, aiding, defends the rights and benefits of their members, members or the community, contributes to the development of country's society and economics."

Therefore, the main difference between partnership and organization is that partnership enterprises are for-profit, while associations are non-profit.

[Question 2] Claims of creditors D, E, F, and G against MT and for its remaining assets

Mr. D, Bank E, F Company and Ms. G can claim damage compensation from MT Company. According to Article 3 of the Contract and Tort Law (2008): "Damages cost is referred to the amount of money, of materials of the person who is responsible to compensate the damages which are arisen to another person."

The rights that they have in the remaining assets, consisting of 10 pieces of carpets and the claim of USD 2,000 against H, are as follows:

-Mr. D has the right, as the owner of the house, to receive the rent of USD 1,000 from MT Company.

-Bank E is the creditor, according to Article 56, Paragraph 3 of the Contract and Tort Law (2008): "Loans of money or assets may bear interest provide that such (interest obligation) is stipulated in a contract. In case there is a delay in the reimbursement that is not beneficial to the lender, it may consider having a service charge if there is a request."

-F Company and Ms. G are creditors.

-To solve such problems, MT Company should sell the remaining assets and distribute money to all creditors. 10 pieces of carpet cost USD 10,000 and the claim of USD 2,000 from H. The total is USD 12,000, it can be distributed as below:

Mr. D: USD 1,000;

Bank E: USD 2,000; and

F Company: USD 6,000.

[Question 3] The individual responsibility of the members of MT for its debt

Ms. A, Mr. B, and Ms. C are not individually responsible for MT Company's debt because MT is a partnership company; as stated in Article 3, Paragraph 3 of the Enterprise law (2014): "Individual enterprise is a form of enterprise created by one person. Individual enterprise conducts business in the interests of an owner. The owner is solely and unlimitedly responsible for the enterprise's liabilities."

2. Transformation of Property Right: Acquisitions of Immovable Property

[Case2] Double Transactions of Immovable Property (Chapter 1, 2.3 above)
[Question] Claim of the first purchaser B against the second purchaser C and vice versa

According to Article 28 of the Property Law (1990): "The acquisition of a property [right] takes place when the asset is granted[1] or received in accordance

---

[1] The reader should refer to Article 29 for the sense in which "grant" is used, which appears to include physical handover and simple giving.

with the laws. Property [rights in an asset] may be acquired under contracts concluded before the act of granting or receiving such asset. If the contract containing the grant of an asset to another individual or such asset has not yet been registered, property [rights] shall commence when registration is completed, even though the act of granting has occurred".

According to the case, even though B agreed to trade that land beforehand, the payment transaction is not yet completed because in the content of the bilateral contract it was mentioned that the transfer of ownership will be successful after making all payment of the land. Thus, there is no legality in land registration between A and B, which enables/allows C to demand B to move out of the land wherewith A has legally transferred the ownership to C.

So, A can be the landholder in righteousness, according to Article 39 of the Contract and Tort Law (2008) on sale-purchase contracts mentioned that: "Buyer becomes the owner of assets that (he or she) has purchased:

-From the time that the buyer pays money to the seller and the seller delivers the assets to the buyers;

-From the time that the buyer has paid money, whether or not the seller has transferred such assets, or from the time that the seller has transferred such assets, whether or not the buyer has paid money to the seller as agreed."

However, B has a possibility to preserve his/her right with A, which is agreed in the contract, because of the full amount paid that make A has the right to use the land. Therefore, two of them have to set the dispute settlement methods.

Regarding Article 101 under the Contract and Tort Law (2008) has stated that "In the event that there is a dispute on the performance of a contact and the request to have a compensation for damages, the contracting parties may seek the method to settle the dispute by themselves or by a mutual conciliation. If the contracting parties fail to reach agreement, they have the rights to submit to the village's dispute mediation unit, or the Economic Arbitration Office or to lodge a claim with the court for consideration to settle the dispute in accordance with laws and regulations."

3. Contractual Liabilities

[Case 3] Debtor's Liability for the Non Performance of Contract (Chapter 1, 2.4 above)

[Question 1] Debtor's liability for the impossibility which occurred after the conclusion of contract (impossibility after contract) due to the natural disaster

B can claim for damage compensation against A. Article 24, Paragraph 1 under the Contract and Tort Law (2008) mentioned that: "Contracting parties must perform a concluded contract in good faith, completely within the period (for performance) and at the location specified by the contract or by the laws".

According to the damages that happened because of the force majeure A can make the defense against B's claim based on Article 33, Paragraph 2 of the Contract and Tort Law (2008), which mentioned that: "If either contracting party breaches a contract, that party must be liable to compensate (the other party) for damages which arise, except if the contract breach occurred as a result of a force majeure."

[Question 2] Debtor's liability for the impossibility which occurred before the conclusion of contract (initial impossibility) due to the natural disaster

B can claim for damage compensation against A because the quality of goods does not satisfy the standard they agreed in the contract. According to Article 40 of the Contract and Tort Law (2008) has mentioned that: "The quality of assets sold must conform to the contents of the contract, if the assets sold are not of the quality provided for in the contract, the seller must be liable for such assets".

In the event that B has the right to request an exchange of the assets sold for some kind of assets which are of the (expected) quality or to request a price reduction or to terminate the contract while also demanding compensation for damages. B can also claim for compensation against A in accordance with the

Contract and Tort Law (2008), Article 91 mentioned that: "In addition to (compensating for) damage, the person causing may also pay for sick-benefits, (such as): the income of the injured person would have earned, (and) additional expenses of the injured person resulting from such wrongful act." – in this situation, by selling canned fruits.

In this case, company A cannot defense itself against B's claim because all of the damages were caused by A, which did not comply with the contract between A and B.

[Question 3] Debtor's liability for the delayed performance of contractual obligation due to the natural disaster

A can make the defense of rights and benefit by declining/denying the damage costs in B's claim. Article 33, Paragraph 2 of the Contract and Tort Law (2008), mentioned that: "If either contracting party breaches a contract, that party must be liable to compensate (the other party) for damages which arise, except if the contract breach occurred as a result of a force majeure" – because A cannot predict that there will be a flood during the delivery of the products.

B Company can re-defense against A's defense in accordance with the same law, but under Article 37, Paragraph 2 that "If there is a breach of contract, the disadvantaged party may modify or terminate the contract unilaterally. Except otherwise the contracting parties agreed."

4. Non-contractual Liabilities, Succession, Status of the Fetus, etc.

[Case 4] Claim for Compensation for Damages Caused by the Traffic Accident (Chapter 1, 2.5 above)
[Question 1] Claim for compensation by the victim A (who was wounded by the accident), B (A's wife who died due to the accident), and D (a fetus who was given birth after the accident)

Based on the Common Case, A can claim the 4 following aspects of compensation for damages against C as follows:
- Physical damages: A can claim for a compensation as his leg was broken as a result of having an accident with C.
- Mental damages: by having to go through the experience, A lost his wife and his only daughter, D, becoming permanently disabled. All of these have an impact on A's overall mental well-being.
- Loss of assets: A's car was broken due to the accident.
- Loss of earnings: A could not go to work, therefore could not earn an income during the period of one month that he was hospitalized.

Calculation of amount of compensation for damages of A's

The amount or ways of calculation of compensation for damages depends on the Judges' decisions as they see fit, where various considerations and characteristics of (1) the case's; and (2) the involving parties' will be taken into account. For examples:
- How much is the regular income of the injured party?
- What else was damaged or broken?
- What is the financial situation of the opposing party? Will he/she be able to pay?

[Question 2] Claim for compensation by the victim D who suffers from after-effect of the accident

Inheritance of rights in compensation for damages of D

Article 3 of Inheritance Law (2008) stated that "...inheritance is every type of assets that belong to the deceased, including rights and obligation." Therefore, purely based on this, D can receive a right and obligation from her mother to claim for compensation – however, there are also others factors that need to be taken into consideration as follows:

Can D really claim for the compensation?

- Legal ability or ability to be a party to a lawsuit: according to Paragraph 1, Article 71, Section V of Civil Procedure Law (2012), stated that for a person to be a party to lawsuit, the person must "(1) be 18 years of age or older; and (2) not mentally ill; otherwise, the person shall be accompanied by parents/guardians." Based on this limitation and what was given in the Common Case, it can be summarized that, despite of D having inherited rights to claim for compensation in place of her mother; she still cannot utilize her rights because she is under 18.
- Prescription of petition: according to Paragraph 1, Article 102, Section IV of Contract and Tort Law (2008), stated that "prescription of petition is 3 years for filings of compensation for damages - starting from the day the damage(s) occur." Based on this, again, by the time D has fully grown into an adult and become 18, the prescription period would had ended.

In short, whether D can or cannot inherit rights to claim for compensation, for her mother, she still cannot claim for the compensation because (1) she does not have a legal ability because of her current age; and (2) the prescription will be long ended by the time she becomes an adult.

If he/she can, then how much?

As it was stated above that D cannot claim for compensation for damages by herself; nonetheless, the amount that she can receive will, again, be up to the Court's decision to make the fairest judgement possible for the involving parties in the case.

[Question 3] Claim for compensation by A against C when the fetus could not be born due to the accident

According to what was mentioned in question 3, D, who is the child, does not have a legal ability to be a litigant due to the 2 facts that were mentioned earlier. As a result, D cannot claim for Mrs. B's, who is D's mother, rights to compensation of damages. However, A, who is the father and husband, can still be a legal representative, for his wife who passed away, in claiming for rights to compensation for damages according to Indent 3, Article 71 of Civil Procedure Law (2012).

Legal capacity of fetus in Laos

There are 3 examples given where there is a legal capacity of fetus in Laos as follow:

1) Illegality of abortion: according to Article 92 of Specific Section under the Penal Law (2005) states, abortion is considered an illegal act and the law also states various penalties for an attempt and an act of doing so.

2) Right to inheritance: a fetus has a right to inherit assets from a deceased while it is in mother's womb, where the mother shall be the one to overlook and protect the assets until the fetus is born, according to Article 16 under the Inheritance Law (2008).

3) Free-of-charge childbirth service: the service is available for children under the age of 5 in designated districts in Xayaboury, northern province of Laos. It is listed in Bullet 1 of the Application of Policy on Free Childbirth Service and Medical Treatment for Children Under the Age of 5 Ordinance (2015).

Changes in rights given by Lao laws when fetus was not born

There are 2 examples to demonstrate of when there are changes in the rights of an unborn fetus, as given by Lao laws, which are:

1) The case of when there are changes in rights: changes will happen when there is an identical or similar situation as in number 2 under the answer of question 5 above, where in the case that a fetus is still alive it will be able to retain its right to inheriting assets from a deceased; however, otherwise, the fetus does not live any longer, these right ends; and

2) The case of when there are no changes in rights: it is an example of the rights to the free-of-charge childbirth service mentioned in number 3 of answer number 5 above, whereby whether the fetus is successfully born

and becomes a person or passes away during the childbirth process, the right to the service for the fetus and mother will still remain regardless of the outcome of the situation.

Chapter 6

USE OF COMMON TOPICS TO IMPROVE COMPARATIVE LAW AND LEGAL EDUCATION:

Application of Thai Law

Munin Pongsapan*
Junavit Chalidabhongse**
(Thammasat University)

1. A Group of Persons as a Subject of Rights

[Case 1] Legal Personality of the Group MT (Chapter 1, 2.2 above)
[Question 1] The nature of MT; the requirements for becoming a legal person; and differences and distinguishing criteria between partnership and association

Thai law grants two types of persons legal personality: natural persons and juristic persons (juridical persons).

Juristic persons can be established under the Thai Civil and Commercial Code, which recognizes five types of juristic persons: ordinary partnership, limited partnership, limited company, association, and foundation, all of which require registration with a competent official to establish. Juristic persons can be established by law or by registration under other statutes (e.g., a public limited company under the Public Limited Company Act). Private juristic persons

---

* Assistant Professor, Faculty of Law, Thammasat University.
** Lecturer of Law, Faculty of Law, Thammasat University.

normally require registration with a competent officer, whereas public juristic persons (juristic persons with governmental power), for example, ministries, departments, provinces, local authorities, Buddhist temples, schools, and universities, can be established by statute or registration with a competent official. Without registration or legal authority, a group of natural persons cannot form a juristic person.

According to Thai law a contract organizing a partnership or company is a contract whereby two or more persons agree to unite for a common undertaking with a view of sharing profits that may be derived therefrom. (Section 1012)

There are three types of partnerships and companies under the Thai Civil and Commercial Code:

1. Ordinary partnership;
2. Limited partnership;
3. Limited company.

(1) Ordinary partnership (Section 1025) is a form of partnership in which all partners are jointly and unlimitedly liable for all obligations of the partnership. There are two categories of ordinary partnership: non-registered and registered. Only a registered ordinary partnership has status as a juristic person with legal personality separate from its partners. A non-registered ordinary partnership has no registration and thus no legal personality.

(2) Limited partnership (Section 1077) is a partnership in which: (1) One or more partners whose liability is limited to such amount as they respectively contribute to the partnership, and (2) One or more partners who are jointly and unlimitedly liable for all obligations of the partnership.

(3) Limited company (Section 1096) is formed with capital divided into shares. The liability of the shareholders is limited to the amount, if any, unpaid on the shares respectively held by them.

There is another type of company—a public limited company—which is established under the Public Limited Companies Act B.E. 2535 (1992 AD).

A public limited company is established for the purpose of offering shares for sale to the public, and shareholders shall have liability limited up to the amount to be paid on shares.

A limited partnership, limited company, and public limited company must be registered to become a juristic person and acquire legal personality.

Under the Thai Civil and Commercial Code an association is another type of juristic person. An association is established to conduct any activity which, according to its nature, is to be done continuously and collectively by persons other than those sharing profits or earning incomes (Section 78). An association must be registered according to the law, and its purpose is not for profit.

Therefore, the only kind of partnership not required to register is the ordinary partnership. An unregistered ordinary partnership has no status as a juristic person and therefore no legal personality in its own right.

From the facts in Case 1, **MT is regarded as a non-registered ordinary partnership according to Thai law.** To be a juristic person MT must be registered to become a registered ordinary partnership.

[Question 2] Claims of creditors D, E, F, and G against MT and for its remaining assets

As a non-registered ordinary partnership, MT is not a juristic person. Creditors D, E, F and G cannot make a claim (or file a lawsuit) against MT, as it has no legal personality. They must instead demand repayment of debts from its partners.

[Question 3] Individual responsibility of the members of MT for its debt

Since MT is a non-registered ordinary partnership, all partners (A, B, and C) are jointly and unlimitedly liable for all of its obligations.

Section 1150 states *"All the partners are bound by the acts done by any of them in the ordinary course of the business of the partnership and are jointly and unlimitedly liable for the performance of the obligations incurred in such management."*

All transactions by B, including the contracts to rent a house from D and to borrow money from E, and all transactions by C, to include buying silk from F and hiring G to produce 30 pieces of carpet, were in the ordinary course of the business of the partnership. Therefore A, B and C are jointly and unlimitedly liable to each creditor according to Section 1150.

Each creditor can demand A, B, or C alone repay the debt owed him fully or partially as it wishes. The partner who has paid more than his share can claim the overage back from the other partners. The share of responsibility of each partner is determined in Section 1044. Section 1044 states *"The share of each partner in the profits or losses is in proportion to his contribution."*

From the fact that each partner contributes equally (US$20,000 each), if A has paid a total of US$12,000 to the creditors altogether, he can claim US$4,000 from B and US$4,000 from C.

2. Transformation of Property Right: Acquisitions of Immovable Property

[Case 2] Double Transactions of Immovable Property (Chapter 1, 2.3 above)
[Question] Claim of the first purchaser B against the second purchaser C and vice versa.

Under Thai law, to sell immovable property, parties normally enter two types of contract: an agreement to sell or buy and a complete sales contract. The agreement to sell or buy immovable property imposes obligations on the parties to enter a second contract, a complete sales contract. The second contract creates obligations to transfer ownership of the property and pay the price. An agreement to sell or buy immovable property does not require a form of contract, whereas the latter must be registered at a land office. Otherwise, the contract becomes void under Section 456 paragraph 1, which states *"A sale of immovable property is void unless it is made in writing and registered by the competent official...."*

Even though A and B entered a sales contract and part payment for the price was made, the contract between them is considered an agreement to sell or to buy because they had the intention to register the sales contract later at the time of making the remaining payment.

Since A was still owner of the land, he had the right to sell it to C or anyone by virtue of Section 1336: *"Within the limits of law, the owner of property has the right to use and dispose of it and acquires its fruits; he has the right to follow and recover it from any person not entitled to detain it, and has the right to prevent unlawful interference with it."* The sale contract between A and C is valid, as it was made in writing and the written contract was registered with a competent official. In terms of property law, Company C's acquisition of the ownership of the land was complete for the same reason, according to Section 1299 paragraph 1, which states *"Subject to a provision of this Code or other laws, no acquisition by juristic act of immovable or of real right appertaining thereto is complete unless the juristic act is made in writing and the acquisition is registered by the competent official."*

Because ownership of the land was legally transferred from A to C, it was impossible for A to perform the obligation to enter a complete sales contract with B. This constitutes impossibility of performance. As a result, B will not be able to enforce the performance specifically. He can only seek compensation for damages arising from A's breach of contract and termination of contract.

The right to claim damages for impossibility of performance is given by Section 218 paragraph 1, which states *"When the performance becomes impossible in consequence of a circumstance for which the debtor is responsible, the debtor shall compensate the creditor for any damage arising from the non-performance."* B also has the right to terminate the contract under Section 389, which states *"If performance becomes wholly or partly impossible by a cause attributable to the debtor, the creditor may rescind the contract."*

Although B cannot enforce his contract specifically due to impossibility of performance, property and obligations law provide solutions that may effectively give him the chance to own the land.

Under property law, Section 1300, B may request cancellation of the registration of the sales contract between A and C if he can prove he is "the person is previously in the position to register a written complete sales contract before other people" with A. To determine whether B is such person, the Thai Supreme Court often examines two conditions. First, it checks when A and B agreed to register a written complete sales contract and whether such time is earlier than the time A and C registered their complete sales contract. Second, it verifies whether B has performed his obligations under the agreement to sell or buy, i.e., made a payment. However, despite that B can prove he is the person previously in the position to register a sales contract before C, B cannot cancel C's acquisition of the ownership of the land if C receives protection from property law. C will receive protection if (1) he registered his sales contract with A; (2) he paid for the acquisition of the land; and (3) he acted in good faith meaning that he was unaware of B's right when C entered the contract with A. Section 1300 states *"Where a transfer of immovable property or real right appertaining thereto has been registered to the prejudice of a person who was previously in a position to have his right registered, he may claim cancellation of such registration, provided that in no case cancellation be claimed against a transferee for value in good faith."*

Although the property law solution does not work for B because C is protected as a third party who acted in good faith, B may resort to a solution under obligations law known as cancellation of a fraudulent act. Section 237 states

The creditor is entitled to claim cancellation by the Court of any juristic act done by the debtor with knowledge that it would prejudice his creditor; but this does not apply if the person enriched by such act did not know, at the time of the act, or the facts which could make it prejudicial to the creditor, provided, however, that in case of gratuitous act the knowledge on the part of the debtor alone is sufficient.

The provisions of the foregoing paragraph do not apply to a juristic act whose subject is not a property right.

If the fact appears that C knew about the contract between A and B at the time of making his contract with A, then B has the right to ask the court for cancellation of a fraudulent act according to Section 237[1].

The Supreme Court has applied the rule of cancellation of fraudulent act to this type of case by considering that the act between A and C could make it prejudicial to B.

C's knowledge of the contract between A and B is important. If C does not know about the contract between A and B, the law will protect C, who acts in good faith and acquires the land for value, and therefore B will be unable to ask the court for cancellation. In such a case, B will have only one option: apply Section 218 paragraph 1 to claim compensation.

3. Contractual Liabilities

[Case 3] Debtor's Liability for Non Performance of Contract (Chapter 1, 2.4 above)
[Question 1] Debtor's liability for the impossibility that occurred after the conclusion of contract (impossibility after contract) due to the natural disaster

Under Thai law the main issue of this case is breach of contract due to impossibility of performance. To solve it, we must determine whether there was impossibility of performance in the contract between A and B. Whether it was impossible for A to perform the obligation to deliver oranges to B depends on whether the damaged oranges were generic goods or generic goods from a specified place of origin.

In Scenario 1, the damaged oranges are merely generic goods. If so, A can find oranges of like quality elsewhere to deliver to B. Therefore it was not impossible for A to perform the obligation.

In Scenario 2, the damaged oranges are generic goods from a specified place

---

[1] Supreme Court Decision No. 6026/2552

of origin. If parties had the intention to sell and buy oranges from a specific garden only and all oranges from it were damaged, A's performance becomes impossible.

According to the given facts, the impossibility of performance appeared to be attributed to *force majeure*, not the debtor's fault, under Section 219, A will be relieved from all liability. Under Thai law, B cannot claim compensation for damage against A. Section 219 states *"The debtor is relieved from his obligation to perform if the performance becomes impossible in consequence of a circumstance, for which he is not responsible, occurring after the creation of the obligation."* B also has no right to terminate the contract, as such right can be obtained only when the impossibility of performance is attributable to the debtor under Section 218.

[Question 2] Debtor's liability for the impossibility that occurred before the conclusion of contract (initial impossibility) due to the natural disaster

Based on the assumption that A and B wanted oranges from a specific garden only, this is a case of initial impossibility. Initial impossibility renders the contract void under Section 150, which states *"An act is void if its object is expressly prohibited by law or is impossible, or is contrary to public order or good morals."* Most Thai judges and scholars long have held that the parties' knowledge is irrelevant to initial impossibility of performance. Therefore, the contract between A and B became void under Section 150.

[Question 3] Debtor's liability for delayed performance of contractual obligation due to the natural disaster

Under Thai law, for B to make a claim against A, B will need to cite Section 204, which deals with delayed performance. It states *"If the debtor does not perform after warning given by the creditor after maturity, he is in default through the warning."*

If a time by calendar is fixed for the performance, the debtor is in default without warning if he does not perform at the fixed time. The same rule applies if a notice is required to precede performance, and the time is fixed in such manner that it may be reckoned by the calendar from the time of notice." However, A may be able to excuse himself from liability, as Section 205 states *"The debtor is not in default so long as the performance is not effected in consequence of a circumstance of a circumstance for which he is not responsible."* The delay was caused by the typhoon, which is considered a *force majeure,* meaning the incident was not attributed to the debtor. Therefore, A was not in default and did not breach the contract. Accordingly, B cannot demand compensation from A.

4. Non-contractual Liabilities, Succession, Status of the Fetus, etc.

[Case 4] Claim for Compensation for Damages Caused by the Traffic Accident (Chapter 1, 2.5 above)

[Question 1] Claim for compensation by the victim A (who was wounded by the accident), B (A's wife who died due to the accident), and D (a fetus given birth after the accident)

As C unlawfully violated A's, B's, and D's rights to life by acting negligently, causing damage to B and D, C committed tort against A, B, and D under Section 420, which states *"A person who, willfully or negligently, unlawfully injures the life, body, health, liberty, property or any right of another person, is said to commit a wrongful act and is bound to make compensation therefore."* Even though D did not have legal personality when the accident occurred, Section 15 states *"Personality begins with the full completion of birth as a living child and ends with death.*

A child en ventre sa mere is capable of rights provided that it is thereafter born alive." According to Section 15 paragraph 2, D had the right to life retroactively. Therefore, his right to life was violated when he was in the womb.

Under the law of succession, A and D inherit B's rights and duties. They inherit B's right to sue C on grounds of tort. A can claim compensation for his injuries, damage to his property, and B's loss of life and income. D also can sue C for loss of maintenance he would receive from B. To determine compensation, a Thai court has discretionary power to determine the scope of damage and award monetary and non-monetary compensation under Section 438, which states *"The Court shall determine the manner and the extent of the compensation according to the circumstances and the gravity of the wrongful act.*

Compensation may include restitution of the property of which the injured person has been wrongfully deprived or its value as well as damages for any injury caused."

However, under Thai civil procedural law, a minor cannot exercise his right in court of law by himself. He needs a legal representative to act on his behalf.

Two related rules of succession are Sections 1599 and 1600.

Section 1599: *"When a person dies, his estate devolves on the heirs.*

An heir may lose his right to the succession only under the provisions of this Code or other laws."

Section 1600: *"Subject to the provisions of this Code, the estate of a deceased includes his properties of every kind, as well as his rights, duties and liabilities, except those which by law or by their nature are purely personal to him."*

[Question 2] Claim for compensation by the victim D, who suffers after-effects of the accident

D also can sue C for medical treatment of his injuries and loss of income he would generate with good health and normal ability. Under Thai civil procedural law, however, a minor cannot exercise his right in court of law by himself. A legal representative must act on his behalf.

[Question 3] Claim for compensation by A against C when the fetus could

not be born due to the accident

A could claim compensation against C on the grounds of tort under Section 420. As the fetus was not born alive, it did not have legal personality and therefore did not have a right to be violated by C. Injuring the fetus is merely injuring an organ of A. Therefore, A is the only victim or injured person.

Chapter 7

USE OF COMMON TOPICS TO IMPROVE COMPARATIVE LAW AND LEGAL EDUCATION:

Application of Myanmar Law (1)

Khin Khin Su*

(University of Yangon)

1. A Group of Persons as Subjects of Rights

[Case 1] Legal Personality of the Group MT (Chapter 1, 2.2 above)

[Question 1] The nature of MT; requirements for becoming a legal person; differences and distinguishing criteria between partnerships and associations

MT may be a partnership or a company under Myanmar law. If MT has registered as a partnership under Section 58 and 59 of the Partnership Act, it is a partnership. If MT registered as a company under Section 4 of the Myanmar Companies Law, it is a company.

Myanmar does not allow partnerships to acquire a separate legal personality, but it allows partnerships to sue and be sued.[1] Moreover, the property of the firm includes all property and rights and interests in property originally brought into the firm or acquired, by purchase or otherwise, by or for the firm, or for the pur-

---

* Assistant Lecturer, Department of Law, University of Yangon.
[1] Order XXX, Rule 1(1) of the Code of Civil Procedure.

poses and in the course of the business of the firm and includes goodwill. Unless a contrary intention appears, property, rights, and interests in property acquired by the firm are deemed to have been acquired for it.[2] Partners are liable for the business activities of the partnership.

The Myanmar Partnership Act and other laws make no provision for a partnership to have a separate legal personality. To obtain a legal personality, MT must obey Section 5(a) (1) of the Myanmar Companies Law.[3] It may become another type of corporation registered under this law (a business association, overseas corporation, other corporation entitled to register as a company by this or other applicable law and such entities as prescribed by the Union Minister from time to time). Therefore, if an association seeks a legal personality, it must register under the Myanmar Companies Law, 2017.

The differences between partnerships and companies are as follows:

1. Partnerships are created by agreement, and the company is created by registration.
2. Partners are bound by their agreement, but shareholders are bound by the constitution of the company.
3. A partnership has no separate legal entity but the company is a separate legal entity distinct from its owners.
4. A partner's liability is usually unlimited. Partners are jointly and severally liable for all debts. In a company, a member's liability is usually limited to the amount unpaid for their shares or to the extent of their guarantees.
5. Apart from professional partnerships, the number of partners is limited to 20 (10 for banks). A private company may have no more than 50 members and a public company any number of members.
6. A change of partner constitutes termination of the old firm and causes the

---

[2] Section 14 of the Partnership Act.

[3] A company will be a legal entity in its own right separate from its members having full rights, powers, and privileges and continuing in existence until it is removed from the Register.

beginning of a new one. Companies continue without cessation by changes of membership.
7. A partner can assign his interest, but the assignee does not become a partner. Company members can transfer their shares.
8. Partners jointly own partnership property. Companies owns their assets. Members cannot own assets of company.
9. Partners may by mutual agreement withdraw capital at their discretion. Capital subscribed by a company's shareholders may be repaid to them only under specific rules.
10. Partners are entitled to participate in management, and they are agents of the firm. A company must have one or more directors. A company's business is managed by or under direction of the board of directors or one director in the case of a single-director company.

[Question 2] Claims of creditors D, E, F, and G against MT for its remaining assets

D, E, F, and G are creditors of MT, and their claims are pecuniary claims, but amounts of each claim differ. In Myanmar, they have the right to attach MT's remaining assets. Its 10 pieces of carpet shall be sold at public auction by Order XXI, Rules 66 and 76 of Civil Procedure Code. Proceedings from sale shall be distributed among creditors. A judge decides amounts to which each creditor is entitled.

If the 10 pieces of carpet can be sold for US$1,000 per piece, the total will be US$10,000. H will collect his claim of US$2,000. Total assets are US$12,000 and shall be distributed as follows: US$1,000 for D, US$2,000 for E, US$6,000 for F, US$3,000 for G.

If the carpets are sold at a price below US$1,000, total assets will be insufficient to be distributed among creditors, and the court will determine priority of payment.

If the 10 pieces of carpet are kept in the building leased from D and are produced by G, D as building owner receives first priority of claim because he holds the possessory lien. As the carpet's producer G is prioritized second. The remaining balance (if any) will be distributed among E and F in proportion to amounts of their claims.

If there is any balance for E and F, they will bring a suit against A, B, and C individually or severally in a case of a partnership firm. They cannot make any claim if MT is a company.

Myanmar makes no provision with regard to priority. Judges hold ultimate discretionary power, although they must rule in accord with principles of equity.

[Question 3] Individual responsibility of the members of MT for its debt

Were MT recognized as a company, A, B, and C would not be responsible for its debt.[4] Were MT recognized as a partnership, A, B, and C are individually responsible for MT's debt because MT cannot be separated from its members.[5]

2. Transformation of Property Rights: Acquisition of Immovable Property

[Case 2] Double Transactions of Immovable Property (Chapter 1, 2.3 above)
[Question] Claim of first purchaser B against second purchaser C and vice versa

In the given case, C claimed against B (the first purchaser, who took the possession of land) on the basis of registered ownership acquired from A.

---

[4] Section 5 (a)(1) of the Myanmar Companies Law states that a company is a legal entity in its own right separate from its members, having full rights, powers, and privileges and continuing in existence until removed from the Register.

[5] Section 25 of the Partnership Act mentions that every partner is liable, jointly with all the other partners and also severally, for all acts of the firm done while he is a partner.

According to the case, A (owner) first contracted with B to sell his land for US$200,000. B paid US$20,000 to A and took possession. The transaction was not registered. Thereafter, A contracted to sell this same land to C for US$220,000. C paid the absolute purchase money, and A gave C ownership of the land by registering the contract.

The disputed subject is land, and land is immoveable. Therefore the case falls under the Transfer of Property Act. Sale is a transfer ownership in exchange for a price paid, promised, or partly paid and promised. Transfer of tangible immoveable property of at least 100,000 Kyats in value can be made only by a registered instrument.[6] Therefore, registration is compulsory in order to be a perfect sale.

Hence, C may presume a right to make a claim against B because B did not register the transaction despite taking possession of the land.

B can successfully prove he made a contract with A before A's contract with C. He also paid US$20,000 A, who delivered possession to B.

Section 53A of Myanmar's Transfer of Property Act contains a provision for partial performance. Protected under this section entails five conditions:

1. The owner contracts for consideration any immoveable property;
2. The contract must be in writing;
3. The contract must be signed by the owner (transferor) or his agent;
4. The transferee must take possession although the contract is not registered;
5. The transferee has performed or is willing to perform his remaining part of the contract.

Thus, if the transferee has complied with those five conditions, the transferor or person claiming under him shall be debarred from enforcing against the transferee. B has satisfied four conditions. He need prove only that he has met or is willing to meet the fifth. If so, he can successfully defend against C's claim.

Moreover, B can bring a suit against A for specific performance of contract under the explanation of Section 12 of the Specific Relief Act, which mentions

---

[6] Section 54 of the Transfer of Property Act.

that the breach of a contract to transfer immoveable property cannot be adequately relieved by monetary compensation. Therefore, he can claim for specific performance of contract.

B also can bring suit against A and C under section 27(b) of that Act.[7] Illustration: A contracts to sell land to B for 500,000 kyats. B takes possession of the land. Afterward A sells it to C for 600,000 kyats. C makes no inquiry of B relating to his interest in the land. B's possession is sufficient to affect C with notice of his interest, and he may enforce specific performance of contract against C.

Thus, if C made no inquiry related to the land and had knowledge of the contract between A and B, B also can sue C.

To enforce specific performance of contract to sell land, the plaintiff (first purchaser) can file claim against the seller and subsequent purchaser under Section 27(b) of that Act. The court can join the subsequent purchaser in the suit as a party under Order I, Rule 10 of CPC.[8]

B cannot sue under the exception of Section 27(b) of Specific Relief Act if C made the purchase in good faith and did not know of the contract between A and B.

---

[7] Specific performance of a contract may be enforced against any other person claiming under him by a title arising subsequently to the contract except a transferee for value who has paid money in good faith and without notice of the original contract.

[8] Maung Tun Wa v Maung Thagadoe 1 LBR 252.

Chapter 7

USE OF COMMON TOPICS TO IMPROVE COMPARATIVE LAW AND LEGAL EDUCATION:

Application of Myanmar Law (2)

Khin Phone Myint Kyu*

(University of Yangon)

3. Contractual Liabilities

[Case 3] Debtor's Liability for Non-performance of Contract (Chapter 1, 2.4 above)

[Question 1] Debtor's liability for impossibility that occurred after conclusion of contract (impossibility after contract) due to natural disaster

B cannot claim against A.

A can defend against B's claim on the basis of impossibility to perform the obligation under contract under Section 56 of the Contract Act.[1]

A has no obligation for non-delivery under the third paragraph of Section 56 of said Act[2] because the orange fields are grievously damaged by a typhoon,

---

* Professor, Department of Law, University of Yangon.

[1] An agreement to do an act impossible in itself is void. A contract to do an act which, after the contract is made, becomes impossible, or, by reason of some event which the promisor could not prevent, unlawful, becomes void when the act becomes impossible or unlawful.

[2] Where one person has promised to do something which he knew, or with reasonable diligence, might have known, and which the promise did not know, to be impossible or unlaw-

which cannot be anticipated by either party. Hence, the contract is automatically void. Frustration is the occurrence of an unexpected event beyond the control of all parties after making a contract but before its completion. If frustration is established, the law deems it fair to excuse parties from their performance obligations, and the contract automatically ends. B cannot make a claim for non-performance of promise.

B in the stated situation has not paid the full amount of purchase. If A claims purchase money from B, B may refuse to pay by asserting that A did not deliver the promised oranges and is unable to do so.

[Question 2] Debtor's liability for the impossibility that occurred before conclusion of the contract (initial impossibility) due to natural disaster

Questions 1 and 2 feature a crucial difference: the time at which the typhoon hit. The typhoon hit the orange field after the execution of the contract in Question 1 but not of that in Question 2.

At the making of the sale contract, A and B did not know about the damage to the oranges caused by the typhoon. So this is a mistake in fact. Under Section 20 of the Contract Act[3] the contract between A and B is void and cannot be binding upon both parties.

For example, A agrees to sell to B a specific cargo of goods supposedly en route from England to Yangon. Before the day of the bargain, the ship conveying the cargo had been cast away and the goods lost. Neither party was aware of these facts. The agreement is void, and B cannot make a claim against A.

In the case of Daw Ohn Sein and three others v. U Ba Tint,[4] land was sold under the condition that both parties believed that it was owned by the vendor. In

---

ful, such promisor must make compensation to such promise for any loss which such promise sustained through the non-performance of the promise.

[3] Where both the parties to an agreement are under a mistake as to a matter of fact essential to the agreement, the agreement is void.

[4] 1970, B.L.R. (CC) 43.

fact, it was not. The mistake was mutual, and the vendor cannot claim the agreed sum. In the given question, A cannot claim the purchase price from B.

If A knew that all the oranges had fallen or had been damaged by the typhoon when he concluded the contract, the condition would differ. According to Section 22 of the Contract Act,[5] the contract between A and B is valid, and if A did not deliver the oranges, B would sue for damages.

[Question 3] Debtor's liability for delayed performance of the contractual obligation due to natural disaster

B can claim compensation if A knew of a contract between B and C, according to Section 73 of the Contract Act.[6] Under this provision, the loss from non-delivery of the oranges arose in the course of natural events, which, the parties knew when making the contract, could result in its breach. Hence it is necessary to prove that A could reasonably foresee a breach that must result in the loss, and his foresight must have arisen "at the time when the parties made the contract." In the given case, B could not manufacture orange cans by the date promised to C, which caused damages of US$1,000 to B. Moreover, it is necessary to consider the inconvenience caused to B by the non-delivery of oranges in calculating compensation under Section 73.[7] Hence, B can claim US$1,000 and compensation for inconvenience.

---

[5] A contract is not voidable merely because it was caused by one of the parties to it being under a mistake as to matter of fact.

[6] When a contract has been broken, the party who suffers by such breach is entitled to receive, from the party who has broken the contract, compensation for any loss or damage caused to him thereby, which naturally knew, when they made the contract, to be likely to result from the breach of it.

[7] In estimating the loss or damage arising from a breach of contract, the means which existed of remedying the inconvenience caused by non-performance of the contract must be taken into account.

According to Section 73, Illustration (i)[8] and (q),[9] B cannot claim the profit he/she expected by manufacturing the orange cans.

A can defend against B's claim for damages on the grounds that A did not know of the contract between B and C.

According to Section 73[10] and Section 73 Illustration (k),[11] B's obligation to compensate US$1,000 is for the remote and indirect loss sustained by reason of the breach. Hence A has no obligation to compensate B on the grounds of not manufacturing the orange cans by the date promised to C.

In calculating damages, B, the injured party, is entitled to compensation only when the loss arises in the natural or direct course of events. If the cause of the loss is remote or indirect, the injured party is not entitled to damages.

---

[8] A delivers to B, a common carrier, a machine, to be conveyed without delay to A's mill, informing B that the mill is stopped for want of machine. B unreasonably delays the delivery of the machine, and A in consequence loses a profitable contract with the Government. A is entitled to receive from B by way of compensation the average amount of profit which would have been made by the working of the mill during at the time that delivery of it was delayed, but not the loss sustained through the loss of the Government contract.

[9] A contract to sell and deliver to B, on the first of January, certain cloth which B intends to manufacture into caps of a particular kind, for which there is no demand except at that season. The cloth is not delivered till after the appointed time, and too late to be used that year in making caps, B is entitled to receive from A, by way of compensation, the difference between the contract price of the cloth and its market price at the time of delivery, but not the profits which he expected to obtain by making caps, nor the expenses which he has been put to in making preparation for manufacture.

[10] Such compensation is not to be given for any remote and indirect loss or damage sustained by reason of the breach.

[11] A contract with B to make and deliver to B, by a fixed day, for a specified price, a certain piece of machinery. A does not deliver the piece of machinery at the time specified, and in consequence of this B obliged to procure another at a higher price than that which he was to have paid to A, and is prevented from performing a contract which B had made with a third person at the time of this contract with A (but which had not been then communicated to A), and is compelled to make compensation for breach of that contract. A must pay to B, by way of compensation, the difference between the contract price of the piece of machinery and the sum paid by B for another, but not the sum paid by B to the third person by way of compensation.

Parties to some contracts stipulate amounts of damages arising through breach—e.g., liquidated damages or penalty. Courts ruling under the principle of equity allow reasonable compensation. The party rescinding the contract is entitled to compensation only when he/she has sustained actual damage.

4. Non-contractual Liabilities, Succession, Status of the Fetus

[Case 4] Claim for Compensation for Damages Caused by the Traffic Accident (Chapter 1, 2.5 above)
[Question 1] Claim for compensation by victim A (wounded by the accident), B (A's wife who died due to the accident), and D (a fetus delivered after the accident)

Criminal and civil action can be brought against C.

The accident was a cognizable offense at the time it happened. Hence the State must initiate the case as plaintiff against C under the following sections:

(a) Section 304(A) of the Penal Code for causing B's death by negligence;[12]

(b) Section 58 of the Automobile Law for inattentive driving;[13]

(c) Section 338 of the Penal Code for his act causing B's leg to break[14].

Under criminal action, C may be imprisoned and fined (paid to the state). Offenses under Section 304(A) are non-bailable and not compoundable. Offenses under Section 338 are bailable but not compoundable.

Civil action is taken by the injured persons. A and D can sue C for B's death under the tort principle and calculate the amount of damages. With regard to

---

[12] Shall be punished with imprisonment for the term which may extend to seven years and fine.

[13] Shall be punished with imprisonment of not more than one month or fine of not more than 50000/ Kyats (about 35 US $) or both.

[14] Shall be punished with imprisonment of either description for a term which may extend to five years and shall also be liable to fine.

damages for death caused by the wrongdoer, only the Fatal Accidents Act, 1885, applies, and victims can claim damages from the wrongdoer under that Act. Since Myanmar observes common law, the common law system in UK can be applied in Myanmar.

Section 1 of the Fatal Accident Act provides as follows:

"Whenever the death of a person shall be caused by wrongful act, neglect or default and the act, neglect or default is such as would if death had not ensued have entitled the party injured to maintain an action and recover damages in respect thereof, the party who would have been liable if death had not ensued shall be liable to an action or suit for damages, notwithstanding the death of the person injured, and although the death shall have been caused under such circumstances as amount in law to a crime.

Every such action or suit shall be for the benefit of the wife, husband, parent and child, if any, of the person whose death shall have been so caused, and shall be brought by and in the name of the executor, administrator or representative of the person deceased and in every such action the court may give such damages as it may think proportioned to the loss resulting from such death to the parties respectively, for whom and for whose benefit such action shall be brought and the amount so recovered, after deducting all costs and expenses, including the costs not recovered from the defendant, shall be divided among the before mentioned parties, or any of them, in such share as the court by its judgment or decree shall direct."

Under this section, A and D can claim damages from C, but there are no provisions for calculating them. Where legislation governing a matter before the courts is absent, English common law rules, which have been developed and adopted in Myanmar case law, are applied. Moreover, judges have the discretion to decide the matter in accordance with justice, equity, and good conscience in the absence of an applicable law. Damages awarded depend on the judge and circumstances of each case.

[Question 2] Claim for compensation by victim D who suffers aftereffects of the accident

Fatal Accidents Act cannot be applied to Question 2 because the victim must be **dead** through the wrongdoer's neglect and only the family of the deceased can claim damages.

In this question, D claims damages for his permanent disability and not for D's mother. Although D cannot claim damages under this Act, his disability resulted directly from injury to his mother and the tort principle applies. D would be entitled to damages that the Court deems appropriate, given the extent of injuries, permanent disabilities, and treatment expenses.

Myanmar requires every vehicle to carry third-party liability insurance required by the Road Transport Administration Department. D can get the damages under the third party liability policy.

[Question 3] Claim for compensation by A against C when the fetus could not be born due to the accident

The answer to Question 3 mirrors the answer to Question 1. A can claim damages against C under Section 1 of the Fatal Accidents Act. In Myanmar, most injured persons prefer to settle out of court rather than proceed to a civil suit.

ON-SITE REPORT

FROM LAW CLASSROOMS IN ASIAN UNIVERSITIES:

A Short Report on the Collaboration Program in Cambodia in 2018

Hitomi Fukasawa*
(Keio Institute for Global Law and Development)

1. Introduction

From March 6 to 9 of 2018, the Keio University Law School (KLS: Tokyo, Japan) conducted a Collaboration Program for Comparative Legal Education with the Pannasastra University Faculty of Law and Political Administration (PUC-FLPA: Phnom Penh, Cambodia). This program consisted of (a) special lectures by Cambodian teachers and Japanese teachers on civil law, business law, arbitration, negotiation, and conflict of laws; (b) presentation by Cambodian students and Japanese students on a common topic; and (c) site visit to the Senate of Cambodia and the NGO, the Contribution of Laws. KLS six students (five J.D. students and one LL.M. student) and two teachers (a professor of civil law and a second one who is a professor of international arbitration, negotiation, and conflict of laws), plus a researcher participated. Around twenty Cambodian students, three teachers, and two staffs took part in the program.

KLS started the collaboration program in the year 2017 with KLS's partner universities from Mekong regional countries. It held joint study programs in Ho

---

This paper is supported by the Keio University Doctoral Student Grant-in-Aid Program.
* Ph.D. candidate, Keio University Graduate School of Law, Researcher, Keio Institute for Global Law and Development (KEIGLAD).

Chi Minh City, Vietnam, and Phnom Penh, Cambodia, in March 2017[1]. In September 2017, it held the second program in Bangkok, Thailand[2]. The collaboration program between KLS and PUC-FLPA was the third joint program, as well as the second program to be conducted in Cambodia.

Since the first program, KLS and partner universities assign the same legal case known as the "Common Topic" to students. The Common Topic was used in the last joint program in Cambodia. What is the purpose of the Common Topic? It is assigned each time the program is conducted because it is believed the assignment assists students to understand the difference between Japanese law and Cambodian law from the perspective of comparative legal study. First, the preparations for a presentation enable students to understand their country's interpretation and application of laws, which dominate the academic discussion and precedents. By listening to submissions from students from other countries, the participants recognize the difference between each country's interpretation and application of laws. During the discussion sessions, students talk about reasons as to why each state has different legal frameworks. The cycle of preparation, presentation, and discussion for a specific legal case is one of the methods that improve the comparative legal study.

In 2017, during the first program in Cambodia, the assigned common topic was about a lessor sold a building which has leased to a buyer. The discussion point was whether a sales contract breaks a lease contract, in other words, can the lessor claim his right of the lease contract to a new building owner or not. Japanese students made the presentation, and Cambodian students gave us comments based on the Cambodian Civil Code. Both students discussed the difference between Japanese and Cambodian laws[3]. However, we could not examine

---

[1] Hiroshi Matsuo=Hitomi Fukasawa, "From Law Class Rooms in Asian Universities Short Report on The Collaboration Program in Vietnam and Cambodia", Comparative Legal Education from Asian Perspective, Keio University Press (2017) pp.157-174.

[2] Hiroshi Matsuo=Hitomi Fukasawa, "From Law Class Room In Asian Universities Short Report on The Collaboration Program in Thailand" Challenges for Studying Law Abroad in the Asian Counties, Keio University Press (2017) pp.169-189.

[3] Supra note 1 Matsuo=Fukasawa pp.164-167.

how Cambodian students analyzed the legal case or how they interpret Cambodian Civil Code nor the manner how the Civil Code, for example, was applied and why both legal systems are different.

After the program, coordinators from both sides analyzed how the program can be improved with both Cambodian and Japanese students making presentations while being involved in discussions. Challenges were observed to be in the program framework itself rather than in the students' capabilities. The 2017 program was the first challenge; therefore, both Japanese and Cambodian teachers in charge could not share the aim and strategy of the program comprehensively. Moreover, students had to prepare the presentation within one month of being selected as participants. It was, therefore, difficult to arrange and discuss the case in such a short time with international students.

In the 2018 program, two changes for the improvement of the program were factored in. First, both Cambodian and Japanese teachers gave a starter lecture for participants. The talk aimed at brainstorming on all necessary legal information required to solve the Common Topic. At the same time, we tried raising students' awareness of the Common Topic. The second change was about creating a mixed group of Japanese and Cambodian students. We expected various interpretations of the laws, and a discussion among each group could be a first positive step for the classroom discussion.

In Chapter 2, I explained about the Common Topic assigned to students in the year 2018 program. In Chapters 3 and 4, I briefly explain the overview of starter lectures and student presentation. In the final chapter, I describe what I learned from the program in 2018.

2. About Common Topic for 2018 Program in Cambodia

We assigned the Common Topic related to association and the order of propriety between creditors in cases where the group defaults. Below are the facts of the case:

Ms. A, a foreign designer, planned to open a boutique of silk products. Mr. B and Ms. C, who are both domestic entrepreneurs, collaborated with Ms. A by investing USD 20,000 respectively for Ms. A's plan. They agreed to establish their group named "Monsoon Textile [MT]" and begun to prepare for the launch. Mr. B rented a house from Mr. D for the office and boutique of MT at a rate of USD 1,000 per month and proceeded to borrow USD 20,000 from Bank E as the operating fund of MT. Mr. B concluded these contracts as a representative of MT. Ms. C bought silk fabric from Company F at the price of USD 5,000 and ordered Ms. G to produce 30 pieces of silk carpet at the cost of USD 200 per piece. Ms. C concluded these contracts as an agent of MT. Ms. G delivered 30 pieces of silk carpets to MT which sold 20 pieces to customers at a price of USD 1000 per piece.

MT defaulted with its remaining asset valued at only USD 5,000 and ten pieces of silk carpets. The creditors of MT were Mr. D for the unpaid rent of USD 1,000; Bank E for the loan money of 2,000; Company F for the price of silk fabric at a cost of USD 5,000; and Ms. G for the unpaid contract price of USD 3,000. The question is what claims can D, E, F, and G make against MT, A, B, and C for the performance of contractual obligations?

Discussion points were three. First was the nature of group MT where various possibilities were considered, for example, partnership and association. We did not specify the nature of MT, because this task belongs to students who are expected to pick the possible nature MT in as many ways as they can. The second was whether the members of the MT, Ms. A, Mr. B, and Ms. C are individually responsible for the debt of the MT or not. The third was the order of priority among each creditor, Mr. D, Bank E, Company F, and Ms. G. In other words, how and how much each creditor gets satisfied from remaining assets, USD 5,000 and 10 pieces of carpets. Both Japanese and Cambodian teachers arranged to articulate these three discussion points. In the next Chapter, I explain the contents of starter lectures before the student's presentations under each teacher.

3. Starter Lectures by Japanese and Cambodian Teachers for Students' Presentations

3.1 The starter lecture by a Cambodian teacher

A Cambodian teacher gave a lecture about business regulations in his country. He explained about the kinds of institutions, types of rules, tax, and how to get information for the establishment of businesses by using a simple example:

Mr. A is Japanese, and Ms. B is Cambodian. They would like to open a restaurant in Phnom Penh. How do they start their business in Cambodia?

The teacher explained the five types of business forms found Cambodia. These include (1) general partnership; (2) a limited partnership; (3) private limited partnership; (4) public limited partnership; and (5) single-member private limited company. A single-member private limited company is distinguished from a sole proprietorship. Business forms (1) to (4) can be used for the example case. Sole proprietorship, public and private limited companies plus general and private partnerships have to be registered. Cambodia's Ministry of Commerce provides an online registration system. An individual has to register the name of sole proprietor, company or partnership, and the type of business being formed. Registration of a name has some regulations. For example, in the case of a private limited partnership, if the name of a person appears in the trade name of the partnership, he is regarded as a general partner, even if he is a limited partner.

The Cambodian government permits 100% foreign ownership of companies; however, the government prohibits foreign companies from holding land ownership. For foreign investors to own land in Cambodia, they need to establish a company with Cambodian citizens or institutions. More than 51% equity capital needs to be held by Cambodian. As for lease agreement, foreign companies can lease land; however, the length of the lease is limited. Maximum length is 50 years (Cambodian Civil Code, hereafter CCC, 244 and 247 (1)). Foreign companies can mortgage this right to a long-term lease for a loan.

Labor and tax laws are other related areas of interest for businesses in Cambodia. The teacher explained about the liability of an owner under these laws through giving actual case scenario, where a Cambodian police officer arrested a manager on charges of violation of labor laws. The company sent employees to work overseas and accommodated them in dormitories. The company prohibited the workers from going outside, and this was viewed as illegality. Any person or legal entities must also pay tax. However, the Cambodian law has some exemptions. For example, according to the Laws related to Commercial Regulations and article 5 paragraphs 1 of Cambodia's Commercial Register, people who only sell the merchandise of their spouses are not considered to be merchants. Therefore, a wife or husband does not need to pay corporation tax individually. This provision has an impact on taxation laws especially article 3, paragraph 6, that defines "sole proprietorship."

A husband, wife, and their dependent children shall be treated as a single physical person if they engage in the same family business. Moreover, employees who support their owners are not merchants (the Law Bearing upon Commercial Regulations and The Commercial Register in Cambodia 5 (2)). In this case, owners of the business are liable to pay tax. However, according to the teacher's explanation, the distinction between employee and owner is difficult in Cambodia because of Cambodian business culture. Generally, they do their business with their friends, family, or relatives. It is not clear if they support their activities as employees or jointly participate in a business or not.

3.2 The starter lecture by Japanese teachers

Two Japanese teachers conducted the lecture where one was a researcher of civil law and the other was a professor of civil law. First, the researcher explained the two only possible ways of starting a business in Japan. First is the establishment of a company through partnership, and the second is by purchasing a company through mergers and acquisition (M&A). Her explanation focused on the first point. She explained about business forms in Japan, and these were sole-proprietorship, partnership, and company. Each type is distinguishable by its establishment procedure and members' liability. Anyone, including foreigners, can establish a company by following the Japanese Companies Act (hereafter JCA) procedures, which gives a company a legal personality after registration. It, therefore, can purchase and register land and buildings in its name. In contrast, a partnership is established by a contract with partners and does not have any legal personality. Therefore, a member of the partnership can conclude a lease or loan contract only in the name of their partner's representative. However, they cannot register for real-estate using the name of the partnership.

The liability of members is different. In the case of a company, JCA stipulates two types of companies: stock company and membership company. In the case of a stock company, shareholder liability is limited to the amount of the subscription price of the shareholder (JCA104). In contrast, for a membership company, JCA lists three types of membership companies: general partnership company; limited partnership company; and limited liability company. General partnership company consists of general members, and the members are liable for the debt of the company.

In contrast, a limited liability company has members whose liability is limited to the amount of the subscription price. The difference between a stock company and limited liability company is that whether a company issues stock or not. Limited partnership company is in between a general partnership company and a limited liability company because it consists of both general members and limited liability members. For the Cambodian case, a limited partnership is similar to a limited partnership company in Japan.

In case of a partnership, the creditor of a partnership may exercise his or her rights against each partner in equal proportions (Japanese Civil Code, hereafter JCC, 675), which means that each partner is individually liable for the debt of partnership. In this sense, the liability of partners is similar to that of general partners in a membership company. However, it differs on one point. A creditor of a membership company shall exercise his or her rights against the members first. Partners shall be jointly and severally liable for the performance of obligations of the member company in cases where the obligations of such membership company cannot be sufficiently performed using the assets (JCA 580 (1) (i)).

Another teacher explained about M&A as another possible way for establishing a business. He introduced the different types of M&A in Japan. These are through a merger, stock transfer, stock swap, acquiring stock by takeover bid (TOB), and corporate spin-off. He explained the structure of TOB and defense plan for a hostile TOB by using Japanese Supreme Court Precedence of the Bull-Dog Sauce Co., Ltd. vs. the Steel Partners case[4]. This judgment was the first decision about hostile TOB defense plan by using poison pills. At the end of the class, Cambodian students asked how taxation offices impose a tax on partnership. The teachers answered that it is the responsibility of each partner to pay the partnership tax obligations because a partnership does not have legal capacity. However, this answer did not satisfy the Cambodian students. Fundamentally, it is related to the taxation system in each country.

4. Presentation by Students
4.1 Preparation for the presentation
Japanese and Cambodian program coordinators divided the students into three groups with membership from both Japan and Cambodia. Group 1 was assigned to make a presentation in case the MT is a partnership. Group 2 presented in case the MT is an association, and Group 3 made a presentation in case the MT is a company. Students had a work day for group preparations. They made a schedule, fixed the meeting time and location all by themselves. One group prepared their presentation from the school library, whereas another group did their work from the coffee shop near the university. Each group discussed how to make a PowerPoint presentation and the difference between Cambodian law and Japanese law during this day of preparation.

4.2 Group presentation
4.2.1 Presentation by Group 1

---

[4] Minshu Vol.61 No.5, p.2215, http://www.courts.go.jp/app/hanrei_en/detail?id=909, last accessed on December 14, 2018.

The Presentation by Students

Group 1 presented about MT case being a partnership. Cambodian students stated that their country has two types of partnership. One is a general partnership while the other is a limited partnership and both are established by a contract. The difference lies in the manner of contribution and the rights of the limited partner. General partners can contribute not only through their money and properties but also through their work and skills too (Law on Commercial Act, hereafter LCA 16 (a), 70 (2)). However, limited partners can only contribute through their money and properties only (LCA 70 (1)). Limited partners do not have the authority to represent the partnership, nor can they become an agent for it (LCA 79 (1) and (4)).

The Cambodian students in group 1 concluded that all members of MT are not limited partners in line with the Common Topic facts. Ms. A's contribution is by her skill, and a limited partner cannot contribute by their skill and works (LCA 70 (1)). Ms. A's contribution is only allowed as a general partner, and this makes her a general partner. Mr. B and Ms. C are also general partners because Mr. B concluded a lease contract with Mr. D and a loan contract with Bank E.

A representative of MT., Ms. C, concluded these sales contracts between Company F and an order contract with Ms. G as an agent of MT. According to LCA 79 (1) and (4), a limited partner does not have an executive authority to act on behalf of a limited partnership and cannot be an agent for the same. Both Mr. B and Ms. C performed activities that are not permissible to limited partners.

Therefore, they concluded that MT is a general partnership under the Cambodian law. In a general partnership, each partner has ultimate personal liability. General partners are jointly liable to creditors (CCC 704). However, creditors of a general partnership shall initially be satisfied from assets of the general partnership (LCE 42 (2)) in the equal portion by following their claim right (CCC 324). They will subsequently claim from general partners to perform their obligations if they cannot be satisfied with the partnership's assets. In case the creditors exhaust executing from each general partner, they can claim all or part of their claim rights to general partners (CCC 324 (4) and 921). General partners should be responsible for the total debt concerning creditors.

Applying these articles to the Common Topic case, creditors firstly execute the assets of MT. The assets divide equally among each creditor by the portion of their claim right. After that, the execution of general partnership assets follows, followed by a claim on the general partners. Ms. A, Mr. B, and Ms. C are therefore responsible for settling the total debt owed to creditors.

Group 1 Japanese students explained about the establishment process of partnership. According to the JCC 667, a partnership is established by a contract. Members of a partnership are individually liable for the debt of the partnerships as per their share of the partnership (JCC 675 (2)). In the Common Topic case, each member's liabilities are divided into one third. Creditors can also execute the assets of the partnership (JCC 675 (1)). The Japanese law does not have execution orders like Cambodian law. It does not prohibit debt execution to partners before the execution of the partnership assets.

The Japanese students explained how the remaining assets of MT are divided among creditors. Under the Japanese Civil Code, some claim rights are prioritized by a statutory lien. Japanese Civil Code article 311 lists the causes of the statutory lien. A claim right caused by a lease contract of immovable property and a sales contract of movable property are listed as a statutory lien over certain movables the obligor (JCC 311 (i) and (v)). In the Common Topic Case, the lessor Mr. D and the seller Company F's claim rights can be considered under statutory lien. The students examined Mr. D's case, Where, under JCC 313 (1), it states that statutory lien for a lease of immovable property shall exist concerning movables furnished to that land or buildings for the use of that land. Whether carpets in the office are recognized as objects for statutory lien or not is a discussion point. They concluded that Mr. D does not have a statutory lien to carpets in this case because these are MT's merchandise not furnished objects. Therefore, Mr. D cannot execute his claim right over any other this merchandise.

As for Company F's claim right for payment of silk materials, the students referred to JCC 321 that relates to the statutory lien for sale of movables. It says that statutory lien shall exist concerning movables, in connection with the price of those movables and interest on the same. They explained that the object of movables for a statutory lien should either be the same or be an alternative product like insurance money for materials, resale money, and so on. On the basis of their interpretation of JCC 321, the students concluded that Company F does not have a statutory lien because it had sold the silk materials that are movable property to MT which has been converted to carpets. In this case, whether the carpets are an alternative product of silk or not is discussable. Though they said the answer is no, because the silk carpets have an increased price due to value added by Ms. G's manufacture, hence cannot be the same as the silk materials.

4.2.2 Presentation by Group 2

Group 2 students presented the case where the MT is an association. The Japanese students explained the necessary elements for the establishment of a general incorporated association. It should be non-profit and has legal personality through its registration. By applying their analysis to the case, MT is not a general incorporated association, because it does not meet the requirements of non-profitability. Therefore, students concluded that MT should be a partnership or a company. However, Japanese students assumed that MT is a general incorporated association for comparing the difference between a partnership and a company. Regarding member's liability, a general incorporated association differs from a partnership as it has a legal personality itself. Members are independent of the association; therefore, creditors of general incorporated association only execute the properties of the association. As for a company, it also has a legal personality. On the basis of these analyses, students concluded that creditors of MT only execute properties of the association, and therefore, the members, Ms. A, Mr. B, and Ms. C are not liable for the debt of MT.

When creditors execute the properties of MT, how will the share be distributed to each creditor? Students explained about statutory lien under the Japanese Civil Code. Their explanation and conclusion was the same as that of Group 1 Japanese students. Properties of MT are equally distributed to each creditor in line with their portion of their claim right.

Group 2 Cambodian students explained about the difference between an association and private limited company under the Cambodian law. Both an association and a private limited company have legal personality once registered, and each member is independent of the association or the private limited company. Therefore, they are not liable to the debt of the association or the company. However, an association and a company differ in terms of their activity. An association activity should be non-profitable, whereas a private limited company engages in profit-seeking operations. Therefore, under the Cambodian legal system, MT is a private limited company and not an association. If the MT is a private limited company, how are the assets of MT distributed to each creditor? Their conclusion was the same as that of Group 1 Cambodian students. The assets of MT are equally divided among each creditor by following their portion of claim right.

4.2.3 Presentation by Group 3

Group 3 presented the case where MT is a company. Japanese students explained an overview of the company system under the Japanese Company Act. Here, a stock company and a membership company are permitted (JCA 2 (1)), and the membership company is further divided into three types. They are a general partnership company, a limited partnership company, and a limited liability company (JCA 2 (1)). Anyone, including foreigners, can establish a company under the JCA, which is then considered a Japanese company. The students explained the differences between the types of companies by focusing on their structure. A stock company issues shares, and stockholders purchase them. The stock company and each shareholder is an independent legal person. Therefore, shareholders are not liable for the debt of the stock company. In contrast, all partners of a general partnership company should have an ultimate liability (JCA 576 (2) ①). A limited partnership company consists of ultimate liability members and limited partners (JCA 576 (3)), whereas a limited liability company consists of only limited partners (JCA 576 (4)). Limited partners are not liable to the debt of a company. Though, under the JCA, ultimate liability members are jointly and severally liable for the debt of a company (JCA 580 (1)). However, unlike a partnership, creditors will initially execute a company's asset for the performance of their obligation. In cases where the obligations of Membership Company cannot be fully executed with the assets of the company or where the execution against the company has not been successful, the ultimate liability members are liable for the debts of the company (JCA 580 (1) ①②).

Group 3 Japanese students also explained the distribution of MT's assets. They mentioned about a statutory lien and the explanation and conclusion were the same as those of the other groups. Group 3 Cambodian students' presentation started with the nationality of a company. Under Cambodian law, a company shall be deemed to be of Khmer nationality only if (a) the company has a place of business and a registered office located in the Kingdom of Cambodia; (b) more than 51% of voting shares of the company are held by natural or legal persons of Khmer nationality (LCA 101). In the Common Topic case, the students concluded that MT is a Khmer nationality company, because Mr. B and Ms. C are of Khmer nationality, and they have more than 51% of voting shares even though Ms. A is a foreign designer. The Students' presentation moved on to the liability of each member, i.e., Ms. A, Mr. B, and Ms. C. They regarded MT as a private limited company without any explanation. They concluded that each member of a private limited company is not liable for the debts of the company. Therefore, creditors of MT can only execute the assets of the company. On the distribution of assets among each creditor, their conclusion was the same as Group 1 and 2

Cambodian students.

4.3 Discussion part

The discussions were facilitated by the Japanese teacher, the Cambodian program coordinator, and the Japanese researcher. They first confirmed the partnership difference in the two countries. According to Japanese Civil Code, a partnership is established by a contract, and the liability of each member is ultimate plus it cannot be registered. However, under the Cambodian law, a general partnership, a limited partnership, and member's liability is different from each partner's status. Moreover, the partnerships should be registered and they have a legal personality. For Japanese students, registration of partnership is unique. Students and teachers took time to discuss the meaning of registration of partnership under the Cambodian law, and we could not reach a conclusion that was agreeable to all during the discussion part of the program. A partnership as explained by the Cambodian students was stipulated in the country's Law on Commercial and Enterprise and not the Civil Code. Partnerships under the Law on Commercial and Enterprise are similar to a partnership company and limited partnership company under the Japanese Company Act. However, facilitators could not lead the discussion towards finding out the difference between a partnership and an association.

Another discussion point was the distribution of the assets of MT to each creditor. Both student's conclusion were the same as the assets equally divide to each creditor according to their portion of claim right. However, the conclusion was different as the Japanese students discussed whether some creditors have statutory liens or not and concluded that no creditors have statutory liens in the Common Topic case.

In contrast, Cambodian students did not discuss this point. Facilitators asked Cambodian students about a statutory lien in Cambodian Civil Code. A student explained that the Cambodian Civil Code has articles about a statutory lien for the lessee of immovable properties and seller of movable properties (CCC 788), and according to his interpretation, no statutory lien is found in the Common

The Class Room Discussion

Topic case. As for a statutory lien for lessee, it exists against movables that furnish the land or building for the use of lease. However, carpets are not furnished for the use of lease but are for sale. As for a statutory lien for the seller of movable properties, it exists for movables on the same. In the Common Topic case, the seller does not have a statutory lien, because silk carpets cannot be considered to be the same as movable silk materials.

The conclusion and manner of analysis was the same for Japanese students because the Cambodian Civil Code statutory lien provisions are similar to the Japanese one. The facilitator introduced Japanese precedence of July 4, 1914[5], that involves a case about a number of statutory liens against movable properties when leasing a house that did encourage the student's discussion. This precedence helped to interpret the meaning of the word "*furnished.*" The Supreme Court of Judicature ruled that movables not only relate to merchandise that has been brought for use in a leased building but also apply to movables that have been brought to a leased building during the period of a lease contract and should be recognized as "*furnished*" movables of the leased building.

This is because a lease contract continues the relationship between a lessor and lessee. Therefore, a lessor's statutory lien applies to movables that are in the leased house, like checks, family member's watch, and jewelry. More ways of interpretation could be given to the students. Unfortunately, there was a time lim-

---

[5] Tai-Shin-In Minji Hanketsu Roku (Record of Great Court of Judicature Civil Caases) Vol.20, p.587.

itation that hindered the discussion. The facilitator also mentioned the Japanese Civil Code article 324, which is a statutory lien for industrial labor that discusses whether this article is analogically applicable to Ms. G, a silk carpet creator or not. Some Cambodian students commented that article 324 is for the protection of workers who are hired and are working at a factory or somewhere. Ms. G is an independent creator, and MT did not hire her. Therefore, it is difficult to apply this article to her case. The teacher asked Japanese students the purpose of the article 324 to further discuss this point. However, we could not exhaust the subject due to time constraints.

5. Conclusion

In this program, we tried to come up with the difference between the Japanese and Cambodian laws throughout the student's presentation and discussion. To achieve this purpose, we introduced starter lectures that focused on how companies are established in both countries through Cambodian and Japanese joint groups. Students presented necessary discussion points about the nature of MT, the liability of members of a partnership, an association and a company, and division in the Common Topics. Therefore, we could discuss the difference in how companies are formed and regulated in both countries.

However, the program framework needs to be improved, first through the choice of the starter lecture topic. By using Japanese court precedence, we explained that M&A is one of the methods for starting a business in Japan. However, these seemed difficult for the Cambodian students to understand because of the difference in the Cambodian market situation vis-à-vis Japan and other developed countries. The notion of the stock market is new in Cambodia, and only five companies are listed on the Cambodian Securities Markets[6]. It is easy to imagine how M&A is not popular in Cambodia, however, a fact that was recognized during the program. More attention needs to be paid to the social and economic

---

[6] Cambodian Securities Exchange, "List of Companies" http://csx.com.kh/data/lstcom/list-Posts.do?MNCD=5010, last accessed on December 7, 2018.

situation of the country in a subsequent lecture.

Second, fundamental legal issues were not adequately tackled, for example, on the difference between a partnership and an association. The reason why Japanese laws do not allow for registration of partnership is because of the difference between its legal nature of partnership and association. If these points could be discussed, it would have made students understand about partnership and association in a much better way. The facilitator's advanced communication skill is required to lead the discussion in a productively. This skill is cultivated through the accumulation of program experiences.

SAMPLES OF TEACHING MATERIALS
FOR CIVIL LAW

JAPAN

1 Textbook

Civil law textbooks cover general principles, property, contracts, torts, and family law. Each chapter explains relevant concepts. For example, chapters regarding the agent system explain its purpose and related legal matters such as apparent and unauthorized agency. The textbook also explains legal theory and Japanese Supreme Court precedents.

* Material Sample: Hiroshi Matsuo, *Minpo no Taikei*, 6th ed., 2017, Tokyo: Keio University Press (ISBN 9784766422771)

2 Casebook

The Japanese Supreme Court publishes an official casebook periodically, "Saikousaibansho Minji Hanreishu (Supreme Court Civil Law Precedents)" and Saikousaibansho Keiji Hanreishu (Supreme Court Criminal Law Precedents). Alongside these official casebooks civil law courses use an unofficial casebook, Hanrei Hyakusen (Journal of 100 Selected Cases). It introduces about 100 essential cases arranged by legal discipline (constitutional, civil, criminal law, etc.).

* Material Sample: *Saikousaibansyo Minji Hanreishu* (Supreme Court Civil Law Precedents)

3 Workbook

A workbook is used to study how conflicts are resolved by application of civil law. Although compiled cases are fictional, they are based on actual cases and essential precedents. Cases present facts and questions. Contributors briefly explain what students need to consider, related legal arguments, and cases. Students learn legal thought processes by studying workbooks. The Law Practice Series is one of the best known for law students.

* Material Sample: Hiroyuki Hirano, *Shin Kangaeru Minpo*, vol.1, 2018, Tokyo: Keio University Press (ISBN 9784766424751)

4 Others

Japanese Law Translation[1] is a website for legal research in English. Books of civil law commentary are used for reference along with databases of cases. The Supreme Court of Japan operates the official database of judgments[2]. It is free to the public and has an English version. West Law Japan[3] and the TKC Law Library[4] are renowned private databases. Private database sites charge fees, but they include Supreme Court precedents and lower court cases.

1 Japanese Law Translation, http://www.japaneselawtranslation.go.jp, last accessed on December 23, 2018.
2 The Supreme Court of Japan, "Judgement of the Supreme Court" http://www.courts.go.jp/app/hanrei_en/search?, last accessed on December 23, 2018.
3 West Law Japan, https://www.westlawjapan.com, last accessed on December 23, 2018.
4 TKC Law Library, https://www.tkc.jp/law, last accessed on December 23, 2018.

VIETNAM

1 The Civil Code (2015-In effect)

The Vietnamese Civil Code is the basic legal document for the private law sector in Vietnam and can be considered to be a fundamental legal code in Vietnam. This code contains basic rules for most of the main behaviors in private legal fields, including civil transactions, contracts, common civil contracts, regulations on inheritance, compensation for damage outside the contract (tort liability), etc. All law students in Vietnam have to study civil law; hence, learning the civil code is inevitable. Civil law is a compulsory subject for students of all major disciplines in legal studies at university, including the Criminal Major track.

2 Textbook 1

In Vietnam, every university has the right to have its own textbooks. Within the Faculty of Economics and Law, Vietnam National University, HCM City, we divide the contents of civil law into two textbooks. The first book includes contents related to the subject matter of civil law relationships (besides natural persons, it includes juridical persons, households, cooperative groups, and other non-natural persons), civil transactions, representation, limits and limitation periods, property, and ownership rights.

This textbook also contains review questions and student homework. Hence, it can also be viewed as a workbook. This textbook has been authored by Prof Nguyễn Ngọc Điện, and it is published by the Vietnam National University, HCM City Publishing House. It is used by many universities in southern Vietnam.

3 Textbook 2

The second textbook contains topics such as civil obligation from different sources (e.g., unlawful possession or use of or receipt of benefits from property, unilateral legal acts, etc.), raising of obligation, termination of obligation, contract (general theory of contract and common contracts), succession, civil liability (from breach of civil obligation and liability to compensation for non-contractual damages (tort liability)), etc.

This textbook also contains review questions and student homework. Hence, it can also be viewed as a workbook. This textbook has been authored by Prof Nguyễn Ngọc Điện, and it is published by the Vietnam National University, HCM City Publishing House. It is used by many universities in southern Vietnam.

At the present moment, with regard to Vietnamese Civil Law, we need to outline and explain the courts' decisions in our teaching; these judgments are also made public on the Internet where everyone can read them.

SAMPLES OF TEACHING MATERIALS FOR CIVIL LAW

LAOS

1 Textbook

Lao studies 2 (2016)

This textbook was published for students in year one at university, periodically introduces the sources and legal systems in Laos, edited by academic professionals from the Ministry of Education and Sports.

* *Lao Studies 2 (2016). Department of Higher Education: Second Strengthening Higher Education Project (SHEP).*

Fundamental of Secured Transaction Law (2015)

Study document in subjects similar to Civil Law.

* *Vixay Sihapanya (2015). Fundamental of Secured Transaction Law. Faculty of Law and Political Science: Luxembourg Development Cooperation Agency (LAO/023).*

Fundamentals of civil law (2007)

Study document in subjects similar to Civil Law.

* *Vixay Sihapanya (2007). Fundamentals Civil Law. 3rd Edition. Faculty of Law and Political Science: Swedish International Development Cooperation Agency (SIDA).*

Civil procedure (2006)

Study document in subjects similar to Civil Law.

* *Ket Kiettisack, Keyoune Yotxayviboune (2006). Civil Procedure. Faculty of Law and Political Science: Swedish International Development Cooperation Agency (SIDA).*

Labor law (2006)

Study document in subjects similar to Civil Law.

* Nouphanh Mahaphom (2006). Labor Law. Faculty of Law and Political Science: Swedish International Development Cooperation Agency (SIDA).

Fundamental of Notary Law (2006)

Study document in subjects similar to Civil Law.

* Khampha Vangduangnapha (2006). Fundamental of Notary Law. 1st Edition. Faculty of Law and Political Science: Swedish International Development Cooperation Agency (SIDA).

Writing Procedural Documents (2006)

Study document in subjects similar to Civil Law.

* Nuanthong Vongsa (2006). Writing Procedural Documents. 2nd Edition. Faculty of Law and Political Science: Swedish International Development Cooperation Agency (SIDA).

Fundamental of Judicial Organization (2005)

Study document in subjects similar to Civil Law.

* Phaimany SAYVONGSA (2005). Fundamental of Judicial Organization. 1st Edition. Faculty of Law and Political Science: Swedish International Development Cooperation Agency (SIDA).

2 Handbooks
Civil Law by JICA (2012)

Legal commentaries, which have been prepared by the Japanese Project for Human Resource Development in the Legal Sector (JICA), in cooperation with the National University of Laos (FLP), Ministry of Justice, Supreme People's Court and Office of the Public Prosecutor. They are rated highly by law practitioners.

* Here are some handbooks published since 2012:

1) *Charts of Civil procedure in Lao PDR;*
2) *Guidebook of Civil Law Procedure in Basis and Resurrection;*
3) *Questions and Answers for Civil Law;*
4) *Overview of Contract Law;*
5) *Overview of Tort Law;*

Etc… (on penal law)

3 Legislation
Amended law on civil procedure (2012)

The Law on Civil Procedure defines in detail the principles, regulations and court procedures for solving civil disputes, commercial disputes, family disputes and cases involving problems in a manner consistent with the reality, laws and justice. The law was amended in 2004, consists of 129 articles, translation endorsed by the Law Committee of the National Assembly of the Lao PDR.

* *Amended law on civil procedure (2012). People's Supreme Court: Japan International Cooperation Agency (JICA)*

4 Reference
Customary law series (1990's)

These Lao customary law books were adapted from ancient palm leaf manuscripts, commenting on social life and customs during the Lanexang period (XIV-XVIII Century). The transliteration project was sponsored by The TOYOTA FOUNDATION in the 90's, rewritten in modern Lao by Grand-Master Samlit Buasisavat.

* List of Lao collection customs, etiquette and folklore.

1) Mūlatantai: Ancient verdict on administrative policies, investigation and prosecution (1992);

2) Sōi Sāikham: Principles comparing to 227 rules of conduct of Buddhism

"Pātimokkha" (1992);

3) Dhāmmāsat Luāng: The Ancient Law, equivalent to the constitution, consists of 431 articles (1993);

4) Souvānnāmoukha: The code of Lao customary law in Bali-Sanskrit, including law on heritage (1994);

5) Rāsasāt: The ethics of Royalists and law enforcement (1995);

6) Phosārath lae Sāngkhāpākob: Prosecution rights of appeal and the punishment against Buddhism violation (1996);

7) 'Anachak lae Thammachak haeng Dhāmmāsat (1997): Cases in society and in Buddhism training-precepts and commitments.

Court Judgement of Civil Law (2012)

Compiling court judgments since 2010, even though Laos is a civil law country and, as such, jurisprudence is not recognized as a source of law and is not part of the legal system. Yet, some court judgments are publicly published for legal professionals, including teaching methods in legal institutions.

* *Court Judgement of Civil Law (2012). People's Supreme Court*

5 Workbook

Japanese civil code (2004)

The Japanese Civil Code was established since 1898, and provided valuable lessons to legal practitioners in Laos for the comparison of legal systems between Laos and Japan.

* *Japanese Civil Code Vol.1-5 (2004). 1st ed. Legal and Judicial Development Project: Japan International Cooperation Agency (JICA)*

6 Others

Legal Terminology in selected laws in civil and commercial law areas (2007)

Dictionary for legal studies on various laws: Property, Contract & Tort, Inheritance, Family & Registration, Secured Transaction, Bankruptcy, Business, Enterprise and other related legislations.

* *Terminology in selected laws in civil and commercial law areas (2007). Ministry of Justice: Legal and Judicial Development Project, supported by Japan International Cooperation Agency (JICA)*

Laws in present (2004)

This book was created under the project "Strengthening Legal Education in Lao PDR" started in July 2000 at the Faculty of Law and Political Science – National University of Laos, funded by the Swedish International Development Cooperation Agency (SIDA) and the Department of Law, Umea University.

* *Richard Powell (2004). Law in present. (S. Sengdouangchanh, Transl.) Umea University: SIDA.*

THAILAND

Thai Civil and Commercial Code

This book contains the full text of the Thai Civil and Commercial Code. The Code provides substantive law, which is the legal foundation for private law in Thailand. It is divided into six Books (chapters): General Principles, Obligations, Specific Contracts, Property, Family, and Succession. The book contains not only original content in the Thai language, but also the English translation. It is a useful reference book for law students, lawyers, and other legal professionals.

* Book detail: *The Civil and Commercial Code, Books 1–6*, complied and translated by Professor Kamol Sandhikshetrin.

Textbook on Contract Law

This book provides extensive, detailed explanation of principles of contract law. It is a main textbook recommended for first-year law students studying contract law. The book covers the principle of private autonomy, basic requirements for contract validity including legal capacity, object, form, and intention. It also contains description on the effect of void and voidable acts, conditions, and time, as well as prescription. In addition, the book explains contract formation, effects of contract, breach of contract, and remedies for breach of contract including termination of contract. Finally, the book provides clear examples and important Supreme Court decisions in contract law.

* Book detail: Sanunkorn Sotipun, *Description of Juristic Acts and Contracts with the Unfair Contract Terms B.E. 2540 and Related Laws*, 22nd ed., 2018, Published by Winyuchon: Bangkok.

Textbook on Obligations

This book describes legal rules of obligations in a comprehensive fashion. It is a main textbook recommended for second-year law students studying obligations. The book explains general concepts of obligations, subject of obligations, and effect of obligations such as nonperformance. It also covers transfer of claims and extinction of obligations. Extensive examples and notable Supreme Court decisions are included.

* Book detail: Daraporn Thirawat, *Obligations: General Principles*, 6th ed., 2018, Published by the Textbooks and Teaching Materials Program under the Faculty of Law, Thammasat University:

Bangkok.

A Practical Guide to Exam Legal Writing

This book is designed to help law students with legal writing, especially writing examinations. It begins with guidance on techniques for studying law. It then illustrates different types of examination questions and demonstrates how to analyze problems systematically. The book offers analytical and writing techniques with extensive examples and practice exercises.

* Book detail: Munin Pongsapan, *A Practical Guide to Exam Legal Writing*, 12th ed., 2018, Winyuchon: Bangkok.

The Reception of Foreign Private Law in Thailand in 1925: A Case Study of Specific Performance

This thesis examines the drafting of Book I on General Rules and Book II on Obligations of the Thai Civil and Commercial Code in 1925, which has largely remained in place. The thesis gives a historical account of establishment of modern Thai civil law. It also gives an overview of and the structure of the Thai Code.

* Book detail: Munin Pongsapan, *The Reception of Foreign Private Law in Thailand in 1925: A Case Study of Specific Performance* (Ph.D. Thesis, University of Edinburgh 2013).

Remedies for Breach of Contract in Thai Law

This book chapter overviews Thai contract law, especially remedies for breach of contract. Some of the chapter's early parts provide some historical accounting and an overview of Thai civil law.

* Book detail: Munin Pongsapan, "Remedies for Breach of Contract in Thai Law" in Mindy Chen-Wishart, Alexander Loke, and Burton Ong, editors, *Remedies for Breach of Contract*, Published by Oxford University Press, 2016.

Useful Websites:

1. http://deka.supremecourt.or.th

This website is administered by the Office of the Supreme Court of Thailand. It is connected to the database of Thai Supreme Court Decisions. The website provides a search engine for finding court decisions available in the Thai language.

2. *http://mratchakitcha.soc.go.th/*

This website is administered by the Secretariat of the Cabinet under the Office of the Prime Minister. It is the official website of the Royal Thai Government Gazette that collects laws, regulatory notifications, and public journals. It is available in the Thai language.

MYANMAR

1 The Burma Code (Volume I - XIII)

Law students and other persons interested in the Myanmar Laws should read and study the Burma (Myanmar) Code. It was published by the Attorney General in English and Myanmar, its 13 non-chronological volumes cover laws enacted and remaining in force from 1818 to 1954. Codes are too old but still in force, for example, Contract Act, Evidence Act, Civil Procedure Code etc. As those Burma Codes are too old, some laws are not presently applicable. Laws that have been repealed and replaced are promulgated and published yearly as the laws of Myanmar.

2 Myanmar Laws (1955 - Present)

Laws enacted after the Burma Codes were compiled are published by the Attorney General yearly in Myanmar, the official language, and occasionally in English. Scholars publish some compiled laws unofficially with commentaries. They are available to students.

3 Law Reports

Teachers of civil law apply court decisions as stipulated in the law reports, which specify what kinds of issues arise and what legal provisions endorse decisions. The Myanmar Supreme Court publishes official law reports annually. Civil and criminal cases are compiled and included in a separate portion of each Law Report. Unofficial reported cases are passed each year and it is also called Digest -- for example, *U Thaung Htun for civil law and criminal law* spanning 1948-1969. Digests complied by scholars, brief decision for each judgment is included. Some Digests are chronological and some arrange cases under the sections of relevant law.

4 Reference Books

Knowledge for Contract Act *1

Civil Procedure Code *2

Scholars have published books related to specific laws (e.g., *Knowledge for Contract Act* by U Thet Pe and *Civil Procedure Code* (volumes 1-3) by U Mya) in which each chapter explains the legal concept of each provision. It also contains rulings of the Highest Court in Myanmar for the whole period. Scholars briefly present facts related to issues and specify which cases students should consider in solving problems. Therefore, students can learn how to think and learn issues in legal sense.

*1 U Thet Pe, *Knowledge for Contract Act,* 1st ed., 1998, published by Sarpaypang Law Book House, Yangon.

*2 U Mya, *Civil Procedure Code,* 2nd ed., 2010, published by Mandalay Law Firm, Mandalay.

Myanmar Customary Law *3

In addition to the Burma Code and Myanmar Laws (statutory law), Myanmar Customary Law is essential for the study of civil law. It concerns family affairs (e.g., marriage, divorce, partition, adoption, succession, inheritance, and matrimonial rights). These largely customs having the force of law concerning family affairs still apply in Myanmar, although those that are obsolete or out of conformity with current customs have been abolished. U Mya Sein explains family affairs in detail and the legal reasoning for resolving relevant issues. Moreover, we also use ancient dhammathats in teaching civil law. This customary law remains in force unless it contravenes statutory law or society's practices. This book introduces students to legal thinking and resolutions of family issues. Many books useful for learning civil law were written by eminent writers such as Dr. Maung Maung and Dr. E Maung.

*3 U Mya Sein, *Myanmar Customary Law,* 12th ed., 2014, published by Gonhtoo Sarpay, Yangon.

INDEX

A
acquisition of property 247
AEC 35, 46
ASEAN 35, 46, 57
Asian Law Student Association 49
association 255

B
barristers 36, 40
Bowring Treaty 165
Brahmanism 167
Buddhism 104, 146, 167

C
case law 121, 133
civil law 4, 32, 35, 50, 53, 61, 66, 70, 107, 135, 144, 184, 201, 245, 250, 265, 313
civil law system 5, 37, 100, 109, 124, 130, 187, 189, 198
claim rights 7
class action 79
coal workers' pneumoconiosis case 81
codification 166, 189
colonization 35
common law 37, 80, 106, 189, 198, 201, 250
common law system 6, 58, 121, 189, 308
Communist Party 100, 142
comparative law 244
comparative legal education 4, 244
Confucianism 104
consumer group litigation 89
contractual liabilities 248
court system 113
customary law 132, 215

D
democratic centralism principle 100
diploma 53
Doi Moi 99, 102
domestic law 61

E
English-taught master of law programs 47
examination 10, 19, 23, 32, 41
extraterritoriality 165

F
factfinding 6
family law 7
fetus 250
force majeure 268
Fukushima nuclear accident evacuees' cases 85

G
general part 7
globalization 33, 103
graduate school of law 13
group litigation 79

H
Hanoi Law University 123
hepatitis C cases 82
Hindu Laws 173
Ho Chi Minh City Law University 123
HPV vaccine cases 87

HRD Program   59, 64

I
inclusive institution   32
inheritance   216
Institutiones   5
interpretation   6, 32
IRAC Method   70
Isahaya bay tide gate cases   83

J
J.D.   13
Japan International Cooperation Agency   70, 106
judges   36, 116
Judicial Committee   40, 42
Justice System Reform Council   6

L
law of lawyers   148
law of the people   147
law school   6, 13
lawyer   41, 118
lecturer   9
Legal Training and Research Institute   6, 31
LL.B.   39
LL.D.   12
LL.M.   12

M
Marxism   142, 146
Myanmar   197

N
National Legal Examination   23
National University of Laos   157
non-contractual liabilities   250

P
Pandekten   5
Paññāsāstra University   69

partnership   255
precedents   110
Preliminary Qualification Examination   23
private law   3, 175, 196
procurators   117
prosecutors   36
public law   129

R
real rights   7
requisite facts   14
rule of law   36

S
socialist law   107
socialist legality   100, 107
statutory law   131
subject of rights   245
subjective rights   133
succession   216, 250
Sustainable Development Goal 16   32
technical law   148

T
Thai Bar   36, 39, 40
Thammasat University   36
transformation of rights   247

U
University of Economics and Law   265
University of Yangon   53
unreasonableness   5

ABOUT KEIGLAD

KEIGLAD - Keio Institute for Global Law and Development

Keio Institute for Global Law and Development (KEIGLAD) was established for the purpose of assisting the promotion of international exchange and international cooperation among researchers, students, and staffs for legal study and legal education. KEIGLAD will promote the concerned projects as follow:

- Promotion of the Program for Asian Global Legal Professions (PAGLEP)
- Collection of information on the concerned comparative law
- Collection of information on the method of legal education
- Provision of materials for legal education
- Provision of information and support for foreign students who will study at Keio Law School and Keio Law School students who will study abroad
- Promotion of the concerned symposiums and research meetings
- Publication of working papers
- Other matters concerned with objectives of KEIGLAD

Through these activities, KEIGLAD aims to contribute to the promotion of "Law-Ubiquitous Society", in which Anyone can access to justice Anywhere and Anytime.

ABOUT THE AUTHORS

Isao Kitai
Dean, Professor, Keio University Law School, Japan

Hiroshi Matsuo
Director, KEIGLAD; Professor, Keio University Law School, Japan

Munin Pongsapan
Assistant Professor, Faculty of Law, Thammasat University, Thailand

Junavit Chalidabhongse
Lecturer of Law, Faculty of Law, Thammasat University, Thailand

Viravat Chantachote
Adjunct Assistant Professor, Faculty of Law, Thammasat University, Thailand

Khin Phone Myint Kyu
Professor, Department of Law, University of Yangon, Myanmar

Kong Phallack
Dean and a professor of law at the Faculty of Law and Public Affairs, Paññāsāstra University, Cambodia

Mao Kimpav
Manager of Law Programs, Faculty of Law and Public Affairs, Paññāsāstra University, Cambodia

Toshitaka Kudo
Associate Professor, Faculty of Law, Keio University, Japan

Phan Thi Lan Huong
Deputy Head, International Cooperation; Professor, Department of Hanoi Law University, Vietnam

Nguyen Ba Binh
Deputy Dean in Charge of Faculty of International Business and Trade Law, Hanoi Law University; Arbitrator at Vietnam International Arbitration Centre (VIAC), Vietnam

Nguyen Ngoc Dien
Associate Professor–Vice rector, University of Economics and Law, Vietnam National University in Ho Chi Minh city, Vietnam

Alounna Khamhoung
Lecturer, Faculty of Law and Political Science, National University of Laos

Doan Thi Phuong Diep
Lecturer and Head of Office of Inspection and Legal Affairs, University of Economics and Law Vietnam National University in Ho Chi Minh City, Vietnam

Khin Khin Su
Assistant Lecturer, Department of Law, University of Yangon, Myanmar

Hitomi Fukasawa
Researcher, KEIGLAD, Japan

MEXT/JSPS Re-Inventing Japan Project (Type B: ASEAN) FY 2016
文部科学省　平成 28 年度大学の世界展開力事業（ASEAN 地域における大学間交流の推進）
タイプ B 採択プログラム